Response to Student Writing

Implications
for Second Language Students

Response to Student Writing

Implications
for Second Language Students

Dana R. Ferris
California State University, Sacramento

LEA LAWRENCE ERLBAUM ASSOCIATES, PUBLISHERS
2003   Mahwah, New Jersey   London

Copyright © 2003 by Lawrence Erlbaum Associates, Inc.

Lawrence Erlbaum Associates, Inc., Publishers
10 Industrial Avenue
Mahwah, NJ 07430

Cover design by Kathryn Houghtaling Lacey

Library of Congress Cataloging-in-Publication Data

Ferris, Dana.
Response to student writing : implications for second language students / Dana R. Ferris.
      p. cm.
      Includes bibliographical references and index.
ISBN 0-8058-3656-X (cloth : alk. paper)
ISBN 0-8058-3657-8 (pbk. : alk. paper)
1. English language—Study and teaching—Foreign speakers. 2. English language—Rhetoric—Study and teaching. 3. Report writing—Study and teaching. 4. Grading and marking (Students) 5. College prose—Evaluation. 6. Second language acquisition. I. Title.
PE1128.A2 .F473 2002
428'.0071—dc21
          2002022519
          CIP

Printed in the United States of America
10 9 8 7 6 5 4 3 2

*To all those students, teachers, mentors
and friends who have given me encouragement
and taught me how to be a better encourager
through my feedback. And to the God of all
encouragement, who daily gives me purpose
and the ability to value others
as I am valued.*

CONTENTS

PART II: PRACTICE

PREFACE

The purpose of this volume is to synthesize and critically analyze the literature on response to the writing of second language (L2) students and to discuss the implications of the research for teaching practice in the critical areas of written and oral teacher commentary, error correction, and peer response.

The primary goal of this book is to present current theoretical perspectives on response. Thus, one important target audience group is researchers in L2 composition who are concerned with one or more aspects of response to student writing. Composition researchers who are interested in the contrast between first language (L1) and L2 writers may also find the book of value. Because the book, though research-based, is of an essentially practical nature, in-service and pre-service teachers of ESOL/EFL writers should find the book useful as well, especially the pedagogical section (chaps. 6–8). Finally, teacher educators concerned with preparing graduate students for the teaching of writing will find the book to be an important resource on a crucial topic. This book can serve as a supplementary text for courses in "Teaching ESL Composition," "Second Language Writing Theory/Analysis of L2 Written Texts," or practica that include writing components.

This book should have considerable value for both practical and theoretical purposes. Response to student writing—whether it takes the form of teachers' written commentary on student content, error correction, teacher–student conferences, or peer response—is an extremely important component of the endeavor of teaching L2 writing. Probably no single activity takes more teacher time and energy. Peer response, done well, can consume a good deal of class time and student energy. Thus L2 writing teachers and students invest a great deal in response—yet there is misinformation and confusion about the best ways for teachers and peers to give feedback.

As research on L2 writing has grown as a subdiscipline of both composition and second language studies (Silva, Leki, & Carson, 1997), a wide variety of studies on response have appeared. These have ranged from discourse analytic studies of the nature and effects of peer response and teacher commentary (e.g., Carson & Nelson, 1994, 1996; Connor & Asenavage, 1994; Ferris, 1997; Ferris, Pezone, Tade, & Tinti, 1997; Lockhart & Ng, 1995a, 1995b; Mendonca & Johnson, 1994; Patthey-Chavez & Ferris, 1997) to surveys of student opinion about feedback (e.g., Ferris, 1995a; Hedgcock & Lefkowitz, 1994, 1996; Mangelsdorf & Schlumberger, 1992; Zhang, 1995) to experimental studies of the effects of response (e.g., Fathman & Whalley, 1990; Kepner, 1991). There have also been numerous treatments of error correction in L2 writing contexts (for reviews, see Ellis, 1998; Truscott, 1996). These studies have been conducted in very diverse contexts, with widely differing student populations, and using methodologies that are difficult to compare. The researcher or teacher who seriously seeks answers about response to student writing will thus benefit greatly from a comprehensive summary, analysis, and synthesis of the research that has been done and an acknowledgment of questions that remain unexplored or inadequately investigated.

OVERVIEW

This text provides a comprehensive summary and synthesis of previous research on response to L2 student writing, paired with careful critical analyses of the strengths, weaknesses, and limitations of the literature as it exists at the time of writing. The studies reviewed were drawn from a wide range of sources, including published books and book chapters, journal articles, printed annotated bibliographies on second language writing, various computer databases, master's theses, doctoral dissertations, and conference papers that became available to me. In an effort to be comprehensive in the review of research, I included both published and unpublished studies. However, recognizing that the inclusion of unrefereed research studies is always potentially problematic, at no point is an unpublished, unrefereed source used by itself to argue for a particular conclusion or pedagogical practice.

The book begins with a theoretical foundations chapter, which overviews both the influence of L1 composition theory and research on L2 response issues and the influence of various L2 theoretical and pedagogical paradigms on the teaching of L2 writing, particularly as they relate to issues of response. The middle section of the volume (chaps. 2–5) focuses on research covering specific subtopics related to response (written and oral teacher response, peer response, grammar feedback, and student views on response). The final section (chaps. 6–8) discusses pedagogical implications of the existing theory and research for the provision of teacher feedback, the facilitation of peer response, and the preparation of teachers to provide commentary on student writing (both content and grammar).

Readers will also find numerous examples of student texts and teacher commentary as well as figures and appendices that summarize research findings and present sample lessons and other teaching materials. The book thus aims to be simultaneously comprehensive in its approach to the existing research and highly practical in showing current and future teachers how this material applies to their everyday endeavors of responding to student writing and teaching composition classes.

ACKNOWLEDGMENTS

I am grateful to my home institution, California State University, Sacramento, for granting me sabbatical leave during the Spring, 2000 semester so that I could concentrate on the writing of this book. I am similarly thankful to the CSUS English Department, especially the TESOL/Applied Linguistics faculty (Linda Callis Buckley, Robby Ching, Marie Helt, Fred Marshall, & Sue McKee), who operated shorthanded while I was on leave.

I am thankful to many ESL writing students and teachers at CSUS who have given me access to textual and classroom data over the years. Though many have helped out, I would be remiss if I did not especially mention the contributions of Shelagh Nugent, Gabriella Nuttall, and Stuart Schulz, all instructors in the Learning Skills Center at CSUS. I am also thankful to the various graduate research assistants and thesis students from the CSUS MA TESOL Program who have worked with me on the research projects described in this book: Susan Pezone, Cathy Tade, Sharee Tinti, Gabriella Nuttall, Hiliry Harvey, Sarah Chaney, Keiko Komura, Barrie Roberts, Luba Schmid, and Christiana Rennie.

I would also like to acknowledge the support of many generous colleagues in the field of second language writing who have read my work, critiqued my research, listened to my conference papers, and otherwise informed my thinking and encouraged my progress. These include Diane Belcher, Jun Liu, Joy Reid, Ilona Leki, Tony Silva, Barbara Kroll, Ann Johns, Lynn Goldstein, Janet Lane, Jan Frodesen, and, of course, John Hedgcock. I especially need once again to thank Robert Kaplan, my PhD advisor and now a valued mentor, for his continuing interest in and support of my work (even when he disagrees with me!).

I want to express special thanks to members of the Thursday evening Bible study group that meets in our home for their encouragement, support, and prayers, as I completed the writing of this book in the midst of various family crises. Finally, most loving thanks and appreciation to my husband, Randy Ferris, and my daughters, Laura & Melissa Ferris, who tolerated my preoccupation and occasional crabbiness with patience and great humor.

PART

I

RESEARCH

<table>
<tr><td>

CHAPTER

1

</td><td>

An Overview of L1 Composition Research on Response and Its Influence on L2 Writing Theory and Practice

</td></tr>
</table>

Response to student writing has been a source of interest and debate in L1 composition theory and research since the early 1970s, when the "process approach" to teaching composition began to take hold in classrooms around the United States (e.g., Elbow, 1973; Garrison, 1974). These scholars, reacting to earlier paradigms in which teachers responded to a finished piece of writing primarily to justify a final grade, strongly suggested that teachers allow students to complete multiple drafts of their papers, encourage substantive revision, and give students feedback while they were in the process of writing rather than at the end of that process. It is also important to note that, even as they advised teachers as to the "when" of written feedback, these scholars expressed doubt as to its usefulness, touting instead alternative forms of response such as teacher–student writing conferences and peer response groups. Significantly, in a recently published essay on "Options for Responding to Student Writing," Elbow (1999) observed that "Writing comments is a dubious and difficult enterprise" and that his suggestions "in the end are least likely to waste our time or to cause harm" (p. 201)—hardly a ringing endorsement for the efficacy of written teacher comments!

In contrast to these discouraging assessments (and others that followed in the 1980s) is the empirical and practical work of the 1990s, most notably by Straub (1996, 1997, 1999; Straub & Lunsford, 1995), which suggests that "students read and make use of teacher comments and that well-designed teacher comments can

help students develop as writers" (Straub, 1997, p. 92). Over the past several decades, an entire vocabulary for talking about teacher response has developed, for instance the distinction between "directive" and "facilitative" teacher comments
(Knoblauch & Brannon, 1984; Straub, 1996, 1997), the issue of control and "appropriation" of student texts by their teachers (Brannon & Knoblauch, 1982;
Sommers, 1982), and distinctions between "teacherly" and "reader response" comments (e.g., Straub & Lunsford, 1995).

In this chapter, I review the most important stages in the history of L1 scholarship
on response to student writing—focusing primarily on written commentary by teachers, which is still "the most widely practiced and most traditional form of response"
(Straub & Lunsford, 1995, p. 1), but also touching on error correction and peer feedback. I then trace the effects of this theoretical and empirical work on the teaching of
writing to L2 students, which exposes another debate—between those who embrace
the findings of L1 research and find them largely applicable to and appropriate for L2
writers (e.g., Zamel, 1987) and those who argue that L2 writers are distinct enough
that pedagogical practices designed for native speakers need to, at minimum, be
closely reexamined before being adopted in L2 settings (Leki, 1990a; Silva, 1988,
1993, 1997; Zhang, 1995). The chapter closes with a summary of the state of the
art—of L1 praxis and its influence on L2 writing instruction, noting the recent convergence of lines of research on response in L1 and L2 writing (e.g., Ferris, Pezone,
Tade, & Tinti, 1997, and Straub & Lunsford, 1995; Ferris, 1995b; Hedgcock &
Lefkowitz, 1994, and Straub, 1997; Patthey-Chavez & Ferris, 1997; Goldstein &
Conrad, 1990, and Newkirk, 1995). This review in turn frames the detailed syntheses
and analyses of L2 research on these topics that appear in subsequent chapters.

TEACHERS' WRITTEN COMMENTARY
AND THE BAD NEWS 80s

In the early-to-mid 1980s, several studies and reviews of research appeared that,
taken as a whole, provided a dismal picture indeed of the state-of-the-art in teacher
commentary. By that point, scholars had been writing for more than a decade about
importance of focusing on writing as a *process* rather than a fixed final product,
with specific implications and applications including the use of multiple-drafting
cycles that emphasized substantive revision and teacher feedback that took place
between drafts rather than only after the final draft had been submitted. It could
have been hoped that as more enlightened pedagogical practices took hold in composition classrooms, subsequent research would have found increased benefits for
teacher feedback on student writing. The scholarship of the early 1980s, however,
yielded no such good news. A now-famous research review by Knoblauch and
Brannon (1981) began with the following "morose" generalization: "Different
types of teacher comments on student themes have equally small influences on student writing. For all practical purposes, commenting on student essays might just
be an exercise in futility" (Marzano & Arthur, 1977, quoted in Knoblauch &
Brannon, 1981, p. 1). The authors went on to outline three implications of previous
research on the effects of teacher commentary: "(1) students often do not comprehend teacher responses to their writing; (2) even when they do, they do not always

use those responses and may not know how to use them; (3) when they use them, they do not necessarily write more effectively as a result" (1981, p. 1).

It is important to note, however, that Knoblauch and Brannon's review does not necessarily reflect research on the best pedagogical practices of the time. Of the 15 references given at the end of the article, 7 were written prior to 1970, most likely predating process pedagogy in any form; others appeared in the early-to-mid 1970s, again probably too early to assess the effects of changes in writing instruction. Further, only 2 of the 15 sources appeared in refereed publications; the remainder were unpublished doctoral dissertations or ERIC documents. With this in mind, it is somewhat astonishing that this piece has been cited as being so authoritative on the "state-of-the-art" of teacher commentary.

Nonetheless, Knoblauch and Brannon (1981) made several observations in their review that have stood the test of time and that proved to be influential in subsequent thinking and research about teacher commentary and its effects. First, despite their grim conclusions about previous empirical work, they argued for continuing the practice of teacher commentary: "responding supportively to student writing is indeed central to enlightened instruction, *despite the apparent weight of evidence to the contrary*" (p. 1, emphasis mine). They observed that previous research has failed to consider two important related issues: (a) that specific teacher comments written on student papers cannot be isolated from "the larger conversation between teacher and student" (p. 1), and (b) that if teacher commentary is proven to be ineffective, the fault may lay with the larger context of classroom instruction rather than with the feedback itself. They concluded by calling for more enlightened research methodologies that do not merely consider the formal characteristics of teacher commentary (e.g., short vs. long comments, marginal notes vs. end notes) but that situate the commentary within the larger classroom context and the ongoing dialogue between teachers and students, of which a single comment or set of comments on a paper provides only a brief glimpse. Knoblauch and Brannon's call for contextualized research on teacher feedback has proven to be highly influential in both L1 and L2 response research over the past two decades (see, e.g, Sperling & Freedman, 1987, for L1; and Conrad & Goldstein, 1999, for L2).

Whereas Knoblauch and Brannon's 1981 review definitely set the tone for discussions of this topic, it was a pair of studies published in 1982 that established the new era of studying response in process-oriented, multiple-draft settings. Published as companion pieces in *College Composition and Communication*, articles by Sommers and by Brannon and Knoblauch stood as indictments of current teacher responding practices and introduced discussion of teacher control and "appropriation" of student texts to the discourse on response.

Sommers began by observing that providing written commentary on student papers "consumes the largest proportion of our time," averaging 20 to 40 minutes per student paper, yet "although commenting on student writing is the most widely used method for responding to student writing, it is the least understood" (1982, p. 148). Ostensibly, we comment for three purposes: (a) to let student writers know whether or not their texts have conveyed their intended meanings; (b) to help students become aware of the questions and concerns of an audience so that they can ultimately evaluate their own writing more effectively; and (c) to give students a motive for revision—for without feedback from other writers, novice writers will typically revise narrowly or not at all (Sommers, 1980).

To investigate the question of whether "teachers comment and students revise as the theory predicts they should" (1982, p. 149), Sommers, together with Brannon and Knoblauch, studied 35 university writing teachers. They examined comments that the teachers wrote on first and second drafts of student texts, interviewed a number of teachers and students, and asked their teacher subjects all to write comments on the same set of student papers. Sommers, contrasting a computerized analysis of one of the student papers with comments given by "live" teachers, characterized the teachers' feedback as "arbitrary and idiosyncratic," and hostile and mean-spirited (p. 149). She reported two major findings: (a) that "teachers' comments can take students' attention away from their own purposes in writing a particular text and focus that attention on the teachers' purpose in commenting" (p. 149); and (b) that "most teachers' comments are not text-specific and could be interchanged, rubber-stamped, from text to text" (p. 152). These two findings—that teachers "appropriate," or take over, students' texts with their feedback and that teacher comments are not text-specific—have had a major impact on subsequent theory, research, and pedagogy.

Sommers defined the problem of appropriation as follows: "Students make the changes the teacher wants rather than those that the student perceives are necessary, since the teachers' concerns imposed on the text create the reasons for the subsequent changes" (1982, pp. 149–150). Such appropriation, Sommers argued, is most likely to occur when teachers focus on errors on a first draft rather than on discovery and development of ideas, and when teacher comments fail to establish a hierarchy of importance of issues for revision. Figure 1.1 provides an example of a "response round" (Sperling & Freedman, 1987)—an excerpt from a student writer's first draft, the teacher's comments, and the same passage from the student's next draft.

In this paper (which is shown in its entirety in Appendix 6B with background information about the writer), the teacher's feedback throughout was focused intensely on getting the student writer, "Antonio," to change the content of his essay

---

First draft excerpt: I understand both of my cultures and this mekes me feel good about my self because I know what my identity is and I feel proud of who I am. Being a minority is like journey, is like a adventure, like story that at the begining you passed by a lot of obstacles but at the end there is a happy ending. Each one of my cultures have special things that I like and enjoy very much. For example the language that is spoken, traditions that each one has, believes, customs, and ideals. I wouldn't change any of this for nothing and I'm very happy with who I am.

Teacher's comment (in margin): *Make this fit your thesis!* → *negative effects.*

Revision excerpt: Being a minority for me is like a bad journey, or like a nightmare with out a ending or like a story that at the beginning you go thru a lot of obstacles. Each of my cultures have a special things that I like and enjoy very much. For example the language that is spoken, traditions that each one has, beliefs, customs, and ideals. I wouldn't change any of this for anything in the world.

FIG. 1.1.   Teacher appropriation in a response cycle.

to "fit his thesis": *Being a member of a minority group has effected me negatively because I being descrimineted so many times that I lost the count.* The rest of Antonio's first draft, in fact, demonstrated that he had experienced both positive and negative effects of being in a new culture, and the paper ended on a very positive note, as seen in the first draft excerpt in Fig. 1.1, which is the concluding paragraph. But rather than simply suggesting that Antonio rewrite his original thesis to express his real views about the topic, the teacher seemed "stuck" on the idea that the thesis statement was apparently set in concrete and that the entire rest of the essay should change. Her feedback in Fig. 1.1 reflects this, and we see the results in Antonio's revision of his conclusion. He obediently tries to change an upbeat, positive conclusion to a negative one, but with only minimal success: He changes the first sentence of the conclusion as the teacher suggests and leaves the rest of the paragraph upbeat. This results in a concluding paragraph that is arguably less effective and logical than the original, and indeed the same could be said for Antonio's entire revision. This response cycle provides a very pointed example of Sommers' claim that "teachers' comments can take students' attention away from their own purposes in writing a particular text and focus that attention on the teachers' purpose in commenting" (1982, p. 149)—instead of helping Antonio to continue unpacking his own views about being an immigrant, the teacher focused on the extremely narrow pedagogical goal of "making the essay match the thesis."

A second example of teacher appropriation is provided in Fig. 1.2. In this example, the teacher is very directive about making changes to entire phrases (he actually struck out the student's original text and wrote in the changes), which may or may not have truly reflected the student writer's original intent. This excerpt, in my view, crosses the line between correcting *errors* and making *stylistic changes*—for instance, the teacher, a native speaker of English, may well have felt that "a *better* future" sounded more idiomatic than "a *more appropriate* future," but the student's version was not grammatically or lexically incorrect, and the teacher might have left the wording there to the writer's discretion. Besides being overly directive, this teacher's emphasis on making such discrete corrections and changes undoubtedly communicated to the student that the *content* of the text was fine, and if the writer merely transcribed the changes the teacher had made, the paper would be ideal. Again, this is a clear example of Sommers' point that a premature focus on word- and sentence-level issues can confuse or misdirect a student writer.

The second major finding discussed by Sommers was that teacher comments were largely generic, rather than text-specific. In Ferris et al. (1997), we attempted to operationalize this factor by defining "text-specific" as "comments which could

---

Student's Original Text: To [immigrants] this country is the place to seek for a more appropriate future not only for them but also for the next generation. But with all this modern conveniences can an immigrant be truly happy in America?

Teacher's Rewrite: To [immigrants] this country is the place to seek a better future not only for them, but also for the next generation. But in spite of their new life, can an immigrant be truly happy in America?

FIG. 1.2.   Teacher appropriation at the word sentence level.

only have been written on this particular essay, versus 'generic' comments which could have appeared on any student paper" (p. 167). An example of a text-specific comment from that sample was the following: "You also need to explain and illustrate the 'hard-to-discover' stumbling blocks that you mention"; and a "generic comment" is illustrated by the following: "Please spell-check and proofread your papers before you give them to me" (p. 167).

The problem with such generic feedback, according to Sommers, is that it often takes the form of "vague directives" and "abstract commands." She observed that "the teacher holds a license for vagueness while the student is commanded to be specific" (1982, p.153). This inconsistency (or even hypocrisy) is not missed by students, according to Straub's (1997) study on student reactions to different types of teacher feedback. So not only is the feedback itself confusing and unhelpful, but it can actually lead to student resentment because the teacher is preaching specificity but definitely not practicing it.

Most significantly, Sommers claimed that teachers who appropriate student texts and who use vague generalities to respond to them "are formulating their comments as if these drafts were finished drafts and not going to be revised. Their commenting vocabularies have not been adapted to revision and they comment on first drafts as if they were justifying a grade or as if the first draft were the final draft" (1982, p. 154). In short, despite the pedagogical shift to multiple-drafting and to between-draft feedback by teachers, the instructors in Sommers' study had not adapted the substance or form of their comments to be formative rather than summative (Moxley, 1989). Sommers concluded that "we need to sabotage our students' conviction that the drafts they have written are complete and coherent. Our comments need to offer students revision tasks of a different order of complexity and sophistication ... by forcing students back into the chaos, back to the point where they are shaping and restructuring their meaning" (1982, p. 154). Specific suggestions offered by Sommers include giving different levels of response to different student drafts (e.g., focusing on ideas and clarity in first drafts rather than correcting errors) and complementing written feedback with in-class activities on revision.

Writing in the same issue of *College Composition and Communication*, Brannon and Knoblauch (1982) used the findings from the research on which they collaborated with Sommers to argue that students have "rights to their own texts." In particular, they claimed that when teachers appropriate student texts as described by Sommers, they remove students' motivation and incentive to write, because the student is now revising merely to satisfy the teacher rather than to express and develop his or her own ideas. They provided a detailed discussion of a particular student paper in which the writer pretended to be making a summation to the jury in the Lindbergh kidnapping trial. A number of the teachers in their study critiqued the paper because of its "blatant use of emotional appeal" (p. 160), not realizing that in transcripts of the actual trial, the real-life prosecutor successfully utilized a similar strategy! The problem, Brannon and Knoblauch argued, is that the teachers were imposing their view of the "Ideal Text"—one that used logical, linear, rational arguments rather than emotional, descriptive language—on the student writer's communicative purposes.

The key point made by Brannon and Knoblauch is not that students' texts are always authoritative or even acceptable in their purest forms. Rather, it is that when teachers wrest control of the text away from student writers, they remove the students' investment, engagement, motivation, and interest in writing. This affective consequence, in the authors' view, is ultimately far more harmful to students' development as writers than any weaknesses left "untreated" in their texts could ever be: "we lose more than we gain by preempting their control and allowing our own Ideal Texts to dictate choices that properly belong to the writers" (1982, p. 159). Although, like Sommers, the authors offered several concrete suggestions about how teacher response and student revision could proceed more effectively, Brannon and Knoblauch were fundamentally arguing for a change in teacher *attitude*—for a letting-go of the notion that instructors' versions of the Ideal Text are more authoritative and more important than the students' own ideas and communicative purposes—and especially that keeping students motivated and engaged in the process of writing is far more important than the shape and outcome of a particular written text.

In examining the research, scholarship, and suggestions for pedagogy that have been produced by L1 and L2 composition experts in the years since the publication of these two articles in 1982, it would be difficult to overstate their impact. Differences among scholars about the role and nature of teacher feedback continue to be discussed to this day (see, e.g., Straub, 1996, and Straub & Lunsford, 1995). The views of Sommers, Brannon, and Knoblauch as laid out in these twin articles about teacher appropriation and student control have shaped teacher training and pedagogy in substantial ways. For instance, since the mid-1980s, most U.S. composition teachers have been trained to give feedback on content on first drafts and save responses about grammar, word choice, or mechanics for the penultimate draft (following Sommers) and to avoid "teacherly" responses by asking questions rather than issuing directives (following Brannon and Knoblauch). Whether these prescriptions are always necessary or even appropriate, especially in the case of L2 writers, has also been a subject of some debate, particularly in the 1990s. These issues are discussed further later in this chapter as well as in subsequent ones.

While acknowledging the importance and the value of these two articles, it is also necessary to consider two major limitations, one methodological and one philosophical. As to methodology, though it appears that Sommers, Brannon, and Knoblauch collected an impressive amount of data that was well triangulated, their methods of analysis and their results are unfortunately reported in very imprecise terms. Readers are provided only with the authors' statements of their major findings, conclusions, or implications, not with any empirically grounded models of analysis or quantitative presentations of their results. For example, when Sommers said that "most" of the teachers' feedback was arbitrary, idiosyncratic, hostile, and mean-spirited, we have no empirical evidence about how she arrived at that conclusion. We are left to wonder uncomfortably whether the sweeping statements that have been so influential were really based on reality or on the authors' subjective impressions (perhaps colored by pre-existing biases) about their data.

Even if we were to give the authors the benefit of the doubt as to their methodology and the accuracy of their results, the philosophical assumption on which their arguments are based is also possibly problematic: That student writers in a composition class are really primarily motivated by the need to communicate or express their ideas and that teacher feedback that is overly directive can truly "remove the incentive to write and the motivation to improve skills" (Brannon & Knoblauch, 1982, p. 165). Many teachers would argue that this represents an overly idealized and romanticized view of the student writer, who after all has most likely been required to take the writing course against his or her will and whose primary motivations may well be to achieve a good grade and to learn to write successfully for other college courses. If the latter view is more often the case for many student writers, this would provide the basis for an argument that is nearly the opposite of that advanced by Brannon and Knoblauch: That the teacher, as gatekeeper of success in academic writing, should do everything possible both in the classroom and through written commentary to inculcate the vision of the Ideal (academic) Text in the student writer and to be clear and even directive as to ways in which student papers fall short of this ideal. Whereas there is most likely truth to be found at both extremes, Brannon and Knoblauch's insistence that student intentions and motivations should always be more important than whether the finished product is successful, is certainly one that requires close scrutiny and reflection—and most teachers would probably opt for a compromise position and attempt to construct feedback that informs and instructs while leaving ultimate choice and authority as to how to utilize feedback in the hands of the student writer.

Though a number of other studies and reviews followed this pair of articles, one in particular is worth discussing because it has also been very influential in the literature and because it raises several important philosophical issues in considering teacher response to student writing. An article written by Sperling and Freedman and entitled "A Good Girl Writes Like a Good Girl," published in 1987 in *Written Communication,* provides an in-depth case study of a high school student, a good writer and "a good girl," in what appears to be the ideal composition classroom taught by an enlightened and conscientious teacher. Despite these optimal circumstances, the authors provided evidence of many miscommunications between the teacher and student and instances in which the student's revisions failed to address the issues raised in the teacher's written comments. Sperling and Freedman concluded that these missteps stem from two major problems. First, the student writer, "Lisa," is unsuccessful in addressing teacher feedback in revision when the comments refer to issues that have not been covered in classroom presentations. For example, in several rounds of feedback on one of Lisa's papers, the teacher gives indirect feedback that he wants Lisa to rewrite a sentence containing a cliché ("grinning from ear to ear") although he had never discussed avoidance of clichés in class. In other words, the teacher makes assumptions that Lisa will understand the feedback even though he has no firsthand basis for these beliefs. This finding suggests that teachers should take care, as they construct written commentary, to give feedback on issues that have been explicitly covered in their class sessions or to find out at the beginning of the term (perhaps by means of a questionnaire or writing sample) what students already know about composition and rhetoric. Even then, it is probably better to be as clear as possible in explaining the problem to the student. (In this instance, the teacher circled the offending phrase and wrote "Another way to say this?" Lisa never did eliminate the cliché, despite several more rounds of feedback and revision.)

Second, there is a mismatch between the teacher's and the student's values regarding teacher feedback and its effects on revision. Whereas "Mr. Peterson" feels that "writing well has to do with developing a personal voice," and that compliance with what *he* wants does not necessarily produce good writing (Sperling & Freedman, 1987, p. 358), Lisa feels that her teacher's comments "reflect his wiser perspective on writing, and for this reason a student would do well to accept them—'always'" (p. 356). Lisa, in fact, believes that learning to "write for other people"—specifically, different teachers every semester—is an important adaptive strategy for student writers (see discussion, pp. 357–358).

Although Sperling and Freedman's article profiles only one teacher interacting with one student, any experienced writing teacher will recognize "Lisa," the "good girl" who is more interested in being compliant and earning a good grade than with standing up for her own ideas even if it potentially means defying the teacher. This paper suggests that some, if not most, writing students attempt to figure out, from the teacher's commentary, what the teacher wants and what they have to do in order to please the teacher, earn a good grade, and succeed in the class. This observation implies that, as noted by Straub some years later (1996), *any* form of teacher feedback can be seen as being "directive" and exerting "control" simply because it comes from the teacher, the final authority as to success and grades. In response to this awareness, teachers can either bend over backward to be as "nondirective" as humanly possible (see, e.g., Straub's 1996 analysis of four composition experts responding to the same paper and demonstrating varying degrees of directiveness, with Elbow's response clearly being the least so) or they can accept the inevitable—that their feedback *will* influence the student's subsequent choices and attempt to make that feedback as respectful, clear, and helpful as they can.

Following the observations gleaned from these reviews and primary research studies, several experts in the latter half of the 1980s offered practical suggestions based on the research as to how to make written commentary both less onerous and more effective. In Hairston's (1986) often-cited book chapter "On Not Being a Composition Slave," she argued that providing excessive amounts of feedback is ultimately harmful to both teachers and students. For teachers, it inevitably leads to burnout, frustration, and resentment. For students, it leads to "cognitive overload" and (psychologically) "defensive barriers" (pp. 120–121). She then provided a list of ideas as to how to make feedback less burdensome for teachers and more helpful for students. Moxley (1989) reviewed the scholarship produced in the 1980s and provided a list of suggestions about written commentary. (The lists given by Hairston and by Moxley are shown in Fig. 1.3.) However, Moxley then went on to argue that audiotaped feedback is preferable to written commentary anyway, and spent the bulk of his paper talking about specific practical mechanisms for audiotaping commentary (see also Anson, 1999). At any rate, the two lists provided in Fig. 1.3 provide a fairly comprehensive summary of the thinking about teacher commentary at the end of a decade of significant activity on this topic.

Adapted from Hairston (1986)	Adapted from Moxley (1989)
1. Read a paper through first without marking anything.	1. Provide "formative" rather than "summative" evaluations.
2. Create a supportive environment in the classroom by using journals and free-writing, sharing your own writing, and duplicating good student writing.	2. Require multiple drafting.
	3. Use peer response groups, training students to evaluate each other's work.
3. Use multiple-drafting and make facilitative comments that deal with one major issue rather than every single error.	4. Avoid appropriating students' texts through commentary.
4. Utilize peer response groups at various stages of the writing process.	5. Role-play the students' intended audience.
5. Prioritize error marking and mark only a limited number of the most serious types.	6. Encourage students to do substantive revision, not mere copy-editing (or "punishment for not getting it right the first time").
6. Give students in-class opportunities to write and revise their papers after receiving feedback.	7. Identify only one or two patterns of error at a time.
7. Give in-class instruction on how to revise.	8. Praise positive attributes in each paper.
	9. Avoid vague, formulaic, abbreviated commentary.
8. Limit written response as follows: (a) mark a few important errors; (b) note several things the student has done well; and (c) suggest one major change.	10. Omit grades on individual papers, opting instead for portfolio assessment.

FIG. 1.3.   Suggestions for pedagogy from 1980s scholarship. (Sources: Hairston, 1986, pp. 122–123; and Moxley, 1989, p. 3).

To summarize, the work of composition scholars in the "Bad News 80s" yielded insights and findings still extremely influential in both L1 and L2 writing today:

- Teacher commentary in the past, focused as it was on errors and justifying grades, was dismally ineffective in helping student writers to improve (Knoblauch & Brannon, 1981).
- Investigations of teacher commentary and its effects need to be considered in the light of the larger classroom context and particularly the ongoing conversation between teacher and students (Knoblauch & Brannon, 1981).

- Teacher feedback can appropriate or excessively control student writing when it mixes commentary on content and error on the same draft and when the teacher uses it to convey the notion of the "Ideal Text" rather than to work with student writers to find out what *they* want to say (Brannon & Knoblauch, 1982; Sommers, 1982).
- Teacher feedback can often devolve to vague directives rather than text-specific commentary (Sommers, 1982).
- Teacher commentary can demotivate students when it is excessively controlling (Brannon & Knoblauch, 1982).
- Students will often value complying with the teacher's wishes, as conveyed through written feedback, over standing up for their "rights to their own texts" (Sperling & Freedman, 1987).
- Teacher feedback may fail to communicate effectively with students if it does not reference issues that have also been covered in classroom instruction (Sperling & Freedman, 1987).
- For their own sakes as well as their students', teachers need to take practical steps to avoid becoming "composition slaves" (Hairston, 1986).
- Teachers should consider a range of feedback alternatives, including peer response, conferencing, and audiotaped feedback (see all sources cited in this section).

FINDING MIDDLE GROUND:
RESEARCH IN THE 1990s

Though clearly influenced by and respectful toward the powerful paradigms that emerged from 1980s research, L1 composition researchers in the 1990s moved toward more empirically grounded descriptions of teacher commentary and consequently a more balanced view of teacher responsibility and student ownership in the response and revision cycle. For instance, studies by Beason (1993) and Sperling (1994), both published in *Research in the Teaching of English,* utilized clear analytic frameworks to discuss characteristics of teacher feedback. Beason developed two different frameworks to examine teacher feedback (1993, pp. 405–406, Tables 1–2), one which identified "aims" of the comments ("Detected Problem," "Advised," "Praised," etc.) and the focus of the feedback ("Focus," "Development and Support," "Organization," "Mechanics," etc.). Sperling focused instead on the teacher-readers' "orientations" to the students' texts as they responded, identifying five different stances the teachers took: Interpretative, Social, Cognitive/Emotive, Evaluative, and Pedagogical (1994, pp. 181–185). In both cases, the researchers not only described the teacher commentary, but related it to the students' actions and to the larger classroom contexts.

These two studies serve as a backdrop for the substantial work produced by Straub and colleagues during the latter half of the 1990s (Straub, 1996, 1997, 1999; Straub & Lunsford, 1995). Straub and Lunsford (1995), in their landmark work *Twelve Readers Reading,* describe an ambitious and creative project in which they enlisted the assistance of 12 composition scholars, all of whom responded in writing to 12 student essays and provided other written materials, including statements about their composition teaching philosophies. As a group, the readers produced 3,500 comments on 156 sets of student papers. The researchers analyzed the written comments by means of a two-part analysis system that included the "focus" and "mode" of the comments (see Fig. 1.4). They moved from the quantitative results of this analysis to a more qualitative description of the different readers' response styles: authoritarian, directive, advisory, Socratic, dialectic, and analytical, which ranged on a continuum from "authoritative" to "interactive," or, to use Knoblauch and Brannon's earlier (1984) framework, "Directive" to "Facilitative" commentary. The purpose of these descriptive analyses was not to judge or criticize any one of the readers or their styles but simply to observe the range of options available to teachers and used by composition experts considered to be enlightened leaders in the field.

Straub followed up this large-scale analysis with several articles dealing with specific issues raised by this study. In the first (Straub, 1996), he examined the issue of teacher control, looking at four of his readers' responses to the same student paper, and analyzing how the various responders ranged from more to less directive in their commentary. Though the four readers' choices were clearly distinct along the directive→facilitative continuum, Straub observed that in all cases, the readers showed respect for the student writer and left revision choices in her hands. He further argued that even in the least directive response, that provided by Peter Elbow,

Focus	Mode
Global	Corrections
Ideas	Evaluations
Development	Qualified Negative Evaluations
Global Structure	Imperatives
Local	Advice
Local Structure	Praise
Wording	Indirect Requests
Correctness	Problem-Posing Questions
	Heuristic Questions
	Reflective Statements
Extra-Textual Comments	

FIG. 1.4.   Categories used in Straub and Lunsford's analysis. (From Straub & Lunsford, 1995, p. 159, Table 3.1).

the very fact that the teacher is responding *at all* exerts at least some measure of control over the student writer. Straub did not take a position on whether any of the four responses is more or less helpful or appropriate or even on whether teacher control is a bad thing—he merely observed that teacher control is always there when teachers provide written commentary and that this control may be realized in a range of ways as to degree and form.

In a 1997 article, Straub extended his analysis by surveying college student writers about their reactions to the various categories of comments he had operationalized in the 1995 study. In general, he found that students preferred comments that were clear, elaborate, and text-specific, and that they did not mind feedback that pointed out problems as long as it also provided explanations and suggested solutions. They welcomed and appreciated praise but did not like teacher commentary that appeared harsh, negative, or authoritarian. In summary, the subjects "preferred comments that offered some direction for improvement but asserted only moderate control over the writing" (1997, p. 112). Thus, Straub's findings support the findings of earlier researchers who criticized teacher commentary as harsh and arbitrary (Sommers, 1982). However, the reactions of his student subjects do not appear to agree with Brannon and Knoblauch's strong argument (Brannon & Knoblauch, 1982; Knoblauch & Brannon, 1984) that directive teacher commentary discourages students and causes them to lose interest in their writing. Rather, the student writers did not seem to mind teacher suggestions as long as they were helpful and framed positively and respectfully.

SUMMARY: L1 WRITTEN RESPONSE
IN THE 21ST CENTURY

In a collection published by Straub in 1999 (*A Sourcebook for Responding to Student Writing*), the still-ambivalent feelings of L1 composition experts at the end of the millennium is captured quite clearly. In the first half of the volume, Straub provided additional sets of written responses to student papers from his 1995 study (*Twelve Readers Reading*) both for pre-service and in-service teachers to examine and to further illustrate the range of responding styles and options utilized by experts and available to teachers. In the second half of the book, nine reprinted or original pieces by scholars on response to student writing are presented, including the previously discussed papers by Sommers (1982), Brannon and Knoblauch (1982), and Straub (1996). This volume demonstrates the range of opinions that coexist on written response to student writing. Of the nine articles, for instance, two are written by Peter Elbow, who simultaneously made specific suggestions about how to respond most effectively to student writing and characterized it as "a dubious and difficult enterprise" (Elbow, 1999, p. 200). In contrast, Straub's article and one by White clearly present written response as an effective means of communicating with and instructing student writers (at least under certain conditions). Whereas Sommers, Brannon, and Knoblauch warned teachers against appropriating student writing by imposing through their written commentary their notion of the Ideal Text, White in contrast enthusiastically endorsed the use of scoring guides in response as a way to show students the criteria and standards they are expected to meet. One extreme argues that student engagement and motivation should be the primary guiding principle of teacher response; the other says that making external institutional criteria explicit to student writers is a worthy technique and goal. Clearly, in the area of written response, reasonable people can and do disagree.

In my view, a fundamental question is raised by Sperling and Freedman's (1987) article "A Good Girl Writes Like a Good Girl." If teachers give students written feedback on their writing, especially at intermediate stages of the writing process, students are more likely than not to pay attention to it and try to utilize it in subsequent revisions of their texts. In fact, it seems probable that they will in most cases be more interested in pleasing the teacher and meeting external standards than in defending their "rights to their own texts." If this observation is true for many, if not most, students, the question is whether this teacher influence is a good or harmful thing for student writers. If, as Sommers, Brannon, and Knoblauch argued, teacher appropriation through written commentary causes students to lose motivation and interest in their writing, then even the most nondirective forms of teacher response may be potentially harmful—because coming as they do *from the teacher*, they have instant ascribed authority. On the other hand, if students are primarily interested in succeeding in the writing course and in developing skills in academic writing that will help them in the future, teacher feedback that provides clear assistance to them in meeting those goals will indeed motivate and encourage them in their writing (as indicated by the subjects in Straub's 1997 study as well as earlier studies of student reaction to teacher commentary). In short, because the teacher *is* the teacher, any feedback is likely to influence what students do subsequently—and experts disagree as to whether this influence is ultimately helpful or harmful.

OTHER ISSUES IN RESPONSE: ERROR CORRECTION AND PEER FEEDBACK

In the course of discussing the effects of teacher commentary on student writing, two other issues arise: The efficacy of error correction and the benefits of peer response groups. The early reviewers and researchers of the 1980s justly criticize teacher commentary for being primarily an error hunt, claiming that premature and excessive focus on errors is confusing and demoralizing to students. It is confusing because teachers would often mix corrections of word choice, punctuation, sentence structure, or style with substantive questions or comments about the content of the text. Why, researchers argue, should students correct errors in passages of text that may be substantively revised, anyway? And given that making local surface corrections is easier than rethinking one's entire argument, if students are provided with both types of feedback, they may act on the easier issues and ignore the more substantive, but more important ones (Faigley & Witte, 1981; Sommers, 1980).

For this reason, most process-oriented scholars urge teachers to save feedback on errors or other local issues for the very end of the writing process—for the editing phase that takes place as the student polishes his or her final draft. In addition, they suggest that teachers be selective in error correction, choosing only one of two of the most important error types for feedback so that students will not be overwhelmed cognitively or emotionally (Hairston, 1986; Moxley, 1989). In addition, it is suggested that error feedback and related grammar instruction be limited (through the use of brief, well-focused mini-lessons) and carefully contextualized (related directly to students' own writing rather than in isolation) (Atwell, 1998; Weaver, 1996). In general, L1 composition experts seem dubious about the efficacy of grammar instruction and error feedback under even the best of circumstances, and argue that concerns with correctness should receive minimal amounts of attention in the classroom and in teacher feedback.

In contrast, nearly all of the scholars discussed in this chapter who express doubts or concerns about teacher feedback simultaneously voice enthusiasm for the use of peer response groups in the writing class. It is suggested that peer feedback offers student writers a more varied and authentic audience than simply writing for the teacher, that careful reading and evaluation of peers' texts builds critical thinking skills that can help students to better assess their own writing, that students will feel less threatened by and resentful of feedback given by peers than by the teacher, and that peer response groups will lighten the teacher's "composition slave" responding load. The differences among scholars in their views of teacher feedback (if we must do it, let's figure out how we can avoid wasting time and doing harm—Elbow, 1999) and their praise of peer feedback are quite striking. As we see later, this nearly unqualified endorsement of peer feedback has had tremendous influence in L2 pedagogy and research.

Thus, as we turn to the examination of teacher commentary, error correction, and peer response in L2 writing, we can trace the following influences from L1 commentary:

- Debate over whether the highest value in written teacher commentary is to be "nonappropriative" or to be explicit and detailed in offering suggestions for revision.
- Consensus as to the limited role and efficacy of error correction.
- Enthusiasm about the benefits of peer response, especially compared with teacher commentary.

In the final section of this chapter, we examine the effects of this scholarly base on L2 pedagogy to date.

THE INFLUENCE OF L1 RESPONSE RESEARCH ON L2 WRITING

It is easy to trace the major effects of L1 composition scholarship on research and teaching in L2 writing. Even today, if one examines research papers on issues related to L2 writing and response, one will often find that a substantial percentage of the items in the reference list come from L1 sources. As L2 writing research becomes more extensive and varied in its own right, this is becoming less and less true, but at this point in time, L2 writing as a separate area of inquiry is still in the early stages.

Zamel (especially 1985, 1987) is one of the most articulate advocates for allowing the insights of L1 research to guide research and pedagogy in L2 writing. For instance, in her influential articles on using the process approach with ESL students and on response to student writing (Zamel, 1982, 1983, 1985), she argued, like Sommers (1982), that ESL writing teachers need to have students write multiple drafts, to give feedback at intermediate stages of the writing process, to give feedback on content only on early drafts, saving form-based feedback for the end of the process, and to utilize teacher–student conferences and peer response. As to error correction and grammar instruction in the L2 writing context, experts have argued that its role should be severely limited (e.g., Krashen, 1984; Zamel, 1985) or even nonexistent (Truscott, 1996, 1999) both because it is ineffective and because it is harmful in that it diverts teacher and student energy and attention away from more important writing issues.

L1 scholarship has also been extremely important in the adoption of peer response groups for L2 writing classes. Whereas there has been relatively little empirical research on teacher feedback on ESL writing, there has been a great deal of work done on the nature and effects of peer feedback in L2 settings (for reviews, see chap. 4 of this volume; Ferris & Hedgcock, 1998.) In addition, various suggestions have been offered as to how to implement peer response successfully (e.g., chap. 8 of this volume; Ferris & Hedgcock, 1998; Mittan, 1989). However, as is discussed later and at length in chapter 4, there has been considerable backlash among L2 scholars as to the appropriateness of peer feedback in L2 writing classes.

Although some L2 experts have argued that L2 writers fundamentally need the same types of instruction as L1 students except that they need "more of everything" (e.g., Raimes, 1985; Spack, 1988; Zamel, 1987), others have claimed that L2 writers are so different from native speakers that every pedagogical technique advanced by L1 composition research needs to be carefully reconsidered as to its appropriateness for L2 students. Early *TESOL Quarterly* essays by Eskey (1983) and Horowitz (1986) pointed out that ESL writers have very real needs to succeed in L2 academic settings and that process approaches that did not deal with L2 writers' linguistic gaps and that ignored their need to learn to write for the L2 academic discourse community could ultimately be "cruelly unfair to diverse students" (Johns, 1995, p. 182). In a series of articles, Silva (1988, 1993, 1997) also challenged the implicit assumption that L1 and L2 student writers are fundamentally the same. In the earliest piece, a response to a 1987 research review by Zamel, Silva quoted Raimes (1985, p. 232) in saying that "most ESL teachers ... sense that the process of writing in an L2 is startlingly different from writing in our L1," and went on to argue that "Although there is certainly much to be learned from developments in L1 composition theory, research, and practice, it seems wise to interpret these lessons very carefully into L2 writing contexts" (Silva, 1988, p. 517). In his 1993 article, Silva reviewed 72 L2 writing studies, concluding that there are "a number of salient differences between L1 and L2 writing with regard to both composing processes ... and features of written texts" (p. 657). Finally, in a piece entitled "On the Ethical Treatment of ESL Writers," Silva (1997) argued that because of the fundamentally distinct nature of L2 writing, "respect" for ESL student writers requires that they be (a) understood, (b) placed in suitable learning contexts, (c) provided with appropriate instruction, and (d) evaluated fairly (p. 359).

Authors of individual studies have also argued that various aspects of ESL writing instruction, particularly those related to response, need to be considered separately from the findings and recommendations of L1 researchers. For instance,

Goldstein and Conrad (1990) pointed out that cross-cultural differences in expectations about teacher–student relationships may affect the nature and outcomes of one-to-one writing conferences. Similarly, several researchers have suggested that differing cultural expectations may influence L2 students' reactions to peer response groups (e.g., Allaei & Connor, 1990; Carson, 1992; Zhang, 1995). As to teacher commentary and error correction, it has been argued that L2 writers are able to simultaneously cope with feedback on both language and content (Fathman & Whalley, 1990; Ferris, 1995b, 1997) and in fact that postponing error feedback until the end of the writing process may deprive L2 writers, who have linguistic deficits more extensive and serious than those of their L1 counterparts, of input they desperately need. It has also been suggested that L2 writers are not offended by teacher criticisms of their writing, even commentary that L1 scholars would call "appropriative." Because L2 students may not be as sensitive to pragmatic distinctions between, for instance, imperatives and indirect requests, they may not be as resentful of a directive tone as L1 student writers might be, and in fact, they might understand more directive feedback better than indirect or hedged commentary (Conrad & Goldstein, 1999; Ferris, 1997; Patthey-Chavez & Ferris, 1997).

WHERE ARE WE NOW? THE CONVERGENCE OF L1 AND L2 RESPONSE RESEARCH

As L2 composition research has rapidly evolved over the past decade, it has been interesting to observe that both L1 and L2 composition scholarship have traveled some similar paths. For example, both L1 and L2 writing researchers began to develop analytic models for examining teacher commentary, arriving at many similar descriptive categories, albeit with different labels. Figure 1.5 shows the correspondences between the L1 analysis model developed by Straub and Lunsford (1995) and the L2 framework created by Ferris et al. (1997). Research on student reactions to teacher feedback also yielded similar trends with L1 and L2 students. For instance, in L2 studies by Ferris (1995b) and Hedgcock and Lefkowitz (1994), it was found that students valued feedback on all aspects of their writing, that they struggled with vague, cryptic comments and/or symbols or abbreviations, and that they appreciated both praise and constructive criticism, conclusions very similar to those of Straub (1997), who surveyed L1 students.

L1 and L2 research in the 1990s on teacher–student writing conferences also yielded independent but similar warnings that conferencing might not yield its presumed benefits without careful planning and preparation (e.g., Goldstein & Conrad, 1990; Newkirk, 1995; Patthey-Chavez & Ferris, 1997; Sperling, 1991). Finally, both L1 and L2 experts are beginning to ask questions about both the uncritical acceptance of peer response groups and the neglect of linguistic accuracy, asking whether we have jumped on the peer feedback bandwagon and off the error correction bandwagon too quickly.

Because of these recent convergences, in a sense L1 and L2 writing research has come full circle—from an implicit view that whatever was good for L1 writers was automatically good for L2 writers, to rejection of that blanket presumption by many L2 scholars, to some newly shared paradigms and concerns about various respond-

Categories Used in Straub and Lunsford (1995)	Corresponding Categories in Ferris, Pezone, Tade, and Tinti (1997)
Negative evaluations	Give information
Qualified negative evaluations	Hedges
Praise	Positive comment
Imperatives	Imperatives
Advice	Make suggestion or request in statement form
Indirect request	Make suggestion or request in question form
Heuristic questions—closed	Ask for information
Heuristic questions—open	Ask for information
Reflective statements	Give information
Corrections/conventions	Grammar/mechanics comments

FIG. 1.5.   Similarities between L1 and L2 analytic models for teacher commentary.

ing issues and techniques. It is unfortunate, however, that L1 and L2 scholarship on writing and response seem to exist in virtual isolation (see Silva, Leki, & Carson, 1997, for an excellent discussion of this issue). For instance, in Straub's recent (1999) "sourcebook," response issues related to diverse students are not even mentioned, and no L2 sources are included either in the compilation of articles or in the selected bibliography. Whereas L2 scholars tend to be more aware of L1 composition research than vice versa, as L2 research increases, it will also be tempting for researchers to read only L2 studies published in journals such as *Language Learning, TESOL Quarterly*, or *Journal of Second Language Writing*. This trend, should it materialize, would be unfortunate. L1 composition research is several decades ahead of the L2 research base, and we have much to learn from the strengths, weaknesses, successes, and missteps of our L1 composition colleagues.

<table>
<tr><td>

CHAPTER

2

</td><td>

Teacher Feedback
on
L2 Student Writing

</td></tr>
</table>

Writing instructors and researchers appear to have a love–hate relationship with the issue of teacher feedback on student writing. As discussed in chapter 1, for several decades, both L1 and L2 scholars made extremely negative pronouncements about the nature and effects of teacher response, especially instructors' written commentary. Research reviews by Hillocks (1986), Knoblauch and Brannon (1981), and Leki (1990a) suggested that regardless of how written teacher feedback was delivered, there was no evidence that it was successful in helping students to progress as writers. Nonetheless, as noted by Ferris and Hedgcock (1998), Hairston (1986), and Leki (1990a), composition instructors invest a great deal of time in annotating student papers with their feedback:

> Writing teachers and students alike do intuit that written responses can have a great effect on student writing and attitude toward writing.... Written comments are time consuming, but teachers continue to write comments on student papers because we sense that our comments help writers improve.... (Leki, 1990a, pp. 57–58).

The alternative to written feedback that is not only suggested but urged in the composition literature is one-to-one writing conferences between teachers and students (e.g., Atwell, 1998; Carnicelli, 1980; Elbow, 1973; Zamel, 1982, 1985). Proponents of the exclusive use of writing conferences point out the considerable advantages of immediacy, negotiation, and opportunity for clarification that are possible with this approach. They further point to the conclusions of research reviews mentioned earlier that written commentary by instructors is ineffective and can even be resented by student writers.

Despite these strongly held views by leaders in L1 and L2 composition research, written and oral teacher feedback continue to coexist in many, perhaps most, L1 and L2 composition classrooms. The reasons for the persistence of written commentary as a method of delivering feedback are both practical and philosophical. These justifications not only serve to explain why written feedback continues to be widely utilized but also to argue for its continued role in the composition classroom. Besides the two most basic options—written feedback and writing conferences—recent advances in technology have opened up other avenues for teachers and students to communicate about writing. These include audiotaped feedback, written comments inserted into students' computer files (e.g., on a floppy disk or using a software program designed to help teachers insert feedback into student texts), and e-mailed feedback.

Because all of these feedback mechanisms are currently available, because there are (in my opinion) reasonable arguments for the use of each, and because it is unlikely that writing teachers will universally opt for one method over all of the others, the various response options are discussed in this chapter. I first review the available research on teacher feedback in L2 student writing, focusing on several key issues. I then examine a number of methodological questions that need to be addressed in order to evaluate the available research base and to make suggestions for further investigations of teacher response to student writing (see Fig. 2.1).

Issues Covered in the Existing Research:

- On what does teacher feedback focus (content, grammar, etc.)?
- What forms does teacher feedback take?
- How does teacher feedback affect revision and improvement in student writing?

Issues of Methodology:

- Who are the subjects, what is their motivation for writing, and what is their background in composition (especially process-oriented classes)?
- What is the institutional context/type of class?
- What kind of writing is being considered?
- What else do we know about the class context?
- What techniques/mechanisms, and so on does the teacher use to give feedback?
- How are effects on revision measured?
- How is "improvement" measured?

FIG. 2.1.   Methodological issues to be discussed.

WHAT ISSUES HAS PREVIOUS RESEARCH COVERED?

Previous research on teacher feedback has focused almost exclusively on written commentary and teacher–student conferences, with the lion's share emphasizing the former mode. As outlined in Fig. 2.1, empirical studies of teacher feedback have looked at three general issues: what the feedback covers, the form and nature of the feedback, and the effects of the feedback on student writing. A fourth issue is student reactions to and preferences regarding teacher feedback; this question is discussed in more detail in chapter 5.

On What Issues Does Teacher Feedback Focus?

Early studies of response to L2 student writing (e.g., Cumming, 1985; Zamel, 1985) noted that ESL writing teachers appeared to think of themselves as primarily language teachers, rather than composition instructors. Thus, they focused mainly, even exclusively, on students' language errors in writing, as opposed to giving students feedback on their ideas or organization. This generalization is supported not only by the data in these studies themselves, but also by the fact that until the 1990s, most of the published research that appeared on response to ESL student writing consisted of empirical (nearly all quasi-experimental) investigations of the effects of error correction (see chap. 3 for a review). Besides the alleged teacher bias toward correcting language errors rather than focusing on students' content, the research base was doubtless affected by the fact that in many classroom contexts, students were not producing multiple drafts of their papers with teacher feedback provided at intermediate stages to help them revise. Because it makes little sense to give concrete suggestions about content or organization on papers that are already finished products (other than as a means for justifying a grade), it is perhaps not surprising that teachers privileged form-based feedback (which could conceivably be generalized to future writing assignments) under these circumstances.

Beginning with studies in 1985 by Cumming and Zamel, several researchers have attempted to describe or classify the focus of feedback given by teachers to student writers. Based on her findings, Zamel claimed that L2 writing teachers "seem to read and react to a text as a series of separate pieces at the sentence level or even clause level, rather than as a whole unit of discourse. In fact, they are so distracted by language-related problems that they often correct these without realizing that there is a much larger, meaning-related problem that they have failed to address" (Zamel, 1987, p. 700). It is important to observe that Zamel's 1985 study has been criticized on methodological grounds. For instance, Silva (1988) characterized Zamel's conclusions as "overgeneralized, unduly negative, and unjustified," noting that there was no data triangulation (in the form of classroom observations or teacher interviews); there was "no attempt … to contextualize the teachers' responses"; only one researcher (Zamel) conducted the analysis; and "data were presented rather selectively" (p. 519). Further, as I have noted elsewhere (Ferris, Pezone, Tade, & Tinti, 1997), Zamel did not specify her method of analysis in her article, rather reporting examples to support the generalizations she had stated. That said, it seems plausible that at least in the early stages of ESL composition instruction and research, Zamel's observations are accurate for at least some teachers and contexts. Given the lack of training available at that time in the teaching of ESL writing (Reid, 1993; Silva, Leki, & Carson, 1997) and the fact that process-oriented approaches to writing instruction were not widespread until the mid-1980s (and their ultimate adoption is doubtless due in large part to Zamel's work and that of Krashen [1984]), it seems not only possible but likely that many L2 writing teachers (trained by linguists rather than rhetoric/composition experts) were responding to single-draft student products as language practice rather than written expression.

However, beginning in 1990, published research indicates that this focus on language in teacher feedback was beginning to change. For instance, in a case study by Cohen and Cavalcanti (1990), it was found that the three instructors provided a range of comments on grammar, mechanics, vocabulary, content, and organization. Other early-to-mid-1990s researchers reported, based on textual analysis and/or student survey data, that teachers were increasingly providing feedback on a range of composition issues (e.g., Caulk, 1994; Ferris, 1995b; Hedgcock & Lefkowitz, 1994; Lam, 1991; Saito, 1994).

In several studies over the past 10 years, researchers have specifically examined the focus of teacher feedback. In a study of over 1,500 comments provided by one teacher on 110 papers by 47 university ESL students, it was found that approximately 15% of the verbal comments (in the margins and in end notes) focused on grammar and mechanics issues (including spelling, double-spacing, etc.) (Ferris, 1997; Ferris et al., 1997).[1] The remaining 85% of the teacher's comments focused on students' ideas and rhetorical development. A recent case study by Conrad and Goldstein (1999) identified a wide range of issues that a teacher addressed in suggesting areas for revision, including coherence/cohesion, paragraphing, content, purpose, lexical choice, and "development" (add examples, facts, or details, explicitness, depth, and explain/analyze) (see Conrad & Goldstein, 1999, Table 6, p. 159, and accompanying discussion).

To summarize, although there may be L2 writing instructors around the world who still adhere to single-draft, error-focused models of writing and feedback, from the research available, it seems clear that in North American academic settings, many teachers have made the shift over the past 15 years from being form-focused and product-oriented to providing feedback on a broad spectrum of issues in a multiple-draft, response-and-revision writing cycle. As is discussed further in this chapter and in chapters 4, 6, and 8, changes in pedagogical approach have also extended to the more widespread use of teacher–student conferences and peer review sessions.

An interesting and related question is *when* in the writing cycle various types of feedback should be given. Following the suggestions given by L1 researchers, Zamel (1985) argued that "we need to establish priorities in our responses to drafts and subsequent revisions and encourage students to address certain con-

---

[1]The instructor also underlined or circled some errors in grammar or word choice. The focus of analysis in this study, however, was only the verbal comments.

cerns before others" (p. 96). Specifically, this has been interpreted as meaning that teachers should address only issues of meaning and content on early drafts of student writing and attend to form only at the penultimate stage (if indeed at all). Generations of writing teachers trained since the mid-1980s have taken it as virtually axiomatic that they should not give feedback on local issues such as grammar, word choice, and mechanics on the first drafts of student papers. The argument for this multistage approach to response and revision is twofold. First, as students should be encouraged to add, delete, rearrange, and otherwise change their content throughout the writing process, it makes little sense to spend time marking up sentence-level problems that may disappear anyway in the course of global revisions. Second, premature attention to error by instructors may short-circuit the students' own ability to attend to macrolevel meaning changes, as it models for students that "cleaning up" their papers is of more importance than continuing to wrestle with development of ideas and the best ways to arrange and present them (Faigley & Witte, 1981; Sommers, 1982; Zamel, 1985).

Although the reasons advanced for separating form- and content-focused feedback onto different drafts seem sensible enough, they may also be criticized on several counts. First, there is no empirical evidence to support the assertion that simultaneous attention to content and form inhibits students from working on both during revision. On the contrary, in several studies in which teachers gave global and local feedback on the same text, L2 students showed the ability to improve their texts in both content and form during revision (Ashwell, 2000; Fathman & Whalley, 1990; Ferris, 1997; Russikoff & Kogan, 1996).[2] A possible explanation for this divergence from L1 composition research is that L2 student writers are well aware that they have linguistic deficits and make errors as they write, but they also know that improving their ideas is important as well (Ferris, 1995b; Hedgcock & Lefkowitz, 1994). Thus they are motivated to address any and all writing problems as attention is called to them.

Second, as I have noted elsewhere (see Ferris & Hedgcock, 1998, p. 132), the distinction between "content" and "form" may well be a false dichotomy, as content determines form, at least to some extent, and faulty form can obscure meaning for a reader. Such issues could properly be considered rather as a continuum, and rigid and somewhat arbitrary prescriptions about the types of comments teachers should give to their students at various stages of the writing process may well be inappropriate and unhelpful. Third, teacher feedback should be constructed according to the most critical needs of individual student writers (Conrad & Goldstein, 1999; Ferris et al., 1997; Reid, 1994). If a student writes a first draft that is exemplary as to ideas, development, and organization, but that is crying out for careful editing, it would seem foolish for the teacher to turn himself or herself inside out trying to find constructive content-based comments to give to the writer merely because it is the first draft and attention to form is judged "premature." Or, at the opposite extreme, a student's first draft may be so riddled with language

---

[2]Russikoff and Kogan reported that subjects who received only content-focused feedback improved their content more substantially than did those who received a combination of both form and content feedback. They argued that, even though students in the latter group did improve their content scores in revision, the attention to form may have inhibited them from even greater improvement.

problems that the teacher cannot possibly provide useful (or even accurate) mean-ing-based commentary until he or she has more clarity about what the student is trying to say (which may well be achievable only through a face-to-face confer-ence, as discussed later in this chapter). In contrast, as any experienced writing in-structor knows, a student may still be very much in need of content-focused response even on a penultimate essay draft. To ignore this need because it is "time" to focus only on grammar again seems counterproductive.

A final argument against waiting until the end of the writing cycle to give lan-guage-related feedback is that L2 student writers have a tremendous need for expert feedback on their written errors. Students in many contexts will fail their writing courses or university writing proficiency examinations solely because of language errors. The linguistic deficits that many bring to the writing class are real and sub-stantial (Leki, 1990a; Silva, 1993) and it is critical that their instructors address them. Choosing to only give form-focused feedback on a few drafts throughout a writing course could be argued to deprive students of critically needed input on an issue that could ultimately make or break them. Suggestions for how (and if) to bal-ance and combine form- and meaning-based commentary throughout the writing cycle are provided in chapter 7.

What Forms Does Teacher Feedback Take?

Most studies of teachers' written response to L1 or L2 student writing have focused on the question discussed previously (*what* teacher feedback addresses) rather than *how* teachers construct their feedback (as to linguistic form, tone, location of com-mentary, etc.). This emphasis is no doubt appropriate (most of us would no doubt agree that the substance of feedback is ultimately of more import than its form); however, there is evidence that the ways in which commentary is provided can af-fect both students' reactions to it and its effects on short- and long-term improve-ment in student writing.

Survey research on student reactions to teacher feedback is discussed in detail in chapter 5. At this point, it is sufficient to say that the existing student survey re-search suggests that student writers are particularly frustrated by, and even resentful of, teacher commentary that is cryptic, vague, and unclear (Ferris, 1995b; Straub, 1997). In addition, there is some preliminary text analytic evidence that the form of teacher feedback may be directly related to its effects on student revision (and on whether concepts addressed in teacher feedback are acted on by students in subse-quent assignments). These two generalizations suggest that some examination of and reflection on the form of teacher commentary may well be warranted. This ob-servation seems especially salient in the case of L2 student writers, whose linguis-tic, pragmatic, and cultural differences (compared to those of L1 writers) may greatly affect their processing of teacher feedback (Ferris, 1999b; Leki, 1990a; Patthey-Chavez & Ferris, 1997).

Analyses of the forms that teacher feedback may take are extremely rare in the L2 literature. When I began my own investigations into this topic (Ferris, 1997, 2001a; Ferris et al., 1997), my colleagues and I found no appropriate analytic models for our study in previous L2 composition research and thus created our own. To my knowledge, only my own studies and Conrad and Goldstein's (1999) study have examined the issue of the forms of teacher commentary in L2 settings in any detail.[3]

The database for the study reported on in Ferris (1997, 2001a) and Ferris et al. (1997) consisted of 110 pairs of student essays (preliminary drafts with written teacher commentary plus revisions) written by 47 ESL writers in a university-level ESL freshman composition course (three sections of the course taught by the same instructor in two different semesters). Over 1,500 teacher comments were analyzed and classified (Ferris et al., 1997), and effects of the comments on student revisions were also traced, using an original rating scale (Ferris, 1997). In a follow-up case study (Ferris, 2001a), complete sets of student texts and teacher comments were analyzed for eight student writers (four "strong" writers and four "weak" writers) to examine in more detail the aspects of teacher feedback that appeared to lead to successful revisions, unsuccessful revisions, or no revisions at all.

The findings of these three studies, taken together, were as follows:

1. The teacher in the study utilized a broad range of commenting strategies. For instance, she made comments both in the margins and at the end of the paper (either on the student text itself, in one semester, or on a standard feedback form, in the second semester). Across the entire sample, she made more marginal than end comments, but the end comments tended to be much longer. Her comments appeared to have a number of communicative aims: to request more information, to make a suggestion or request, to give information to the student writer, to give positive or encouraging feedback, and to comment verbally on issues of grammar and mechanics. They also took a variety of linguistic forms (e.g., questions, statements, imperatives, hedges, etc.).

2. The teacher's feedback also varied according to the type of essay assignment being considered, the point in the semester at which the feedback was given, and the relative strengths of the student writers.

3. Certain types of comments appeared to lead to more effective revisions than other types. In this study, the students made the most effective changes in response to information questions, imperatives, and comments about grammar or mechanics. In contrast, it was noted that questions or statements that challenged the students' thinking or argumentation (rather than suggesting a specific item of information to be added or a word- or sentence-level change) were more likely to lead to ineffective revisions or to the deletion of problematic material, if not ignored entirely by the student writers.

In a case study of two essay cycles (drafts, teacher–student conferences, written teacher commentary) for three student writers, Conrad and Goldstein (1999) identified five formal characteristics of teacher feedback that led to successful student re-

---

[3]Zamel's (1985) study also provided some description and examples of the forms of teacher feedback and of its apparent effects (or lack thereof) on student revision. Her findings are presented anecdotally rather than systematically, so they are not discussed in detail here. However, several of her examples are included as illustrative of generalizations suggested by the later studies.

visions. In addition, similar to Ferris (2001a), Conrad and Goldstein found that the nature of the problem to be revised was highly predictive of the students' ultimate success or failure in addressing that problem in their revisions. Specifically, "if the problem to be revised focused on explanation, explicitness, or analysis, the resulting revisions were almost never successful. In contrast, if the directive focused on details, examples, coherence/cohesion, purpose, paragraphing, or lexical items ... almost all revisions were successful" (p. 160). The authors concluded that "it is misleading to focus on formal characteristics of the feedback without incorporating discussion of the type of revision that is being requested" (p. 157), and suggested that certain types of revision problems may be best addressed by a face-to-face teacher–student writing conference rather than through written commentary.

These two analyses, taken together, suggest both that the forms that teacher feedback take may be important in students' ability to understand, process, and utilize it, and that there may be real limits on the types of revisions written teacher commentary can be reasonably expected to effect. For instance, brief, cryptic questions or imperatives in the margins such as "Why?" "Relevance"? or "Explain!" may simply provide too little information to student writers. A classic example is provided by Zamel (1985), quoting a teacher in her study: "Some of your statements are so general that I don't know what you mean" (p. 91); Zamel noted that this comment "ironically underscores the fact that we are not very good models for our students" (p. 92). For L2 writers especially, teacher indirectness may add another layer of difficulty. Conrad and Goldstein (1999) defined as indirect any comment in which the teacher's purpose (as to revision) is not explicitly stated. As an example of a "direct" comment, they offer the example *"I'd like you to work on your support some more"* (p. 179). Both their study and the studies by my colleagues and me provide numerous examples of "indirect" comments, using Conrad and Goldstein's definition. For instance, the teacher in our study went through the following sequence with a student writer:

FIRST DRAFT EXCERPT:
Finally our graduation and our decision, which university to attend, we went in different directions and don't know of each other any more.

TEACHER COMMENT:
Is this really a crossroads friendship if you're not in contact?

REVISION EXCERPT:
Finally our graduation and our decision, which university to attend, we went in different directions. We write to each other on our birthday and on special occasions.

The teacher's comment is indirect in several ways. Its intent is really to challenge the writer's use of the term "crossroads friendship" (used in an essay by Judith Viorst in Spack, 1990) to describe her relationship with a high school friend. Yet it misleads the student writer into simply providing more information about her ongoing contact with her friend ("We write to each other on our birthday and on special occasions") without reexamining Viorst's definition of a crossroads friendship and whether it applies to this relationship. The teacher's question is also indirect in that, though it is presented in question form, it is really a directive to the writer to reconsider her logic and her use of specific terminology. No revision strategy is presented or asked for by the teacher. It seems apparent from this exchange that the teacher's indirectness is not an optimal strategy and that it did not lead to the desired result.

Besides commentary that is too cryptic or too indirect, teacher use of rhetorical or linguistic jargon can be problematic for student writers trying to process feedback they have received. Writing teachers in general are fond of marginal shorthand such as "Thesis?" "Add transition!" "Tense?" "Agreement," and so on. Zamel (1985, pp. 89–90) offered a number of examples of this, together with excerpts of student revisions showing how unhelpful such direction can be, including the following:

Student Original:
But is was unbelievable that when I visited New York City.

Teacher Comment:
INC SEN (But is was unbelievable that when I visited New York City.)

Student Revision:
It was unbelievable that when I visited New York City.

It is not apparent from this example whether the student knew what "INC SEN" meant (we assume "incomplete sentence," or sentence fragment), but it is absolutely clear that this teacher feedback did nothing to enable the student writer to correct the sentence fragment problem!

As noted by Reid (1994; see also Sperling & Freedman, 1987), such shorthand may be appropriate and even effective if it refers students to concepts that have been explicitly covered in classroom discussions and/or in the textbook. However, teachers may often erroneously assume extensive student prior knowledge of rhetorical and grammatical terminology that students may have never had presented to them formally (or even if they have heard it before, they may not remember it or know how to apply it effectively). One example (possibly from the apocryphal or "urban myth" category) that makes the rounds at conferences is of a young man, an ESL student writer, who was told by his teacher in a written comment to "add an introduction" to his paper. His next draft began as follows: "Let me introduce myself. My name is Le. I am 19 years old. I have black hair. I have a girlfriend named Kim...."

Although the formal characteristics of teacher feedback may indeed be significant—particularly in instances in which it confuses or misleads the student writer—the case study analyses by Ferris (2001a) and by Conrad and Goldstein (1999) suggest that there are certain writing and revision issues that may be too complex for teachers and students to address in written commentary. As already noted, Conrad and Goldstein suggested that when revision problems are of a more global, abstract nature, they are best tackled in face-to-face discussions between teachers and students. Ferris (2001a) asked the (probably unanswerable) question:

Can teacher feedback foster the development of critical thinking skills without any tangible evidence of this development on student revisions? ... the mere fact that a student does not address a teacher's suggestion in revision hardly means that the teacher's comment was "bad" or "unsuccessful"—it may simply mean that the writer has chosen to go in a different direction with his/her text, which is a healthy sign of independent thinking, not cause for alarm.... Similarly, it is quite possible, and even likely, that teacher feedback can help students think more clearly and critically long before they are able to produce evidence of such improved thinking in their texts. (p. 312)

It is important to observe, however, that evidence on the effects of the formal aspects of teacher commentary is extremely scarce. Conrad and Goldstein's (1999) study considered only two sets of papers from three student subjects, and the final analysis of teacher commentary on which they based their major finding (that type of revision problem was more significant than the form of teacher feedback) considered only 32 teacher comments (see Conrad & Goldstein, 1999, Table 7, p. 161). And although the analyses in my own studies were based on a larger sample of students (47), texts (220), and teacher comments (1,526), they were still based on the responses of only one teacher in one context. And even considering those limited samples, the findings are not consistent, as noted, across assignment types, student ability levels, and point in the semester at which feedback and revision were undertaken.

How Does Teacher Feedback Affect Revision and Improvement in Student Writing?

As mentioned at the beginning of this chapter (and in chapter 1), a number of L1 and L2 researchers have claimed that there is little evidence that teacher feedback helps students at all. Worse, some claim that students resent teacher feedback, that it misleads them, and that it models poor priorities about the process of writing. In the most bleak analyses, written teacher feedback not only takes considerable time and energy on the part of instructors (or "composition slaves," as Hairston, 1986, has termed them), but it may well do more harm than good. These conclusions, which proliferated in the L1 literature in the 1980s (e.g., Brannon & Knoblauch, 1982; Hillocks, 1986; Knoblauch & Brannon, 1981; Sommers, 1982) and that were echoed by early L2 writing researchers (Krashen, 1984; Zamel, 1982, 1985, 1987), raise the critical question to which we turn next: Does written teacher commentary help students at all?

The short answer, which is based on recent investigations that have taken place in the multiple-draft, process-oriented writing classes of the past 10 to 15 years, is that yes, indeed, teacher feedback certainly can and often does help student writers to improve their writing from one draft to the next and over time. Again, however, the evidence on this question is unfortunately quite limited, particularly as to longitudinal analyses. Students themselves definitely feel that teacher feedback is valuable to them and that it helps them to improve their writing (see chap. 5; also Cohen & Cavalcanti, 1990; Ferris, 1995b; Hedgcock & Lefkowitz, 1994, 1996).

The earliest published research linking teacher feedback and student revision is a controlled quasiexperimental study by Fathman and Whalley (1990). In this study, 72 ESL student writers wrote a composition in class and then received one of four feedback treatments: (a) no feedback; (b) feedback on content only, described as "general comments that were not text specific" (p. 182); (c) feedback on grammar only; and (d) feedback on both content and grammar. The papers were then returned to students, who were asked to rewrite their compositions on the spot. It was found that all four treatment groups showed statistically significant improvement in their content scores on their revisions, but the two groups who received content feedback improved their scores substantially more than did the two groups who received no content feedback.

In a follow-up study, Russikoff and Kogan (1996), replicated Fathman and Whalley's study except that students wrote their papers and revisions outside of class with no time constraints. Russikoff and Kogan's findings were very similar to those of Fathman and Whalley as to increases in content scores related to treatment groups: All four groups improved their content scores, and the two groups receiving content feedback improved the most. One distinction between the two studies was that the content-feedback-only treatment group in Russikoff and Kogan's study improved its mean content score far more substantially than did the content-plus-grammar-feedback group, which had a mean content improvement only slightly higher than the no-feedback and grammar-feedback-only groups.

A longitudinal case study analysis by Lam (1991) showed that five student subjects were able to make successful revision changes in both "content and mechanics" in response to teacher feedback on various types of writing assignments throughout the writing course. Lam reported that teacher feedback was utilized more frequently by students in revision when it was more explicit. Another longitudinal study (Kepner, 1991) showed that student writers who received "message-related comments" (in contrast to error correction) on out-of-class journal entries produced significantly more "higher level propositions" at the end of 12 weeks than students who had only their errors corrected. Though Kepner did not measure "improvement" from the beginning to the end of the data collection period, her data at least suggest that content feedback helped the student subjects who received it to make meaning-level progress over time.

Several researchers have looked simultaneously at the effects of peer and teacher feedback on student revision. (Their findings as to peer feedback are discussed in chapter 4.) In all cases, it was found that teacher feedback had a greater impact on revision than peer response. Connor and Asenavage (1994) reported that their subjects' revisions could be traced to teacher comments in 35% to 37% of the cases but that suggestions from peer feedback accounted for only 1% to 6% of the changes. They also report that, regardless of the source of feedback, the majority of student revisions were at the surface level, rather than being "text-based changes." A recent study by Paulus (1999) adopted much of Connor and Asenavage's methodology but reported more encouraging conclusions. Paulus found that both peer and teacher feedback influenced student revisions, that students made both surface- and meaning-level changes, and that the quality of students' texts improved significantly between first and third drafts.

The previously discussed studies by Conrad and Goldstein (1999), Ferris (1997, 2001a), and Ferris et al. (1997) also shed light on the question of whether teacher feedback indeed impacts student revision. Ferris (1997) looked specifically at the influence of teacher commentary on student revision, finding that when "positive" comments were excluded from the calculations, some 76% of the teacher's responses were taken up by the students in their revisions.

Although this finding certainly demonstrates that the student subjects paid attention to their teacher's feedback (confirming survey data reports collected at the same institution and reported on in Ferris, 1995b), saying that students utilized teacher comments in revision is not the same as saying that it helped their writing. This study (i.e., Ferris, 1997 and the case study reported in Ferris, 2001a) addresses the issue of the quality of revisions as well. It was found that over half of the comments (53%) led to changes that had positive effects, 13% of the comments led to revisions with mixed effects, and 34% of the revisions influenced by teacher commentary had negative effects on the texts.[4] This latter finding, that about one third of the teacher comments resulted in revisions judged as having negative effects on the student texts, suggests that the influence of teacher feedback can be a two-edged sword and that researchers (and teachers) should certainly examine it carefully.

Conrad and Goldstein's (1999) case study also reveals a complex picture of the interaction between teacher feedback and student revision. They found that although their three subjects revised in response to 36 out of 44 teacher comments, "over a third of the attempted revisions were not successful" (p. 156). As already noted, they attributed students' lack of success in revision primarily to the type of revision problem being considered, rather than to any formal characteristics of the teacher feedback.

To summarize, the available research to date linking teacher feedback to L2 student revision (and/or to short- or long-term improvement of students' texts), suggests the following generalizations:

- L2 student writers attend to teacher feedback and frequently attempt to incorporate teacher suggestions in their revisions;
- Revisions made by students in response to feedback may range from surface-level to meaning-level changes, and this appears to be largely attributable to the types of feedback they have received from their teachers;
- Students who receive content-based or meaning-related feedback appear to improve the content of their texts from one draft to the next and over time;
- Not all revisions made by students in response to teacher feedback are successful, and some may actually harm the overall quality of a student text;
- Students' success in making effective changes in their texts in response to teacher feedback may vary depending on the type of change being suggested and/or the ability level of the individual student writer.

In summary, the empirical evidence available both from controlled experimental studies (e.g., Fathman & Whalley, 1990; Kepner, 1991) and from longitudinal text analyses appears to support the findings of student survey research: Students say that they value teacher feedback, that they pay attention to it, and that it helps them to improve their writing. Whereas the database on this question again is fairly lim-

---

[4]These calculations are taken from Ferris, 1997 (Table 2, p. 324), but with the following adaptations: (a) marginal and end comment totals are added for more streamlined discussion; and (b) the 320 positive comments were removed from the analysis, leaving a total of 1,206 comments on which the aforementioned percentages were calculated.

ited, the evidence thus far appears to refute (or at least cast grave doubt on) the grim conclusions of early L1 and L2 composition researchers.

METHODOLOGICAL ISSUES

The foregoing review of previous research on written teacher commentary, the issues it has addressed and its findings raise a number of methodological questions that must be considered in assessing the state of the field to date and in designing future research programs that investigate this critically important subtopic in ESL writing instruction. These questions are discussed in turn.

Who Are the Subjects, What Is Their Motivation for Writing, and What Is Their Background in Composition (Especially Process-Oriented Classes)?

Both L1 and L2 researchers and instructors have bemoaned the fact that student writers seem to have little appreciation or understanding for the process of revision, which is described by various scholars as sending writers back into the messiness or chaos of their thinking and asking them to "see again" what they have written and to ask themselves hard questions about what needs to be added, deleted, explained, rethought, or moved in their texts.[5] It has been noted elsewhere that teachers of L2 writers who have been educated outside of the United States (i.e., international visa students or EFL students) may have a hard time convincing their students of the necessity for multiple drafts, teacher feedback, and revision (Ferris, 1999b; Leki, 1992). (An international student of my own acquaintance described her writing teacher at a U.S. university with some bewilderment and frustration: "She makes us work very hard. We have to *write the same thing THREE TIMES!*")

Composition as a separate field of study is relatively rare outside of North America. Students pursuing English language studies in other countries, when they write in English at all, do so typically either to practice the grammar and vocabulary they have learned or to demonstrate prowess in literary analysis. Writing is not necessarily always valued as a means to succeed academically, to solve problems and develop critical thinking skills, or to develop fluency and confidence in the target language. Process-oriented writing instruction, including emphases on prewriting or planning, revision, multiple drafting, collaboration, and feedback at intermediate stages of the process, is for the most part not utilized. United States–trained writing instructors who travel to teach in such settings or whose students come to the United States without a background in process-based composition may have some adjustments to make in their expectations and teaching strategies. That said, in the same way that American schoolchildren can be taught to compose and revise, EFL and international students certainly can develop these skills too, given proper training and teacher patience (and a dose of marketing, as well).

---

[5]It has been pointed out to me that not all writing tasks *should* require revision. This point is well taken; however, it seems fair to say that in many (most?) instances, whether in writing classes or in "real-world" composing, revision activities are valuable to the writing process and to written end products.

Another group of L2 student writers whose backgrounds and motivations must be considered are English-speaking students in college-level foreign language classes (Hedgcock & Lefkowitz, 1994). Such students are arguably more analogous to EFL students in their own countries than to either international or immigrant students in English-speaking tertiary institutions. The former group must only acquire enough L2 language and writing skills to succeed in their language classes, whereas the latter group needs language and writing skills that will serve them throughout their academic careers and perhaps in their working lives beyond the university. In other words, the former groups of students (EFL and American FL students) may not be as interested in developing their L2 writing abilities—because doing so may have little relevance to their short- or long-term goals—and thus may not be as highly motivated to put forth the considerable effort needed to improve their L2 academic literacy abilities (including both reading and writing, which are interconnected).

Even if we assume that the latter groups (ESL students in English-speaking countries) will be more instrumentally and intrinsically motivated to improve their L2 writing skills, it is important for researchers, reviewers, and teachers to be aware of their background in composition. As previously discussed, teacher feedback may be problematic for L2 writers because of their linguistic and pragmatic differences, a point that may be overlooked or underestimated by their English-speaking writing instructors. We cannot assume that such students will know specific rhetoric/composition jargon or the concepts behind the terminology, even if the students have received part or most of their formal education in the United States. Teachers particularly cannot assume that ESL writers will have had any prior exposure to terms or rules related to English grammar, as such instruction, when it occurs at all in American public schools, tends to be aimed at the needs of native speakers of English, which can be substantially different from those of second language learners.

This is all to say that in conducting or reviewing research on feedback to second language writers (or designing instruction for them), we must look carefully at who the learners are, what their motivations for writing in the L2 might be, and what prior composition instruction they may (or may not) have had. We cannot assume that all L2 writers have the same motivations and backgrounds simply because they are all composing in a second language.

What Is the Institutional Context/Type of Class?

The type of institution in which instruction and data collection take place is also an important consideration in evaluating research on response to student writing. For instance, although Intensive English Programs (IEPs) are often housed on university campuses and are typically preacademic (college preparatory) in nature, the goals of the students who enroll in them may vary considerably, even within the same class. Some students may be very serious and highly motivated to improve their English and academic writing skills, yet others may simply be enjoying a short stay in an English-speaking country at their parents' expense and may be resentful of too many teacher demands (homework, multiple drafting, etc.). Students in adult education or community college programs similarly may have a wide range of goals and educational backgrounds that may affect both their willingness and ability to cope with academic writing tasks, teacher feedback, and revision. Students at 4-year colleges or universities, on the other hand, could reasonably be expected to appreciate the importance of academic writing skills for their current and future purposes.

In addition to considering the type of institution in which students are matriculated, the specific type of class in which data are being collected is important. If the class is an integrated course that covers listening, speaking, reading, writing, and grammar, teachers and students may not be able to spend as much time in writing instruction and workshop activities as in a "pure" writing class. Another important consideration is the class level and what it represents about students' second language and writing proficiency. Many of the studies reviewed in this chapter took place in ESL freshman composition courses at U.S. universities. L2 students at this level typically have fairly advanced abilities in English writing. However, other studies were conducted in either university preparatory programs (IEPs) or in university courses a level or two below freshman composition (i.e., remedial or developmental courses). This factor is significant because students at the college level (freshman composition) may have better developed reading, writing, thinking, and revision skills than students in remedial or basic skills courses. This may in turn affect their ability to handle teacher feedback successfully and utilize it in higher order revision processes.

What Kind of Writing Is Being Considered?

In most of the studies discussed here, the type of writing being produced by students, responded to by teachers, and examined by researchers is some variation of expository and/or persuasive academic writing. However, there is some variation, and studies by Ferris et al. (1997) and Ferris (2001a) suggest that these distinctions may be important. For instance, Kepner's 1991 study focuses on students' journal entries, writing that was not revised (and is typically very expressive and focused on fluency and ideas rather than on rhetorical or syntactic form). The students in Fathman and Whalley's (1990) study were writing a descriptive composition based on a picture sequence, which is a very different endeavor than my subjects' analyses of other authors' argumentation.

Several aspects of genre and text type appear to be especially salient in considering the effects of teacher feedback on writing quality and revision. Most likely, students will process teacher feedback differently depending on whether it must be (or can be) revised (see Ferris, 1995b; Hedgcock & Lefkowitz, 1994). Writing tasks that require personal narrative or descriptive writing elicit specific types of information, which may be different from the demands of expository or persuasive writing. In turn, these distinction may suggest variation in teacher feedback. In Ferris et al. (1997), it was found that the instructor asked many more information questions in response to personal narrative essays (i.e., asking for information that only the student writer would know) than on argumentative tasks. The authors noted that where feedback that elicits more detail may be necessary and appropriate for a narrative or descriptive task, the same response could be actually counterproductive for a persuasive essay, in which extraneous or irrelevant details could weaken the writer's argument. Finally, student writing and instructor response may vary depending on whether or not students must draw on ideas or words from other authors' texts. In short, researchers and reviewers should consider the specifications of particular writing tasks and text types in the analysis of teacher feedback and its effects.

What Else Do We Know About the Class Context?

Researchers and reviewers have criticized existing research on teacher response because it has been largely decontextualized, following one of three dominant research paradigms: (a) controlled experimental designs (e.g., Fathman & Whalley, 1990; Kepner, 1991); (b) text analysis (e.g., Ferris, 1997; Ferris et al., 1997; Zamel, 1985); or (c) student survey research that considers only student reactions and preferences to teacher feedback without either examining student texts or checking student perceptions against those of their teachers (e.g., Cohen, 1987; Ferris, 1995b; Hedgcock & Lefkowitz, 1994). Although all of these research designs have their benefits and have added to our knowledge, teacher feedback takes place within a larger classroom context that includes instruction, discussion, modeling, collaboration, and an ongoing personal relationship between the teacher and each student. Reid (1994) observed that an outside researcher who simply collected her own students' texts with her written commentary would doubtless find much to criticize about her feedback, but that if the researcher had observed in-class presentations and discussions, the commentary she gave would appear much less idiosyncratic and problematic.

To assess instructor response and its short- and long-term effects on student writing, it is important to consider the following aspects of the classroom context: (a) whether multiple drafting is encouraged or even required; (b) whether revision strategies are taught and modeled or whether it is simply assumed that students can revise effectively on their own; (c) whether teachers provide instruction about composing processes and rhetorical strategies (to which they can then refer in their written feedback); (d) whether the teacher adheres to consistent and clear feedback procedures and whether these procedures have been made explicit to the students; (e) whether students are allowed or encouraged to question the teacher about feedback they have received; (f) whether students are held accountable for at least considering teacher feedback as they revise; and (g) whether what the teacher says in class is consistent with what she or he models in written or oral feedback (e.g., does the teacher *say* that substantive content revision should precede microlevel editing but then mark primarily on only language problems on student essay drafts?).

It is important to note that in several studies of teacher feedback (Cohen & Cavalcanti, 1990; Conrad & Goldstein, 1999; Paulus, 1999), researchers have indeed attempted to triangulate data collection (e.g., by using observation and interviews to supplement written texts) and to contextualize their findings. However, these studies are all case studies with few subjects and relatively small amounts of textual data, doubtless because of the labor-intensive nature of such in-depth investigations. Yet precisely because both teacher feedback and student processing of feedback can be so idiosyncratic, it is important to consider as much data as possible from as many subjects (teachers and students) as feasible to arrive at any useful conclusions. Future researchers need to seek ways to better contextualize their investigations but still collect adequate amounts of data.

What Techniques/Mechanisms, and so on Does the Teacher Use to Give Feedback?

As discussed earlier in this chapter, research on teacher feedback has focused more on *what* teachers cover (content, grammar, etc.) in their responses and on the effects of feedback than on the actual form of feedback. Several researchers have looked at the effects of variation in linguistic form (questions vs. statements, use of hedges, etc.), with somewhat conflicting conclusions about the relevance of these formal characteristics (Conrad & Goldstein, 1999; Ferris, 1997, 2001a; Ferris et al., 1997). More investigation of these questions is necessary, but promising avenues for analysis appear to include student processing of teacher feedback in question form (especially indirect questioning), the use of rhetorical or grammatical jargon or terminology, the length or brevity of written comments, the effects of teacher hedging (which may either confuse an L2 student writer because of lack of pragmatic awareness or communicate that the teacher is not really serious about the comment because it was not strongly stated), and the pairing of statements or questions about the text with explicit suggestions for revision.

Several other mechanical issues about the provision of feedback have not been investigated at all in L2 writing. For instance, is it better to write comments in the margins, at the end of a paper, or a combination of both? Does teacher feedback and its effects vary if a separate feedback form (perhaps with a checklist or rubric) is used? Is it important to evenly balance encouraging comments and critical ones? Does it make a difference if the teacher addresses the student by name and signs his or her own name at the end of a note? Students, teachers, and researchers may have various opinions about these issues, thus it is important to be aware that they have not been investigated empirically.

How Are Effects on Revision Measured?

As I have discovered in my own work, it can be difficult indeed to quantify and categorize both teacher feedback and its effects on revision. As noted in Ferris et al. (1997) and Conrad and Goldstein (1999), it can be challenging, in looking at teacher feedback, to determine where a specific comment or feedback point begins and ends. It is arguably even more difficult to determine the effects of teacher feedback on subsequent student revisions. As students make additions and deletions, rearrange ideas or change them altogether, it can be hard to say with any certainty what the influence of a particular teacher comment may have been.

Two approaches to the question of measuring revision after feedback have been taken in the studies reviewed in this chapter. The first line of research follows from a well-known L1 revision taxonomy by Faigley and Witte (1981), in which student texts and their revisions are compared and all changes made categorized as either "surface changes" (with the subcategories "formal changes" and "meaning preserving changes") or "text-based changes" (divided into either "microstructure" or "macrostructure" changes). Studies that used this scheme or an adapted version of it include Connor and Asenavage (1994), Hyland (1998), Lam (1991), and Paulus (1999).

This revision categorization scheme, which has been extensively used in L1 and L2 revision research in either its original or adapted versions, typically leads to the finding that student writers make more surface than text-based changes and more microstructure than macrostructure changes. This finding has in turn been used to argue that student writers are poor revisers and that they need instruction in how to revise as well as exhortation to let go (at least temporarily) of the need to make surface changes and focus instead on text-based changes. It has also been claimed that teacher feedback that itself is overly focused on surface issues will lead students to focus (prematurely) on these problems (e.g., Connor & Asenavage, 1994).

Although Faigley and Witte's (1981) taxonomy has stood the test of time and has led to a series of studies yielding useful information on student revising processes, the effects of teacher and peer feedback, and the effects of the word processor on revision, it nonetheless has its limitations. First, the taxonomy can mislead researchers into simple counting schemes that may not capture the complexity of revision. For instance, in a student essay of 500 to 1000 words in length, only a few "text-based, macrostructure changes" may be possible or necessary, where there may be dozens or even hundreds of possible "surface formal changes" within a text of the same length. If one simply counts the raw numbers of both types of revision, it should not be surprising that one will find more instances in the latter category. Yet such arguably inevitable results are viewed with alarm and suspicion, and yield allegations that students "don't know how to revise" or that teachers are "obsessed with form-focused feedback." Secondly, although the taxonomy provides a detailed categorization of the *types* of changes writers may make in revision, it says nothing about the *effects* of such changes in improving the overall quality of the students' texts.

In response to these issues, the second line of research that links feedback with revision has focused specifically on linking teacher commentary to changes in student texts and assessing the effects of the changes on overall writing quality (Conrad & Goldstein, 1999; Ferris, 1997, 2001a; Hyland, 1998; Paulus, 1999). Though specific procedures and labels vary across studies, the basic procedure is that each written teacher comment is identified and labeled, and its effects traced through the next draft of the student's paper using a scheme such as "Not revised," "Successful revision," and "Unsuccessful revision" (Conrad & Goldstein, 1999).[6] This second approach more directly addresses the influence of teacher feedback and its effects not only on the types of revisions students make but on whether those changes actually improve the quality of the students' texts, but it also has its limitations. Most notably, it requires that researchers make post hoc assumptions about why student writers made changes in their texts. It might be most beneficial to have students complete either

---

[6]Hyland (1998) and Ferris (1997) used more detailed schemes to describe the students' revision responses. Paulus (1999) added a holistic rating of overall essay quality between first and third drafts to her design.

think-aloud protocols as they use teacher feedback to revise and/or retrospec-
tive interviews in which they examine their own revisions and discuss the effects
of the teacher commentary on their decision making.

How Is "Improvement" Measured?

Few researchers have assessed whether teacher feedback actually helps students to
improve their writing. The experimental studies by Fathman and Whalley (1990)
and Russikoff and Kogan (1996) clearly measure "improvement" in content scores
from one draft of a paper to the next; Paulus' (1999) study also includes a holistic
measure of essay quality between students' first and third drafts. Kepner's (1991)
analysis found that students who received content-focused feedback had a significantly higher number of "higher level propositions" in their week 12 journal entries
than students who had received only error correction. Although this finding suggests that the "message-related comments" received by the former group had a positive effect on their thinking and writing skills, because there was no pretest
measure (i.e., initial journal entry or writing sample), "improvement" per se cannot
be assessed. None of the other studies reviewed in this chapter measured improvement in either the short or long term.

Clearly, this is a glaring gap in the research base. Teachers spend many hours
providing written feedback to their students, ostensibly because they believe it
helps their students; students feel that such responses are of value to them. It certainly would seem important to find out if these assumptions are indeed true or
whether students can learn just as much or even more if they are given adequate instruction and modeling and the opportunity to rethink and rewrite their own work
with little or no textual input from their instructors (Elbow, 1973; Fathman &
Whalley, 1990). Does written teacher feedback inhibit student development by
causing them to focus on what their teacher wants instead of their own purposes for
writing? Does it make them overly dependent on teacher input, to the detriment of
building independent, autonomous self-evaluation skills? These are difficult questions, and researchers and teachers should quickly turn their attention to trying to
discover the answers.

To summarize, examination of issues in research methodology and a review of
available research suggests the following parameters for future research on written
teacher response to student writing:

• The nature of the student writers, including their language education and composition backgrounds, their motivations for learning L2 writing skills, and the types
of institutions in which they are enrolled need to be carefully considered in research
design. Research projects on the nature and effects of teacher feedback and student
revision may be most salient in settings in which students have strong reasons for improving their L2 writing skills (e.g., in academic ESL courses) and in which there is
adequate time for and teacher/student investment in the response-and-revision cycle.

• The larger classroom context, especially what is being taught and modeled
for students and the nature of the relationship between instructor and students,

needs to be carefully observed and accounted for in data analyses. If students improve in their writing skills or fail to progress, written teacher commentary may well be only one of many factors that can explain their development.

• Analysis of feedback and revision also needs to consider the characteristics of the various text types that students are producing and to which teachers are responding, rather than assuming that teachers and students approach all tasks in the same way.

• The formal characteristics (including linguistic/pragmatic questions and mechanical issues) of teacher feedback need to be considered. If students are not revising successfully or improving in their writing skills over time despite receiving regular feedback from teachers, perhaps there is a problem with student processing of the feedback because cross-linguistic pragmatic constraints make it unclear to them.

• Studies of the influence of feedback on short-term revision and long-term improvement must include carefully designed and operationalized schemes to measure these effects.

All that said, the current state of research on the nature and effects of written teacher commentary is promising, especially considering the relatively small number of available studies. Several models have been designed and tested to quantify and categorize teacher feedback; others have been implemented to examine student revision after receiving feedback. Researchers have identified important contextual issues for future investigators to consider. Although we still have a long way to go in examining teacher feedback, we are not without some direction as to how to get there.

OTHER TEACHER FEEDBACK DELIVERY SYSTEMS

As noted at the beginning of this chapter, many early reviewers and researchers expressed grave doubt about the efficacy of written teacher commentary. One result of this trend was increased interest in both peer response and teacher–student conferences. Peer feedback is discussed in detail in chapters 4, 5, and 8. In this section, I look at teacher–student writing conferences and at other alternative teacher feedback mechanisms, specifically audiotaped and e-mailed commentary.

Teacher–Student Writing Conferences

Dating back to the advent of process-oriented composition instruction in the 1970s, many L1 scholars have enthusiastically endorsed the face-to-face teacher–student writing conference as the ideal approach to both instruction and feedback. Some have suggested in-class writing workshops (Elbow, 1973) that include on-the-spot mini-conferences between teacher and students as students work individually (Garrison, 1974). Others have argued that perhaps classroom instruction should be dispensed with altogether in favor of one-on-one conferences in the instructor's office (Carnicelli, 1980). In addition, campus writing centers, in which students can receive one-to-one or small group tutoring from trained peer (student) tutors, may have a significant influence on students' writing development. Some experts favor writing conferences especially over written feedback because they allow for two-way negotiation rather than teacher appropriation of the students' texts through one-sided written directives (Brannon & Knoblauch, 1982; Sommers, 1982; Zamel, 1985). Finally, it has been suggested that certain types of writing problems (analysis, argumentation, sentence structure, lexical errors) are simply too complicated to be addressed through written feedback and require dynamic in-person discussion to be efficient and effective (Conrad & Goldstein, 1999).

Despite all of this enthusiasm, there has been very little empirical work done on the nature and effects of writing conferences in L1 writing classes, and almost nothing in L2. The few L1 studies that have been conducted have focused on the description of the interactions between teachers and students (Freedman & Katz, 1987; Freedman & Sperling, 1985; Jacobs & Karliner, 1977; Newkirk, 1995; Sperling, 1994; Walker & Elias, 1987); some have further identified differences in conference dynamics between high- and low-achieving students.

Two studies focusing at least in part on ESL writers have also linked the nature of conference discourse with students' subsequent writing (Goldstein & Conrad, 1990; Patthey-Chavez & Ferris, 1997). In Goldstein and Conrad's (1990) study, three ESL writers' texts, conference transcripts, and revisions were examined to assess both each student's participation patterns and the apparent influence of these patterns on their revisions. It was found that there was considerable variation among the three students as to their willingness and ability to nominate topics for discussion and give other input, to set the agenda, and to negotiate meaning. The researchers also found that when changes had been negotiated between teacher and student in the conferences, the resulting revisions were likely to be successful ones. They concluded that conference dynamics may be influenced both by individual student personalities and possibly by cultural differences, which may "play a role in the students' perceptions of their [own] and their teachers' roles in a conference" (p. 456). They concluded that:

> We cannot expect that students will come to writing conferences understanding the purposes of such conferences, the rules of speaking, and the respective roles of the participants. Since the quality of their conferences and revisions can be affected by participant expectations, we must teach students the purposes conferences can serve, and stress that the discourse and the teacher-student relationship can vary greatly between a conference and a classroom. In a sense, we need to give students permission to break the rules they may have learned previously and we need to teach them new rules for a new speech event. (p. 457)

Goldstein and Conrad's warning that we cannot expect that students will automatically become engaged and slip naturally into the role of active, equal participants in writing conferences simply by virtue of the fact that conferences are taking place echoes that given by several thoughtful L1 researchers (e.g., Newkirk, 1995). They add to the picture the awareness that cross-cultural differences in expectations about teacher–student relationships may add a layer of complexity and even awkwardness to conferences between teachers and L2 writers.

Patthey-Chavez and Ferris (1997) examined first drafts, conference transcripts, revisions, and first drafts of the next essay assignment for eight students, four of whom were ESL writers, and four of whom were native English speakers. In addi-

tion, the eight students were subdivided into strong and weak writers. They report the following findings: (a) The conferences between the teachers and the weaker students were shorter and more teacher-dominated; (b) there were no measurable differences in the conference dynamics between the L1 and L2 writers; and (c) all eight of the student writers revised their texts in ways that could be directly traced to the conference input, though the stronger writers' revisions showed more autonomy and sophistication. The authors concluded that writing conferences may be a powerful pedagogical tool, and that quantitative and qualitative differences in conference transcripts across student writers should be expected and even welcomed as an indication that the teacher is adjusting his or her instructional strategies to the needs, abilities, and personalities of individual student writers.

Though the evidence on the effects of writing conferences is extremely limited, especially with regard to ESL writers, it seems relatively uncontroversial to say that teacher–student conferences can be helpful and very effective in some circumstances. What the previous research reminds us, however, is that we should be sensitive to differences across cultural expectations, personality, and language and writing proficiency in conducting conferences with ESL writers. There are several practical implications of these research observations. First, we need to be aware that a one-on-one interaction with a writing instructor may be extremely stressful for some students. This could affect their willingness to participate in the conference, their ability to comprehend what the teacher is saying during the conference, and their retention of key points after the conference is over. Secondly, writing conferences, unlike written teacher feedback, place additional burdens on L2 students' aural comprehension and oral fluency. Considering these potential problems and drawbacks, teachers may wish to make conferences optional rather than required (for those students for whom such an interaction might be truly upsetting), have three-way conferences (two students with one teacher, for a hybrid peer response/teacher conference session), or have the student writer (or the teacher) take notes on and/or audiotape conferences so that the student can review and remember points discussed later.

Other Feedback Delivery Systems

One alternative that has been suggested is for teachers to provide oral feedback on audiotapes rather than written feedback. Although it seems unlikely that this option will save teachers much time, it may benefit auditory learners and eliminates the problem of teacher handwriting interfering with the clarity of feedback. Another option that is rapidly gaining in popularity is the use of computer-based teacher feedback, whether through e-mail, the transfer of a floppy disk, or use of a software program that allows teachers to insert comments or codes directly into student texts. Computerized alternatives are likely to be more and more frequently used as teachers and students become increasingly computer-literate and as technology becomes more widely available on campuses and in students' homes. Research on the effects of alternative delivery systems is still in its early stages, however. Anecdotally, it seems apparent that when students e-mail papers to their instructors and teachers e-mail them back with comments, the result is generally that students get greater quantities of feedback (on a per-word basis) and that they receive it more frequently. Whether more is better, however, remains an open and important question yet to be explored empirically.

In the case of all of these alternatives to handwritten feedback—conferences, audiotapes, and computers—it also needs to be pointed out that they are not equally practical and available to all teachers and students. Zealous proponents of writing conferences tend to be those with relatively few students, and adequate space and time to conduct conferences. The plight of the part-time college or university lecturer who may teach as many as five or six writing courses at two or more institutions without office space or office hours is rarely considered. Reviewers of some of my own research articles on written teacher feedback have expressed surprise at the fact that I am investigating what in their minds is an impractical, passé form of response. Nonetheless, because it may always be more convenient for hardworking writing teachers to write comments directly onto student papers (which can be taken with them wherever they go!) than to schedule conferences, speak into a tape recorder, or sit at a computer, it remains important to ask questions about the optimal ways to provide such feedback. Suggestions that teachers abandon written commentary for other alternatives not only overlook real-world constraints on many (most?) writing teachers, but they may not even serve the best interests of the students, many of whom (see chap. 5) prefer written feedback to other methods because of personality, cultural expectations, or learning style.

CONCLUSION

In this chapter, I have examined numerous issues related to teacher response to student writing, looking closely at available research and what we have learned from it, identifying and commenting on a range of methodological issues that need to be considered in evaluating past research and designing future studies, and looking at the various alternative modes through which teachers can respond to their students' writing.

At the very least, this in-depth examination of teacher feedback suggests its continued importance, even centrality, in the teaching of L2 student writing. Teacher feedback may represent the single biggest investment of time by instructors, and it is certainly clear that students highly value and appreciate it (see also chapter 5). Though there is a lot to be learned about the best ways in which to give feedback and about how (and if) it facilitates students' writing development over time, we "composition slaves" can surely take comfort in the mounting evidence that our efforts are not in vain.

CHAPTER

3

Error Correction

THE HISTORY OF ERROR CORRECTION RESEARCH

As previously noted, the earliest L2 research on response to student writing dealt almost entirely with error correction, defined by Truscott (1996) as "correction of grammatical errors for the purpose of improving a student's ability to write accurately" (p. 329). Depending on the instructional context, Truscott's definition can be broadened to include lexical errors, including word choice, word form, and collocations, and mechanical errors such as spelling, punctuation, capitalization, and typing conventions. Between 1976 and 1986, there was a fair amount of research activity on questions related to error feedback (and related instructional issues) in L2 writing classes. Many of the studies discussed and analyzed in this chapter were published during this time period. From 1986 to 1996, there are few published studies on this topic, due no doubt to the prominence of the process-writing paradigm in ESL writing classes at the time with its consequent de-emphasizing of sentence-level accuracy issues (see chapter 1). In addition, as is discussed later in this chapter, a number of L1 and L2 researchers and reviewers concluded that error correction was ineffective as a means of improving student writing. These two factors—a powerful pedagogical model that actively discouraged a focus on form and a conflicting and somewhat discouraging research base—may well have convinced would-be error correction researchers that error correction in L2 writing was a "dead" issue, as out of vogue as previously trendy L2 teaching approaches like the Silent Way and Suggestopedia (or what Brown [1994] calls "The designer methods of the spirited seventies").

However, as the process approach ascended as a pedagogical model, ESL writing specialists became increasingly aware of and concerned about students' lingering problems in written accuracy (see, for example, Eskey, 1983; Horowitz, 1986; and Reid, 1994). L1 and L2 process advocates implied (and even stated outright in some cases) that if students' content were emphasized, appropriate form would follow naturally, as it does in children's L1 oral acquisition (Krashen, 1984; Sommers, 1982; Zamel, 1982, 1985). Yet as time went on, it became clear to many L2 writing teachers that students' errors were not disappearing as a natural consequence of a focus on students' ideas and writing processes, that students' lack of accuracy might well be held against them in various academic and professional contexts, and that students themselves were frustrated by the lack of grammar feedback instruction. In response to these concerns, a number of editing texts and how-to articles on dealing with student writers' language problems appeared during the same period of time (Ascher, 1993; Bates, Lane, & Lange, 1993; Ferris, 1995c; Fox, 1992; Frodesen, 1991; Lane & Lange, 1993; Raimes, 1992).

Perhaps frustrated by the stubborn refusal of error correction to disappear from the pedagogical landscape entirely, John Truscott (1996) reopened the debate in a controversial article published in *Language Learning*. Based on a three-part argument, Truscott advanced the thesis that "grammar correction has no place in writing courses and should be abandoned" (p. 328). His major points are (a) that the existing research on grammar correction provides no evidence that it helps student writers; (b) that grammar correction as it is currently practiced ignores important insights from second language acquisition (SLA) research; and (c) that insurmountable practical problems related to the abilities and motivations of teachers and students mandate against the practice of grammar correction ever being effective. Truscott's thesis and conclusions were criticized as being premature and overly strong in articles by Ellis (1998) and Ferris (1999b); Truscott reiterated and defended his argument in a 1999 rebuttal to Ferris. The major points of disagreement raised by Ellis and Ferris are that (a) the research evidence on error correction is not as uniformly negative as Truscott asserts; and (b) that even if it were consistent, it is nonetheless inadequate. The remainder of this chapter focuses on these two points. First, I establish an analytic framework for looking at the previous studies on error correction in L2 writing and use it systematically to provide detailed and comprehensive analyses of the studies available at the time of writing.[7] Then I address the inadequate research base and make detailed recommendations about questions and paradigms for further research on this topic. Chapter 7 then applies this analysis to specific suggestions for teachers on error treatment for second language writers.

---

[7]These primary research sources, as discussed in the beginning of this volume, include published studies, conference papers, ERIC documents, master's theses, and doctoral dissertations. However, no finding from an unpublished source is considered conclusive unless it is corroborated by evidence from a study published in a refereed journal.

A FRAMEWORK FOR ANALYZING
ERROR CORRECTION STUDIES

In examining the body of research that exists on this topic, it is immediately apparent that the studies have very little in common. In some cases, the subjects are English speakers in college-level foreign language classes in the United States. Even among those studies, disparities exist: Some students are merely completing foreign language general education requirements, whereas others are foreign language majors, not all of whom are studying the same L2. Other studies examine EFL learners studying outside of the United States, again in a range of cultural and linguistic contexts. Still others study ESL students in university contexts in the United States. The number of subjects ranges widely as well, from 3 to 134.

Besides differences in the nature and number of subjects, the research exhibits crucial variation on two other important levels: instructional methods and research paradigms utilized. In some studies, error feedback was given on freewrites and journal entries rather than on entire compositions. Students were required to revise or edit their writing after receiving error feedback in some cases; in others they were not. Some researchers report using detailed error correction schemes, whereas others are vague about what kind of feedback students received and even who provided it to them. Methods of data collection and analysis range widely as well, with some studies utilizing control groups and others not (and, as is discussed, even the term "control group" meant different things in different studies), some reporting baseline or pretest data and others not; some explicitly describing their analysis system (including reporting interrater or intercoder reliabilities) and others leaving their analysis procedures to the imagination of the reader.

Because of these distinctions, it is necessary to establish a framework for analyzing the studies themselves in order to assess the validity of their findings and conclusions. This three-part model is adapted from questions and issues posed by Ferris (1999a); Ferris and Hedgcock (1998); and Polio (1997). Part 1 of the model (Basic Parameters) addresses such fundamental issues as subject characteristics, sample size, and duration of instructional treatment and/or data collection. Part 2 (Instructional Procedures) looks at what the teacher(s) and students were actually doing: types of writing considered, context for writing (e.g., in-class or out-of-class), the nature of feedback given to the students (including who gave feedback, what categories of error were considered, and how the feedback was delivered), and what students were expected to do after receiving the feedback. Part 3 (Research Design) examines various methodological questions: Is the construct of "error" defined and operationalized for the purposes of the study? In experimental designs, was there a control group and a pretest/posttest comparison? How was linguistic accuracy measured, were multiple raters or coders involved, and are appropriate interrater reliabilities reported? Each part of the model is described and justified before I turn to the analysis of individual studies. Figure 3.1 summarizes the framework.

Part I: Basic Parameters

- Subject (students and teachers) characteristics: SL/FL, language majors or nonmajors, L2 proficiency, background in writing (process vs. product), formal grammar knowledge
- Sample size (including the size of treatment groups into which subjects were divided)
- Duration of instructional treatment and/or data collection

Part II: Instructional Procedures

- Type of writing considered (e.g., freewrites or journal entries vs. multiple-draft compositions; in-class vs. out-of-class)
- Larger instructional context: Were students given grammar instruction or resources for processing error feedback? Did they track their progress, and were they given increasing responsibility for self-editing?
- The nature of error feedback: Who provided it? What linguistic issues were addressed? What mechanisms (direct/indirect feedback, codes, etc.) were used for giving feedback?

Part III: Research Design

- Was an appropriate quantitative design employed (control group, pretest/posttest, accurate statistics, confounding variables accounted for)?
- Were multiple raters or coders used, were interrater reliabilities calculated and reported, and was it clear to what those reliability coefficients referred?

FIG. 3.1. A framework for analyzing error correction studies (adapted from Brown, 1991; Ferris, 1999b; Ferris & Hedgcock, 1998; Polio, 1997).

Part 1: Basic Parameters

Subjects. As noted earlier, subject populations and numbers have varied widely in previous research on written error correction. This is significant because the nature of the instructional context may well affect both teacher and student attention to accuracy in student writing. Hedgcock and Lefkowitz (1994) argued that there are two potentially crucial distinctions between second language (SL) and foreign language (FL) writers: (a) the purposes for which they are writing; and (b) the pedagogical contexts in which they have acquired L1 and L2 literacy. As to the first point, it would not be unreasonable to assume that students in foreign language classes who are merely fulfilling a graduation requirement rather than pursuing a major in that language and perhaps a career as a teacher or scholar of that language might be less motivated to improve their L2 writing and attend to teacher feedback about their errors. Similarly, it seems likely that ESL students, who will at minimum complete their education in English and may perhaps even pursue their careers in English-speaking countries or in disciplines in which a strong command of written English is critical for professional advancement, will take seriously the overall need to improve their writing and the specific need to attend to teacher feedback so that the accuracy and clarity of their writing will improve. EFL students, on the other hand, studying English in non-English-speaking countries, may well demonstrate the same varying degrees of motivation as FL students in the United States (i.e., dividing along English major/non-major lines).

Hedgcock and Lefkowitz (1994) also pointed out that L2 writers' prior educational backgrounds may affect their attitudes toward L2 writing in general and toward the role of teacher feedback in particular. Specifically, if students have been previously exposed to "product-centered instruction" (p. 143), in which they received feedback primarily to justify a grade but not to help them revise the text under consideration (or, in other terms, when teacher feedback is summative, rather than formative), they may not be highly motivated to attend to error correction (see also Cohen, 1987; Ferris, 1995b; and chapter 7 of this volume). Hedgcock and Lefkowitz further noted, based on their own previous research (Hedgcock & Lefkowitz, 1992), that writing in many American FL classes is "not a core element of the curriculum, but rather an ancillary component" (1994, p. 143). In contrast, in many North American college and university ESL programs, writing is a major concern of the curriculum, and students' final assessments will be based on direct tests of writing.

Even among ESL writers, who arguably have similar motivations for improving their writing, there is a crucial (and until very recently, largely overlooked) distinction between student populations: International (visa) students and immigrant (long-term resident) students. Such students may not only exhibit the disparities in prior educational training discussed earlier (i.e., process- vs. product-oriented instruction), but may also have widely differing levels of formal and acquired knowledge of the L2, which will have direct bearing on their ability to process and utilize error correction (Ferris, 1999a; Reid, 1998a). Specifically, international students may have a firm grasp on formal terms and rules of English grammar but little acquired sense of how to apply these concepts to their own writing, whereas immigrant student writers may rely on their own acquired knowledge of the L2 to self-correct their writing but have little or no ability to reference the formal system of grammar elicited by teacher error correction (Roberts, 1999).

Two final issues to consider about student subjects are their L2 proficiency level and their individual learner characteristics. SLA research makes it clear that there are developmental sequences related to the acquisition of various syntactic, morphological, and lexical structures. The degree to which learners have acquired these structures will undoubtedly affect their uptake of teacher error correction, whether for editing of the text under consideration or avoidance of errors in the future. Similarly, it would seem obvious that relevant learning styles such as field dependence and independence, tolerance or intolerance for ambiguity, and inductive and deductive input preferences would affect students' ability to process various types of feedback. However, it is difficult in the available body of research to assess the effects of either of these factors. In the case of learner proficiency, few studies are explicit as to the L2 level of the subjects. (Some describe their subjects as, for instance, "Japanese college freshmen" [Robb, Ross, & Shortreed, 1986, p. 85], but there is little or no reference to how their English language proficiency might relate to that of other learners in other contexts.) As to the issue of individual learning styles, there is virtually no published work on the relationship between these learner characteristics and student writers' ability to profit from error correction. So whereas we can certainly speculate as to the effects of these variables on the development of accuracy in student writing—and include them as part of an agenda for future research on this topic—neither of these factors is discussed further in the review of existing research.

Finally, the missing "subject" in most of these reports is the teacher or teachers. Almost never is any background information given about instructors—their training, prior teaching experience, grammatical knowledge, philosophies or strategies regarding error feedback, and so on. Instead, instructors in these research designs are treated as interchangeable. For instance, in the aforementioned Cohen and Robbins (1976) study, it is stated that "The papers were corrected by one of three people, the instructor or one of the two volunteer classroom aides" (p. 50). In other studies, in which treatment groups consisted of intact classes, the feedback (and other instruction) was provided by the different classroom teachers. Only rarely, however, is there any discussion of how differences across instructors were controlled for; we can only gather that the researchers assumed that the instructors were all giving their students quantitatively and qualitatively similar feedback without ever assessing whether they in fact really did so. In a recent study in which nearly 6,000 corrections given to 92 ESL writers by three teachers (Ferris, Chaney, Komura, Roberts, & McKee, 2000), substantial differences were found across teachers in the amount of feedback they gave students, in their feedback strategies, and in the short- and long-term effects of the feedback on students—*despite the fact that the teachers had agreed to give feedback, for the purposes of the experimental design, according to a uniform error checklist!* As Truscott pointed out in some detail (1996, pp. 349–351), there are a number of ways in which teacher feedback can and does go wrong. Ferris (1999b) asserted that "poorly done error correction will not help student writers and may even mislead them" (p. 4). The fact that the "teacher variable" is almost never addressed in the literature is a substantial problem in assessing the existing research, and the significance of this problem should not be underestimated.

Sample Size.   In the research available at the time of writing, sample sizes ranged from three case study subjects (Cohen & Robbins, 1976) to 141 students (Semke, 1984). Clearly, most of the research on this topic has been conducted on a rather small scale. This is important for at least three reasons. First, in the case of qualitative case study research, readers, researchers, and reviewers need to take care that overly inflated claims are not advanced—even to the point of becoming canonical—on the basis of so few subjects. The case study of Cohen and Robbins (1976), which has been widely cited in subsequent error correction research, is a good example. For instance, Robb et al. (1986), in discussing the previous study, remarked that "Such feedback as Cohen and Robbins (1976) report *negates any positive effects of error correction*" (p. 84, emphasis added).[8] Truscott (1996) also cited Cohen and Robbins' study as being persuasive evidence in support of his thesis that

---

[8]In fairness to Robb et al., they did make it clear in the following sentence that Cohen and Robbins studied only three ESL writers. However, the point is that they made an extremely strong statement about the value of the feedback given in that study—and with three subjects, any findings and conclusions must be viewed as informative rather than definitive!

"grammar correction does not work" (pp. 329–330), despite both the small sample size and the authors' own explanation that the teacher feedback was not well executed and that this was most likely the reason why it did not appear to help the case study subjects. Secondly, in the case of quantitative studies utilizing an experimental design, an already small sample is often subdivided into as many as four different treatment groups. It can be difficult to establish statistical significance for differences in populations when small sample sizes are considered. Thus we have cases in which the raw numbers shown in tables show clear differences among treatment groups that are "not statistically significant" (e.g., Kepner, 1991). This finding (of no statistically significant differences) is then given great weight in the authors' own discussions and in citations in subsequent articles. This is not to challenge the notion of statistical significance in quantitative research but rather to point out that small sample sizes and treatment groups may complicate matters and make results harder to interpret meaningfully.

Third, it is important to interpret the discussion and conclusions of individual researchers carefully in light of sample size considerations. It is all too common in the literature for "sound bites" from the abstracts or conclusions of previous studies to be cited or quoted as being authoritative by later researchers or reviewers, yet when one examines the primary data, one finds that some very strong assertions have been made on the basis of very limited data (see Spack, 1997, for an excellent discussion of this phenomenon of string-cite sound bites). One case in point from the error correction literature will illustrate this danger. A 1990 study by Chastain, published in *Modern Language Journal,* examines the effects of error correction on graded and ungraded student compositions. On careful reading, one finds that Chastain had a subject population of only 14 students and that the data collected included only two papers (one graded, one ungraded) from each student.[9] Yet Chastain, after reporting no differences in student accuracy between the ungraded and graded compositions, provided the following sound bite conclusion and pedagogical recommendation:

> Except with regard to length and sentence complexity, the work on graded and ungraded compositions of motivated students appears to be quite similar. *Therefore, busy instructors can continue to assign writing tasks without expanding their own work load beyond the breaking point or without feeling guilty for not grading the compositions.* (1990, p. 14, emphasis added)

Duration of Instructional Treatment and/or Data Collection.   The existing research on error correction ranges from one-shot experimental treatments (e.g., Fathman & Whalley, 1990) to data collection that took place over the course of an academic year[10] (Robb et al., 1986). Duration of treatment or study is obviously an important factor to consider, as both SLA theory and common sense hold that it takes awhile for students to acquire linguistic structures and for instructional

---

[9]The researcher in this case was apparently also the instructor, although this is not entirely clear.

[10]This "year-long" description is somewhat misleading. Robb et al. pointed out that the "academic year" for this Japanese EFL class consisted of only 23 90-minute meetings for a total of 34.5 hours of instructional time, or less contact time than the typical American university semester- or quarter-length course. In addition, there was one 2-month break and one 2-week break during the course.

techniques to take hold and actually help students. One important recommendation for future research would be for truly longitudinal studies (say over the course of several years) to be conducted in order to assess how much feedback students need for how long in order to improve in written accuracy or whether it is necessary at all because students will improve gradually over time through regular L2 reading and writing activity.

Part 2: Instructional Procedures

Types of Writing Considered. One issue that is never mentioned by Truscott or other reviewers is the nature of the writing that students were doing. In the same way that the overall context of instruction (SL, FL, major/non-major) may yield significant information about students' purposes and motivation for attending to error feedback, student attitudes, attention, and effort may vary according to both the type of writing being considered and what they are expected to do with the text after receiving feedback.

For instance, two studies that report no significant positive effects for error correction (Frantzen, 1995; Kepner, 1991) deal with students' free-writing and journal entries, respectively. Free-writes and journals have typically been utilized in SL/FL classes to provide students with "no-risk" opportunities to practice their written English and to improve their fluency and confidence (Ferris & Hedgcock, 1998; Krashen, 1984; Zamel, 1982, 1985). If students have been told to express their ideas freely without worrying about grammar and mechanics, it might appear to students as a "bait-and-switch" if such texts are then returned to them marked for errors.[11] More importantly, it may well be the case that error correction is most effective for both short- and long-term improvement in accuracy when students are required to revise their texts after receiving feedback. As discussed in chapter 7, student subjects in at least one study claimed to pay more attention to teacher feedback on preliminary drafts of compositions that would be revised than on final, graded drafts that would not be further revised (Ferris, 1995b).

Another distinction related to writing type is the difference between in-class writing completed under time constraints and out-of-class writing. Several researchers have examined this issue from various angles (e.g., Fathman & Whalley, 1990; Ferris, 1995a; Kroll, 1990; Polio, Fleck, & Leder, 1998). Clearly, it is necessary in some experimental designs to obtain maximum control over students' writing and editing processes (through in-class writing and editing) in order to accurately compare the effects of various feedback treatments. However, it should be obvious that the nature and quality of student editing may vary depending on the time constraints, and this point is rarely considered in research reviews.

---

[11]On the other hand, it should be noted that in student survey research, L2 subjects have expressed disappointment when such "fluency-based" activities are NOT corrected (see, e.g., Leki, 1991). Thus, error correction in such circumstances may not be as negatively perceived as teachers might believe.

A final consideration with regard to the classroom context of giving and receiving feedback is whether error feedback is embedded in an overall approach to addressing issues of linguistic accuracy. For instance, in the particular writing or language class(es) being studied, is accuracy important to overall student success, and is its importance communicated to students (e.g., through grading schemes, in-class editing sessions, strategy training, etc.)? Are students provided with any in-class instruction or out-of-class resources to learn more about problematic structures? Are students held accountable for progress and are they encouraged to track their own progress? Error feedback is, of course, only one component of writing instruction, and only one part of a focus on form in a writing course. The degree to which these other instructional components are part of the classroom may add to or detract from the effects of teacher error correction on student writing.

The Nature of Feedback Given to Students.   Probably the most crucial issue to examine in the research base on error feedback is *what kind of feedback* was given to the students in the study. As discussed in the previous section, it would not be surprising to find that poorly designed error feedback did not help student writing and may even have caused harm (Cohen & Robbins, 1976; Ferris, 1999b; Truscott, 1996). To examine error feedback carefully, at least three questions need to be considered: (a) *Who* provided the feedback? (b) *What linguistic issues* did the feedback cover, and how were those structures selected? (c) *What specific mechanisms* were used for giving feedback?

In most error correction studies, the classroom instructors provided the feedback. Exceptions include the previously mentioned study by Cohen and Robbins (1976) in which the teacher and "two volunteer classroom aides" rotated giving feedback and Kepner's (1991) study in which the researcher constructed the feedback and the classroom teachers copied it in their own handwriting so that the students wouldn't be confused or put off. Also, in most studies there were two or more different instructors involved in providing error feedback and other types of related instruction. Yet rarely is "instructor" a variable that is considered in analysis or conclusions, and only in a few cases did the researcher(s) spot-check the error feedback given by the instructors. On the contrary, it seems taken as a given that all of the instructors were equally consistent, accurate, and effective in constructing error feedback. But the little research evidence there is on this point suggests that there may be tremendous variability across instructors in how they give error feedback, even when they have been asked to adhere to a particular system of correction for research purposes (Cohen & Robbins, 1976; Ferris et al., 2000; Truscott, 1996; Zamel, 1985).

In assessing the usefulness of error feedback, it is also important to know what linguistic structures were addressed by the instructors or researchers in providing error correction. As has been noted by SLA researchers and by L2 reviewers on error correction, the notion of "error" is not always well defined. For instance, if a teacher thinks that a different word or phrase inserted in a student text would express the student's idea more precisely or elegantly, is that feedback really "error correction," or a stylistic suggestion, to be acted on or ignored depending on the will of the writer? SLA research has also identified developmental sequences for acquisition of various lexical, syntactic, and morphological forms. If a researcher does not carefully define error and identify the categories of error being considered, it would be possible to blame error correction for "failing" to produce more accurate student writing when in fact the structures being marked by teachers were beyond the L2 developmental level of the students. Other important distinctions have been made in the literature between "global" and "local" errors (Bates, Lane, & Lange, 1993; Corder, 1967; Ferris & Hedgcock, 1998; Hendrickson, 1978; 1980), the former being errors that interfere with communication and the latter being more minor errors that do not obscure the comprehensibility of the text. Finally, as a pedagogical distinction, Ferris (1999b) noted the difference between "treatable" and "untreatable" errors, with treatable errors related to rule-governed structures (so students could consult a grammar book to solve the problem) and untreatable errors being idiomatic or idiosyncratic structures such as prepositions, collocations, and other lexical or syntactic problems that defy classification or explanation. Because all errors are not alike in their difficulty for L2 learners, their severity in impeding written communication, and their ability to "respond to treatment," the researchers' and teachers' decisions about which errors to mark are of vital importance in evaluating the effectiveness of the treatment and interpreting the findings. In error correction research, some authors are quite explicit in reporting how they define "error," operationalize error categories, and relate findings to specific error types, whereas others are quite vague, noting only that "errors were corrected" (Semke, 1984, p. 196), or that "all categories of lexical, syntactic, and stylistic errors" were covered (Robb et al., 1986, p. 86).

Finally, the mechanisms or strategies used to give feedback are important to consider. There has been some disagreement among researchers and teachers as to whether selective or comprehensive correction is preferable. Advocates of selective correction (choosing several major patterns of error in a student paper to mark rather than trying to address all types of error) argue that this more limited approach allows students to focus on their more serious writing problems without overwhelming them and their teachers (e.g., Ferris, 1995c; Hendrickson, 1978, 1980; Krashen, 1984). Those who argue for comprehensive error correction (e.g., Lalande, 1982) argue that students need such detailed feedback in order to improve, primarily because they may be misled about the correctness of their writing if teachers do not mark all errors. In understanding error correction research, it is necessary to know whether teachers and researchers were practicing selective or comprehensive error correction.

Another important distinction is between direct and indirect feedback, to borrow terms used by Hendrickson (1978, 1980). Direct feedback is provided when the teacher writes the correct form onto the student's paper; if the student is required to edit the text after receiving feedback, such "editing" consists mainly of transcribing the teacher's contributions into the paper. Indirect feedback, on the other hand, requires the student to engage in "guided problem-solving" (Lalande, 1982) when the teacher indicates that an error has occurred through underlining, circling, highlighting, or otherwise noting the error. If error correction codes are provided, the student can (ostensibly) use that information to figure out what the correct forms should be. If no codes or labels are used, the student is required not only to self-correct the error, but also to identify the type of error indicated. Most researchers agree that indirect feedback has more potential than direct feedback for long-term student

↳ Inconsistent in teachers' feedback

improvement because of increased student engagement and attention to forms and problems. However, there is some debate as to whether indirect feedback is appropriate under all circumstances. Hendrickson (1980) suggested that direct feedback may be more helpful on final graded versions of student papers (which the students themselves will not be editing) so that the student writers get input about the correct forms at the end of the process. It has also recently been suggested that direct feedback may be useful for "untreatable" (non-rule-governed) errors as a means of giving students input on errors that they might not be able to self-correct (Chaney, 1999; Ferris, 1999b). Because the terms "direct" and "indirect" feedback are not used consistently in the literature, it is necessary to ascertain what exactly is meant by them in a particular study. For instance, in one study, the group designated as the "control" or "no-feedback" group was actually given indirect (underlined, but not coded) feedback (Frantzen, 1995)!

Beyond the broad distinction between direct and indirect feedback, the specific mechanisms used for giving feedback may be significant in understanding whether or not they helped students. There is some evidence from case study and survey research that L2 writers may be confused by teacher strategies with regard to circling, underlining, color-coding, or abbreviations attached to their errors (Cohen & Robbins, 1976; Ferris, 1995b). If student writers fail to progress in accuracy despite receiving feedback, it may be because they did not understand the feedback and that an improved delivery system (fewer error categories and codes, using words rather than symbols, etc.) would provide students with better information and help them more in the long run.

Part 3: Research Design

Specific questions related to research methodology in error correction studies are similar to those posed about any quantitative or quasi-experimental study (see Brown, 1988, 1991): Was there a control group? A pretest/posttest design? Were potential confounding variables adequately controlled for (or otherwise accounted for)? Were the appropriate statistical procedures applied, and were they interpreted appropriately? Many of these issues, particularly those related to subject characteristics, sample size, and the operationalization of "error" as a research construct, have been addressed in the previous sections of this chapter, but one extremely important issue in text analysis research is the use of independent raters or coders and the calculation and reporting of interrater reliability coefficients.

As discussed by Polio (1997) in her excellent article, there are a number of ways to measure linguistic accuracy. These include error counting, ratios of errors to number of obligatory contexts of a particular structure, and ratios of errors to measures of length and syntactic complexity such as number of words, clauses, T-units, or error-free T-units. Because of the complexity and variability of English grammar, nearly all of these measures involve some degree of subjective judgment. This is why it is important to have at least two different raters or coders look at a sample or subsample of the texts being analyzed to make sure that the system of analysis being used is followed as precisely and consistently as possible. If multiple raters are used, it is important to calculate and report interrater reliability coefficients; these statistics assess the internal consistency of the raters and the overall reliability of the analysis.

Most of the quantitative studies on error correction do indeed report interrater reliability results. However, as Polio correctly noted, it is not always clear what is measured by those coefficients. For example, if two raters independently analyze the same paper for errors and both report finding a total of 25 errors, the researcher could report 100% reliability between raters. But did the two raters mark the same 25 errors, and did they categorize them in the same way? As Polio reported from her own studies, minor discrepancies along these lines may prove to be unimportant in the final analysis. Still it is helpful to note whether researchers have calculated reliabilities and whether it is clear what those statistics mean.

REVIEW OF ERROR CORRECTION STUDIES

Figure 3.2 provides a brief snapshot of each error correction study reviewed, presented in chronological order.[12] In the review that follows, I focus on the most salient details and findings of each study, highlighting specific strengths and weaknesses related to the analytical framework I have presented.

The earliest study cited is that of Cohen and Robbins (1976), which is a case study of three ESL students at a U.S. university. Data consisted of all writing done by the students over a quarter and interviews with the students. The authors report finding no relationship between teacher correction and student production of errors over time. This study has several major limitations: (a) it considers only three students; (b) it considers only one category of error (verb form errors); (c) feedback was given by three different instructors, two of whom were volunteers, and was, according to the authors not "systematic nor enlightened enough" (p. 45); and (d) students did not consistently revise their writing after receiving feedback.

Lalande (1982) studied 60 German FL students at a U.S. university, analyzing the difference between a "traditional" error correction system (direct correction of all errors) and a "guided learning and problem-solving" approach, in which students received indirect, coded feedback, the opportunity to correct errors in class immediately after receiving feedback, and error charts on which their progress was measured over time. Lalande reported that the experimental group students made significantly fewer errors over time than the control group students. The design of this study appears fairly sound. The major criticism that has been made of Lalande's study by Truscott (1996) and VanPatten (1988) is that there is no true control group that received no feedback at all. Thus, Lalande's study demonstrates the superiority of one treatment over another treatment, but does not show that students do better over time with error correction than without it. Another possible weakness is that the error feedback was given by the different classroom instructors, and there was no reported independent checking by the researcher to make sure that each instructor provided equally accurate and comprehensive feedback.

---

[12]For this section, only studies that specifically looked at error correction (provided by teachers and/or researchers) and its effects on student accuracy were considered. Studies that simultaneously considered teacher feedback on content or form are also discussed in chapter 2.

FIG. 3.2. Summary of error correction studies.

Study Name(s)	Basic Parameters	Instructional Procedures	Research Design Issues
Cohen & Robbins (1976)	Three "advanced" ESL students at U.S. university; one 10-week quarter.	Writing studied: In- and out-of-class essays; grammar exercises; some rewrites of essays. Only verb form errors studied. Feedback given by instructor and two volunteer aides using a correction checklist, but correction procedures were not consistent across responders.	Case study approach: Interviews plus text analysis. No statistics reported
Lalande (1982)	Sixty "fourth quarter (intermediate-level)" German FL students at U.S. university. Fifteen students in each of four classes; two classes designated "control groups" and two "experimental groups" (i.e., two comparison groups of 30 students each).	Five in-class essays and three in-class rewrites. Both control and experimental groups had "extensive grammar review" in class. Feedback provided by the four classroom instructors; control group instructors more experienced. Control group received direct correction of all errors. Experimental group received indirect coded corrections using a checklist of 20 symbols (12 grammatical and orthographic errors in German usage). Both groups rewrote (controls) or corrected (experimental) essays in class. Experimental group also charted errors over time.	Distinct control and treatment groups with pretest/posttest design. T-test and ANOVA scores reported. Interrater reliabilities reported for "pilot study" of the four teachers; it is not clear to what exactly reliability scores refer.
Semke (1984)	One hundred forty-one first-year (third quarter) German students at U.S. university; one 10-week quarter. Students were in eight different sections; two sections each in four different treatment groups. Treatment group sizes ranged from 30 to 46.	Students' weekly journal entries on assigned topics were given four different feedback treatments: (a) comments only; (b) direct corrections only; (c) direct corrections with comments; (d) indirect (coded) correction. All feedback was given by a German instructor who was not one of the classroom instructors and spot-checked by the researcher. No specific information about error types or in-class instruction was provided. Group 4 (indirect correction) was also required to rewrite their compositions.	Four different treatment groups (no controls) with a pretest/posttest design. Tests consisted of a 10-minute freewrite and a cloze test. No reliability scores reported.

Robb, Ross, & Shortreed (1986)	One hundred thirty-four Japanese college freshman (EFL composition classes) assigned to four different sections for one academic year (23 classes; 34.5 contact hours with two lengthy vacation breaks). The four treatment group sizes ranged from 30 to 37.	Classroom activities consisted of editing sample student compositions, sentence combining exercises, and preparation for weekly essay assignments. Composition assignments included narrative, expository, and descriptive essays; weekly essays had to be revised based on feedback given by instructors. Two classroom teachers rotated among the four classes and provided instruction and feedback. Error categories not specified. Feedback types included: (a) direct correction; (b) indirect coded feedback; (c) indirect highlighted feedback (no codes); (d) indirect marginal feedback (number of errors per line totalled and noted in the margins).	Five "narrative test compositions" written at equal intervals; the first served as a pretest. No control group. Three raters graded the test papers on 19 different measures. Interrater reliabilities reported for both objective and subjective measures, calculated for pretest papers.
Frantzen & Rissell (1987)	Fourteen fourth-semester Spanish students at a U.S. university. Semester-long study.	For three compositions during the semester, students received indirect, uncoded feedback on all errors. Students were then given ten minutes in class to correct (not recopy) the compositions.	Students' ability to self-correct various Spanish constructions was analyzed. No second rater was mentioned; no reliabilities reported.
Chastain (1990)	Fourteen third- or fourth-year Spanish majors at U.S. university in intact class. Two papers (one graded; one ungraded) collected for each student near the end of the semester.	"Process"-oriented composition class; weekly compositions with two drafts each. Every third paper was graded; the other two were ungraded. Some grammar study included in class. It is not clear whether they received between–draft feedback of any type; final drafts were graded with ¼ of the grade based on grammar. No error types specified for either feedback for analysis.	Researcher/instructor provided all feedback and did all analysis independently. No control group; no pretest/posttest. T-tests used for comparisons between graded and ungraded compositions.

(FIG. 3.2 continued)

(FIG. 3.2 continued)

Study Name(s)	Basic Parameters	Instructional Procedures	Research Design Issues
Fathman & Whalley (1990)	Seventy-two "intermediate" ESL students at two U.S. colleges. Subjects were divided into four treatment groups with sizes ranging from 14 to 22. The duration of the study was "a few days" (p. 182); it was a one-time experimental treatment.	Students wrote 30-minute in-class compositions based on a picture-story sequence. Papers were given one of four feedback treatments: (a) no feedback; (b) grammar feedback only; (c) content feedback only; (d) grammar and content feedback. Students then had 30 minutes in class to revise their papers. Grammar feedback consisted of "underlining all grammar errors" (p. 182)—that is, indirect, uncoded feedback. It is unclear whether the teachers or the researchers gave the feedback.	A "no-feedback" control group was included in the design. Pretest and posttest data consisted of original and revised compositions; t-tests used to measure differences. No interrater reliabilities reported.
Kepner (1991)	Sixty "intermediate" Spanish (non-major) students at a U.S. college, divided into two treatment groups of 30 subjects each. Duration of treatment was one semester.	Eight journal entries written over the course of the semester. One group received error correction feedback; the other received "message-related" comments. Students not required to revise journal entries after receiving feedback. The sixth journal entry was selected for analysis and comparison. Feedback was provided by the researcher. Error categories not specifically defined.	No control group. No baseline measure of students' writing abilities prior to the study. Interrater reliabilities reported for both types of feedback.
Sheppard (1992)	Twenty six "upper-intermediate" ESL students, divided into two treatment groups of thirteen each, at a U.S. college. Ten week treatment period.	Two narrative essays were compared as pretest/posttest. One group received comprehensive coded error correction; the other group received written "requests for clarification" in the margins of their papers. Both groups then had conferences with the teacher/author. The correction group then rewrote their papers. The two groups otherwise had identical instruction.	No control group (two different treatments being compared). No other rater was used; no reliabilities reported. Pretest/posttest design. No control for the effects of the one-to-one conferences.
Ferris (1995a)	Thirty advanced ESL writers at a U.S. university. Semester-long study.	Final drafts of three out-of-class essays and two in-class essays were analyzed for instances of five major error categories. All students received generalized error feedback (endnote + selective indirect feedback) on first drafts from the instructor/researcher. In-class activities included mini-lessons on the major error categories, peer- and self-editing activities, and maintenance of an error log.	No control group; no pretest; progress measured longitudinally over a semester. Interrater reliabilities reported.

Frantzen (1995)	Forty-four Spanish majors at a U.S. university divided into two treatment groups of 22 each. Semester-long study.	Students wrote four in-class and five out-of-class essays. The "grammar" group received regular in-class grammar instruction and direct correction of all errors. Specific Spanish grammar points were covered in the in-class instruction. The grammar group had to revise their essays after receiving correction, and grammar was part of their final grade. The "non-grammar" group received indirect feedback on errors, did not have to revise their essays, and were graded on content only. It is not clear whether instructors or the researcher provided the feedback. The first and fourth in-class essays were analyzed as "pretest" and "posttest." Twelve specific error categories were analyzed.	No true control group, as "non-grammar" group also received error feedback. Pretest/posttest design. Ratio of errors to obligatory contexts ("correct usage ratio") was calculated. Analysis done partly by computer program; no additional raters or reliability analysis reported.
Ferris (1997)	Forty-seven ESL students at a U.S. university. Semester-long study.	Three two-draft essays were analyzed. Teacher feedback included comments on content and endnotes with indirect textual corrections on grammar. Students revised after receiving feedback. No specific error categories were identified.	Longitudinal study. Interrater reliabilities reported.
Polio, Fleck, & Leder (1998)	Sixty-five ESL students at a U.S. university, divided into two treatment groups. Seven-week treatment within a semester-long study.	Both groups wrote four journal entries per week for a 7-week period. The control group received no feedback. Experimental group students had in-class editing instruction and error correction and revised one journal entry per week. In-class essays written at the beginning and end of the semester were used as pretests and posttests. Error correction techniques are not described, and it is not stated whether the researchers or the instructors gave the feedback.	Control group was used with a pretest/posttest design. Error analysis explicitly defined. Interrater reliability procedures and results are reported.

(FIG. 3.2 continued)

(FIG. 3.2 continued)

Study Name(s)	Basic Parameters	Instructional Procedures	Research Design Issues
Chandler (2000)	Thirty ESL students at a U.S. college, divided into two treatment groups. Semester-long study.	Students wrote five autobiographical essays; the first and fifth essays were analyzed and compared. Control group students received essays back with errors underlined; experimental group students were required to revise their papers after receiving feedback. Feedback was given by the instructor/researcher. No specific error definitions or categories were discussed.	No true control (no-feedback) group. No other raters included; no reliabilities recorded. Number of errors per 100 words was calculated.
Ferris et al. (2000); Ferris & Helt (2000)	Ninety-two ESL students at a U.S. university, divided into two treatment groups. Semester-long study.	Students wrote four three-draft essays. Second drafts of first and fourth essays were analyzed. Students received a combination of direct and indirect feedback from their instructors and revised after receiving feedback. Sixteen specific categories of errors were marked and analyzed. Experimental group students completed a log of their errors; control groups did not maintain a log.	No true control (no-feedback) group. Longitudinal design. Interrater reliabilities calculated and reported for analysis of long-term improvement only.
Ferris & Roberts (2001)	Seventy-two ESL students, divided into three treatment groups. Experimental design.	Students wrote an in-class essay which then received one of three treatments: (a) no feedback; (b) errors underlined; (c) errors underlined with error codes attached. During an in-class editing session, they attempted to correct as many errors as they could.	Not longitudinal; had a control group with pre/post-treatment design.

Semke's (1984) study also considered German FL students in the United States. One hundred forty-one students were divided into four groups, each of which received a different feedback treatment: comments only, direct correction, direct correction with comments, and indirect (coded) correction. Only the final group (indirect correction) was required to revise papers after receiving feedback. Semke reported no significant differences among the four treatment groups in written accuracy on a posttest and concluded that "corrections do not increase writing accuracy ... and they may have a negative effect on student attitudes" (p. 195). However, Semke's subjects received feedback on journal entries, which, as previously noted, are typically not revised (thus, students may not attend to corrections). Further, the posttest on which the analysis and conclusions are based consisted of a 10-minute freewrite, which arguably does not provide students with an adequate framework (in terms of time or task) to demonstrate any progress in written accuracy. As in Lalande's study, there was no control group that received no feedback at all, nor were any interrater reliability scores reported.

Robb et al. (1986) studied 134 Japanese EFL university students, divided into four treatment groups that received progressively less explicit feedback (ranging from direct feedback to totals in the margin). All students were required to revise their essays after receiving feedback. Although all four groups improved on various accuracy ratios over time (e.g., ratio of error-free T-units to total T-units), the authors argued that there is no apparent benefit attached to more-explicit versus less-explicit correction methods, arguing that the time and effort expended by instructors to provide direct feedback or coded feedback is not justified by the results. Robb et al. used so many different measures of accuracy that the results are a bit hard to interpret, but a couple of comments can be made:

1.   Again, there was no control group. We can assess the relative merits of the four correction methods utilized, but not whether correction is justified at all.

2.   According to Robb et al.'s Table 1 (p. 89), there were sizable differences in accuracy among the four groups on the pretest measure. Thus, students in the different groups had substantially different "change" scores between the beginning and end of the course—but this is confounded by the fact that students in some of the groups had further to go in the first place, so more dramatic short-term improvements could be observed.

It is also important to note that although the Robb et al. study had the longest duration (the class took place over a 9-month academic year), there was relatively little classroom contact time.

Frantzen and Rissell (1987) examined the ability of 14 Spanish FL students at a U.S. university to self-correct errors after receiving indirect, uncoded feedback. The focus of the study was to create a "hierarchy of correctability" with regard to various Spanish constructions. It was found that student ability to self-correct after receiving feedback varied dramatically depending on the morphological or syntactic construction being considered—ranging from 100% accurate self-correction of masculine and plural article errors to only 20% for subjunctive use. This study is limited again by the small sample size (14 students, three papers) and by the apparent lack of another independent rater. (The first author/teacher seemingly provided all the corrections and did all of the analysis.)

Fathman and Whalley (1990) studied 72 ESL students at two U.S. colleges. They looked at the effects of both content-based (see chapter 4) and form-based feedback on papers that the subjects immediately revised under controlled experimental conditions. They found that the two treatment groups who received indirect, uncoded grammar feedback reduced their number of errors significantly on the rewriting task but that the other two groups (content-feedback only and no feedback) did not. Truscott (1996), commenting on Fathman and Whalley's study, pointed out that demonstrating students' ability to reduce errors on a rewriting task does not prove that their accuracy will improve over time given the same treatment; his point is well taken. Still, Fathman and Whalley's study is useful in that a true no-feedback control group was included (so we can assess at least the short-term effects of correction vs. no correction) and that it provides evidence that students can process feedback on content and form simultaneously (contrary to the assertions of various L1 and L2 researchers).

Kepner's (1991) study of college-level Spanish students in the United States is often cited as persuasive evidence that error correction does not help students over time (cf., Polio, Fleck, & Leder, 1998; Truscott, 1996). The 60 students in this study were divided into two treatment groups, one of which received direct error correction and the other of which received "message-related" comments. Kepner reported that the group who received "message-related" comments had greater incidences of "higher level proposition counts" whereas there were no significant differences in accuracy between the two feedback groups. However, Kepner's study is so riddled with design and validity problems that it bears some close scrutiny.

First, Kepner's subjects were Spanish nonmajors. Second, the writing that received feedback consisted of journal entries that students were not required to revise. These two factors taken together suggest that the students were likely not highly engaged or investing in dealing with their Spanish writing at all or with error feedback in particular. Third, there was no baseline or pretest measure of errors or propositional content in the students' entries. Kepner analyzed the sixth set of journal entries (out of eight total) for comparison purposes, but she did not look at the first set of journal entries to see where the students started out on this type of writing. Fourth, there was no control for the length of the journal entries (which were written outside of class), a variable that could affect both error and proposition counts.

Another study frequently cited as evidence against error correction is that of Sheppard (1992). Sheppard compared two narrative compositions by 26 college-level ESL students in the United States (divided into two treatment groups of 13 each) in order to assess the effects over a 10-week quarter of two different feedback treatments: comprehensive indirect (coded) error feedback versus general marginal comments about the clarity of the writers' ideas. Both groups had follow-up one-to-one conferences with the teacher/author and the error correction group was required to rewrite their papers after the feedback and conference. (Sheppard did not state whether students in the other treatment group revised as well.) Sheppard reported that on two measures of accuracy (use of verb forms and sentence boundary markers), both groups improved in accuracy over time, but that only the "punctuation" measure yielded statistically significant differences between the two groups (with the "comments" group showing greater improvement than the "corrections" group. Sheppard's study is obviously limited by the small sample size (particularly the size of the two treatment groups). There are also several methodological issues that are problematic:

1.   The author was also the teacher and no other rater was apparently utilized in analysis.

2.   No data were collected or analyzed about the effects of the teacher–student conferences conducted after written feedback was given (Thus, it is unclear whether the effects of treatment are based upon the written feedback, the conferences, or a combination of the two).

3.   The error correction group received comprehensive correction, but only two specific measures of accuracy were analyzed (verbs and sentence markers), which may mean that students who received error correction improved in accuracy on other syntactic or morphological structures not analyzed and/or that correction of all errors and not only the two being analyzed may have confused or overwhelmed the students, causing the corrections to have less effect than if they had received selective correction of the two measures under consideration.

Given these issues, Sheppard's conclusion that "… students who negotiate meaning in a conference with a teacher are unlikely to do so at the risk of diminished accuracy; *indeed, they are more likely to be accurate in their use of the language than students whose attention is constantly drawn to surface-level inaccuracies and repair techniques*" (pp. 107–108, emphasis added) seems excessive.

Ferris (1995a) examined 136 papers written by 30 university ESL students in the United States. These included both in-class and out-of-class essays. The out-of-class essays received both peer and teacher feedback on various drafts; the teacher feedback consisted of selective indirect (uncoded) correction targeted to each individual student's most prevalent patterns of errors chosen from five major categories. Ferris looked at student progress in these five categories from the beginning to the end of the semester and at the differences in accuracy between in-class and out-of-class writing. The results indicated that nearly all (28 of 30) of the students showed at least some improvement from the beginning to the end of the semester, though progress was not consistent across all error categories and all assignments. In addition, students were substantially more accurate on out-of-class essays than on in-class writing. There was no comparison group; thus it is impossible to know whether similar improvement would have occurred if students had received no error feedback.

Frantzen (1995) examined the writing of 44 Spanish majors at a U.S. university. The "control" group received indirect (uncoded) feedback on errors, did not revise their papers, and were not graded on accuracy. The "experimental" group received direct correction of errors and in-class grammar instruction, they were required to revise their essays after receiving feedback, and they were graded (in part) on the accuracy of their writing. She reported no benefits of error correction for the "grammar" group; in fact, on one construction, their accuracy worsened (p. 336, Table 2).

The results of this study are challenging to interpret because there were so many differences in treatment between the two groups: (a) One group received indirect feedback, whereas the other received direct feedback; (b) One group revised their papers whereas the other group did not; (c) One group was graded on accuracy whereas the other group was not; and (d) One group received in-class grammar instruction whereas the other group did not. Factors (b), (c), and (d) would seemingly predict a favorable outcome for the "grammar group"—they had revision opportunities, higher motivation to improve in accuracy, and more input about grammar. However, if indirect feedback benefits long-term growth in accuracy more than direct feedback (as in Lalande's study), Factor (a) would predict that the "control" group would do better. With four different comparison factors operating simultaneously, it is also impossible to isolate the relative effects of any of them, and to resolve the conflicting predictions about the outcome of the experiment.

Ferris (1997) looked at the effects of teacher commentary on student revision (see chapter 4) on 110 pairs of essays written by 47 university ESL students in the United States. Though this study primarily looked at teacher response to content, about 15% of the teacher comments dealt with grammar and mechanics issues, primarily through the use of end or marginal verbal comments paired with selective underlining of errors. The influence of the teacher feedback on students' revisions was traced, and it was found that these comments were taken up and utilized by students to make positive changes in their revisions. No specific definition of "error" was provided, and no control group was included in the design.

Polio, Fleck, and Leder (1998) studied 65 ESL students at a U.S. university. The students wrote four journal entries per week over a 7-week period. A control group received no feedback; the experimental group received direct correction of errors and revised one journal entry per week. The researchers reported no significant differences in accuracy between the two groups on a posttest. This is one of the most carefully designed and clearly reported studies reviewed. Nonetheless, a couple of possible limitations should be noted. First, students were writing journal entries as opposed to more substantive texts. Second, the study was relatively short in duration (7 weeks). Third, the posttest measure was an in-class essay, not comparison of journal entries at the beginning and end of the treatment.

In a recent study by Chandler (2000), 30 ESL students at a music conservatory in the United States were divided into two treatment groups as they completed five autobiographical essays over a 10-week period. One group received indirect, uncoded correction of their errors and was required to revise their papers after receiving feedback. The other group also had errors underlined but did not revise their work. Chandler reported a statistically significant difference in accuracy between the two groups at the end of the 10-week period, with the experimental group having reduced their errors by more than one third while the control group actually increased their error ratios. In interpreting Chandler's results, it is important to keep in mind her small sample size, the fact that she was both teacher and researcher, and that no other raters were utilized (so no reliabilities were reported).

In another recent study (Ferris et al., 2000; Ferris & Helt, 2000), 92 ESL writers at a U.S. university received error feedback from their teachers, who used a coding system that included 15 error categories, over the course of a semester (four three-draft assignments). All students revised their essays after receiving error feedback on the second drafts; half of the students maintained an error log to assess their progress on the various categories of errors. Though the teachers had agreed to use a consistent marking system, in reality their corrections included a mixture of direct feedback, indirect coded feedback, indirect uncoded feedback, and verbal notes in the margins and at the end of the essay. The authors report the following findings:

1. The vast majority (91%) of error feedback of all types was addressed by students in revision.
2. The vast majority (81%) of the changes made by the writers in response to feedback were correct.
3. A subsample of 55 students made statistically significant reductions in errors from the beginning to the end of the semester (Ferris & Helt, 2000).
4. Over time indirect feedback appeared to help students improve in accuracy more than direct feedback.
5. Students who maintained error logs reduced their error ratios more than those who did not.

Finally, in a follow-up to Ferris et al. (2000), Ferris and Roberts (2001) conducted a quasi-experimental study to assess differences between coded, uncoded, and no-feedback treatment groups in 72 university ESL students' ability to self-edit. They found no significant differences in editing success ratios between students who received coded feedback (errors marked and labeled with an error code) and those who received uncoded feedback (errors marked but not labeled). In contrast, students who received no error feedback were significantly less able to find and correct their own errors.

SUMMARY OF STUDIES

As the studies reviewed in the previous section considered different populations and a range of research questions, it is helpful to attempt to synthesize the approaches and findings. At least five major research issues were addressed by this body of studies. Figure 3.3 outlines these issues and summarizes the findings on each question from the various applicable studies (not all studies addressed all five questions). In discussing the findings of the studies, it is important to note that I have placed the various studies in the "Yes" or "No" categories based on my own foregoing analysis of the individual study, not simply on the interpretations of the authors (though these were carefully considered). For instance, as I have already discussed, Kepner (1991) claimed that her findings demonstrate the futility of error correction. Yet my own re-analysis of her tables showed that her "corrections" group had an advantage in accuracy nearly equal to the advantage that her "content" group had in higher level content propositions. Thus, as to the question "Does error correction help student accuracy?" my own best judgment is that Kepner's study belongs in the "Yes" column.

The first question is of course the most important one: Does error correction help student accuracy in revision and/or over time? This is the question that Truscott (1996, 1999) addressed in his review and critique of error correction practices. De-

Research Question	Studies & Findings
Does error correction help student accuracy in revision and/or over time?	Yes: Lalande (1982); Robb et al. (1986); Frantzen & Rissell (1987); Fathman & Whalley (1990); Kepner (1991); Sheppard (1992); Ferris (1995a); Frantzen (1995); Ferris (1997); Chandler (2000); Ferris et al. (2000); Ferris & Helt (2000) No: Cohen & Robbins (1976); Polio et al. (1998) Unclear: Semke (1984)
Do direct and indirect feedback have different effects on accuracy?	Yes: Lalande (1982); Frantzen (1995); Ferris et al. (2000); Ferris & Helt (2000) No: Semke (1984); Robb et al. (1986)
Do students respond better to feedback on certain types or categories of error?	Yes: Chaney (1999); Ferris (1995a); Ferris et al. (2000); Ferris & Helt (2000); Frantzen, 1995; Frantzen & Rissell (1987); Lalande, (1982); Sheppard (1992) No: Chastain (1990)
Is there a difference in outcome depending on whether indirect feedback is coded or uncoded?	Yes: Sheppard (1992)Maybe: Ferris et al. (2000); Ferris & Roberts (2000) No: Robb et al. (1986)
Does revision after correction help student accuracy?	Yes: Lalande (1982); Frantzen & Rissell, 1987; Fathman & Whalley (1990); Chandler (2000); Ferris et al. (2000) No: Polio et al. (1998); Frantzen (1995) Maybe/Unclear: Cohen & Robbins (1976); Semke (1984); Sheppard (1992)
Does maintenance of error logs lead to improvement in accuracy over time?	Yes: Lalande (1982)*; Ferris (1995a); Ferris & Helt (2000)*
Does supplemental grammar instruction (along with error correction) make a difference in student accuracy?	Yes: Lalande (1982); Frantzen & Rissell (1987); Ferris (1995a) No: Frantzen (1995); Polio et al. (1998)

*Lalande's study is difficult to interpret on this point because there were other ways in which the two treatment groups differed (direct vs. indirect feedback, in-class editing activities), so it is impossible to isolate the effects of error logging. In the case of Ferris and Helt (2000), the two groups differed in treatment only in that one group maintained error logs and one did not. However, as the students all received error feedback, it is impossible to tell whether improvements occurred solely as a result of keeping error logs.

FIG. 3.3.   Major issues in error correction studies.

spite the fact that most of the studies reviewed in this chapter ended up in the "Yes" column in Fig. 3.3, the answer to this question is not nearly as conclusive as it might seem. In many cases, there was no comparison between students who received error feedback and those who did not, but rather between those who received differing types of feedback treatment. A "Yes" answer to a particular study merely indicates *that student subjects who received feedback made numerical gains in accuracy over the duration of the study.* (In nearly all cases, the gains were statistically significant, based on reported pretest/posttest measures.)

With regard to this question (error feedback vs. no error feedback), there are really only three studies—two in the "Yes" column (Fathman & Whalley, 1990; Kepner, 1991) and one in the "No" column (Polio et al., 1998)—that clearly address the issue. Fathman and Whalley's results are the most convincing—they demonstrate a statistically significant advantage in accuracy for the two groups who received error feedback over the two groups that did not (the content-only group and the no-feedback group). However, as previously noted, this is a short-term result, and we have no idea whether these distinctions would hold over a longer period of time and would result in long-term improvement in accuracy. It is ironic that Kepner's study, which Truscott used to advance his "abolish grammar correction" argument, actually provides the only longitudinal evidence that error correction leads to fewer errors than no error correction. However, the differences (at least according to Kepner) are not statistically significant, and other design and analysis flaws render this finding unreliable. Polio et al. (1998) presented findings that clearly argue against any advantage for error correction, and their study is carefully designed and executed. However, one 7-week study of 65 students in one context can hardly be construed as an overwhelming body of evidence against error correction in writing, and in fact, the authors themselves in their discussion warn readers against jumping to that conclusion. Thus, Truscott was right in his assertion that evidence demonstrating a clear-cut advantage for error correction versus no error correction is scant indeed, primarily because virtually no research has been conducted that has framed the issue in those precise terms. However, he overstated his argument when he claimed that the available evidence convincingly demonstrates no benefits of error correction. (Ironically, the one study I have discussed that clearly supports his thesis [Polio et al., 1998] had not been published at the time he wrote his initial argument.)

The rest of the questions outlined in Fig. 3.3 deal with various practical issues regarding feedback: direct versus indirect feedback, codes versus no codes, and the merits of error logs and in-class grammar instruction. A glance at Fig. 3.3 should make it apparent that research on these specific questions is limited indeed. It has been suggested by both error correction researchers (e.g., Ferris, 1995c; Hendrickson, 1978; Lalande, 1982) and by SLA studies (see James, 1998, for a review) that indirect feedback has greater potential long-term benefits for student improvement in accuracy because it provides students with the feedback they need to engage in problem solving and move toward becoming "independent self-editors" (Bates, Lane, & Lange, 1993) of their own writing. The findings of Lalande's (1982) study clearly argue in favor of indirect feedback, paired with guided self-correction techniques, over direct feedback. Similarly, Ferris and Helt (2000) found clear-cut evidence that student writers who received primarily indirect feedback made more long-term gains in accuracy than those who received primarily direct feedback. On the other hand, Robb et al. (1986) and Semke (1984) found no significant differences among error feedback treatments. As previously discussed, Semke's results are problematic because of the type of writing the students were doing and because the posttest written accuracy measure consisted only of a 10-minute freewrite. Robb et al.'s findings are more compelling because the study was more carefully done and considered multiple drafts of completed compositions. If we accept their conclusion—that there was no observable difference in accuracy among treatment groups—one possible interpretation is that indirect feedback is at least as good as direct feedback in helping students improve in accuracy over time. Thus, the results of this study should not be taken as direct counterevidence to the findings of the other studies that suggest an advantage for indirect feedback.

A number of studies have identified particular syntactic and lexical constructions marked by instructors and/or analyzed for accuracy, primarily as a means to define what is meant by "error" in a particular study. In all studies reviewed but one (Chastain, 1990), researchers reported varying gains in accuracy depending on the error type or linguistic construction being considered. Chastain's study only considered two papers each by 14 students and only identified a few very general categories of error (e.g., "lexical" error vs. "morphological" error), so his findings should not be considered substantial counterevidence to the argument that error type or category is a significant issue to consider in evaluating the effectiveness of error correction treatments (Ferris & Hedgcock, 1998; Truscott, 1996).

Only a few studies have examined whether it makes a difference if indirect feedback is coded (specifying type of error) or uncoded (an error is underlined or circled but not coded or labeled in any way). As pointed out by Robb et al. (1986), uncoded feedback is easier for the teacher to provide; if research evidence indicates that the presence or absence of codes makes no difference, teachers might as well dispense with them. On the other hand, survey research suggests that students and teachers feel that unlabeled indirect feedback does not provide student writers with enough evidence to edit their work (Leki, 1991; Roberts, 1999). It has also been pointed out by student writers that error codes and marks can be confusing to them (Ferris, 1995b; Roberts, 1999). As previously noted, the study by Robb et al. suggests that the level of explicitness in error correction makes no difference in student accuracy over time. In a recent study by Ferris et al. (2000), it was found that when students received uncoded feedback (or even feedback with an *incorrect* code), they were still able to edit the error successfully nearly as often as when they received indirect coded feedback (see also Komura, 1999); this somewhat incidental finding was replicated in a controlled quasi-experimental study by Ferris and Roberts (2001).

Another important question in analyzing error correction studies is the impact of required revision after feedback on student gains in accuracy. Both SLA and L2 writing research suggest that giving students time to revise and holding them accountable for doing so will help them to attend better to feedback they receive (and ostensibly to incorporate the information and thinking processes into their acquired knowledge of the L2) (Ferris, 1995b, 1997; James, 1998; Zamel, 1985). A number of studies discussed in this chapter provide evidence that when students revised after receiving feedback, their accuracy improved in the short- or long-term. On the other hand, two studies discussed (Frantzen, 1995; Polio et al., 1998) found no benefits for error correction plus revision. It is important to qualify any discussion of these studies by noting that none of the studies specifically compared students who revised versus those who did not after receiving equivalent amounts and types of feedback. (Lalande's experimental group revised whereas the control group did not, but they also received substantially different types of feedback.) Thus it is hard to assess the effects of the feedback, the revision, or the combination of both treatments.

As to the final two questions (maintenance of grammar logs and supplemental in-class instruction), there is so little research evidence on the effects of these treatments that it is difficult to draw any conclusions. SLA research suggests that instruction on form can help students to progress through developmental acquisition sequences more quickly (Ellis, 1998; James, 1998). Second language writing researchers have suggested that error logs and classroom grammar instruction supplement error feedback and help to make it more salient and effective—in the case of error logs, by keeping students informed of their progress (or the lack thereof), and in the case of instruction, by giving students information to help them self-edit after receiving feedback (Bates et al., 1993; Ferris, 1995a, 1995c; Lalande, 1982). Only two studies to date have investigated the use of error logs (Ferris & Helt, 2000; Lalande, 1982), both reporting that students who maintained error logs made better progress in accuracy over time than those who did not. The results of the few studies that have investigated the effects of in-class grammar instruction have been conflicting and not always well designed or clearly described (especially as to the nature of the classroom instruction).

FURTHER RESEARCH AGENDA

The foregoing discussion makes it clear that there are many questions in error correction of student writing that have not been adequately researched. The most critical need, of course, is to contrast the effects of error correction over time with the effects of no error correction, with all other variables (see Figs. 3.1 and 3.2) held constant. Of course, this is challenging to accomplish on at least two counts. First, classroom teachers and researchers question the ethics of providing no error feedback at all to their students over an entire writing course, wondering if they will frustrate and anger their students and if they will actually harm their students' development by withholding error feedback. Second, it is always challenging in longitudinal classroom studies to isolate the effects of any one variable, such as feedback. Nonetheless, until this question is addressed head on in a series of well-designed, replicable studies, Truscott's (1996, 1999) challenge to grammar correction in the writing classroom cannot be effectively supported or refuted.

All of the other issues outlined in Fig. 3.3 assume a commitment to error feedback. (If one does not believe that error correction does any good, it is of course irrelevant whether such feedback is direct, indirect, coded, or supported by revision activities, error logs, and instruction!) For those who believe that error correction for second language writers is not only valuable, but necessary, these five questions speak to the issue of how best to provide effective feedback, including not only the nature of the feedback itself but how the feedback is embedded in an overall approach to error in a writing class. Clearly, a program of research that addresses these issues in isolation and in combination would be most helpful to teachers wanting to know how best to help their students deal with language errors in their writing.

As the six research issues outlined in Fig. 3.3 (and other issues as well) are addressed in a body of studies, it is critical that the various parameters (subjects, sample size, duration, classroom variables, and research procedures) outlined in this chapter (see Fig. 3.1) be carefully considered and accounted for. Only then can researchers and instructors make informed decisions as to the relative merits of feedback procedures and other aspects of error treatment in the writing class.

<table>
<tr><td>

CHAPTER

4

</td><td>

Research
on
Peer Response

</td></tr>
</table>

As discussed in chapter 1, one of the most common suggestions to come from L1 scholarship on the process approach in composition instruction is the use of collaborative peer review in writing classes. As L2 writing specialists began to embrace the process approach, the implementation of peer response in ESL writing classes was rapid and widespread, especially in the United States. Unlike discussions of teacher feedback (especially as to error correction), L2 researcher and instructor views on peer response were, at least initially, almost universally enthusiastic and optimistic. However, as time went on, many ESL writing instructors began to express reservations about the efficacy of peer feedback for L2 writers. These evolving attitudes were bolstered by research findings during the 1990s that suggested, for instance, that peer feedback was not only ineffective in accomplishing its purposes (to help students revise and improve their writing quality) but also perhaps inappropriate given students' range of cultural norms and expectations about group dynamics, the role of the teacher, and face-saving.

In the field of ESL writing, peer response is a relatively well-researched phenomenon. Over the past 15 years, numerous position papers touting its benefits, "how-to" articles suggesting procedures, and research reports evaluating its nature and effects have appeared in journals and books. As we will see, the advantages of peer review are apparent to students and to instructors in classrooms in which the technique is implemented carefully and systematically (see also chapter 5 for further discussion of student views on peer response). Still, there exists to this day considerable ambivalence among L2 writing instructors and scholars about whether peer feedback does more good than harm and whether its benefits justify the time required to utilize it effectively. Thus, it is important to look carefully at the strands of research evidence available, asking many of the same questions about these studies as were posed in chapter 2 (on teacher feedback) and chapter 3 (on error correction).

PERSPECTIVES ON PEER RESPONSE

In addition to the strong support from L1 composition scholarship for peer feedback in writing classes as a means to provide between-draft feedback and a more varied audience than the teacher alone (Emig, 1971; Flower & Hayes, 1981; Sommers, 1982; Zamel, 1982, 1985, 1987), there are several other theoretical arguments in its favor. One, advanced by Bell (1991), comes from research on the education of adult learners: that adults need to be "self-directed" and have opportunities for "critical reflection" (p. 65). Second language acquisition researchers have long argued that interaction among L2 learners in classroom settings is critical to their continued development of communicative competence (e.g., Long & Porter, 1985; Pica, 1984). Finally, peer review tasks derive support from the view that writing (and indeed all learning and knowledge) are socially constructed activities (Belcher, 1988; Bruffee, 1986; Carson & Nelson, 1994), which in turn follows from the Vygotskyan notion that "cognitive development results from social interaction" (Carson & Nelson, 1994, p. 18; cf. Mendonça & Johnson, 1994; Vygotsky, 1962/1986).

From these theoretical perspectives, a number of practical benefits of peer response for L2 writers have been suggested by various authors:

1. Students gain confidence, perspective, and critical thinking skills from being able to read texts by peers writing on similar tasks.
2. Students get more feedback on their writing than they could from the teacher alone.
3. Students get feedback from a more diverse audience bringing multiple perspectives.
4. Students receive feedback from nonexpert readers on ways in which their texts are unclear as to ideas and language.
5. Peer review activities build a sense of classroom community.

On the other hand, researchers, teachers, and student writers themselves have identified potential and actual problems with peer response. The most prominent complaints are that student writers do not know what to look for in their peers' writing and do not give specific, helpful feedback, that they are either too harsh or too complimentary in making comments, and that peer feedback activities take up too much classroom time (or the corollary complaint that not enough time is allot-

Type of Paper
"How-Tos" or Position Papers: Belcher (1988); Bell (1991); Davies & Omberg (1986); Ferris & Hedgcock (1998); Grabe & Kaplan (1996); Hafernik (1984); Huntley (1992); Hvitfeldt (1986); Jones (1995); Leki (1992); Linden-Martin (1997); Mittan (1989); Moore (1986); Reid (1993).
Empirical Research on the Characteristics and Influence of Peer Response: Berg (1999); Carson & Nelson (1994, 1996); Connor & Asenavage (1994); Hedgcock & Lefkowitz (1992); Lockhart & Ng (1995a, 1995b); Mangelsdorf & Schlumberger (1992); Mendonça & Johnson (1994); Nelson & Carson (1998); Nelson & Murphy (1992, 1993); Paulus (1999); Rothschild & Klingenberg (1990); Schmid (1999); Stanley (1992); Villamil & de Guerrero (1996).
Studies of Student Views on Peer Response: Arndt (1993); Berger (1990); Jacobs et al. (1998); Leki (1990b); Mangelsdorf (1992); Zhang (1995).

FIG. 4.1.   An overview of sources discussing advantages and disadvantages of peer response.

ted by teachers and the students feel rushed). A summary of sources examining these proposed benefits and drawbacks is shown in Fig. 4.1.

RESEARCH ON PEER RESPONSE

To evaluate fairly the arguments for and against the extensive use of peer feedback in L2 writing classes, it is necessary to look carefully at the various strands of research evidence available. As I have noted elsewhere (Ferris & Hedgcock, 1998), research results on the effects of peer response have been mixed and even conflicting. As noted by McGroarty and Zhu (1997), a primary reason for this lack of clarity is the absence of triangulation of data collection methods and analysis procedures in many studies on this topic. In comparing studies and synthesizing findings, it is important to ask a number of procedural questions, outlined in Fig. 4.2.

Subjects and Setting

As in any meta-analysis of a body of classroom studies, it is important to be aware of how many student subjects (and teachers) were being studied, group sizes (in experimental designs), the instructional context (e.g., ESL vs. EFL settings, undergraduate vs. graduate courses, focus of writing tasks, etc.), and the relative ability levels (as to both L2 proficiency and composition skills) of the student writers. It may also, as discussed later, be important to understand how the cultural backgrounds of the students may inform their expectations and condition their behaviors during peer feedback sessions.

Subjects & Setting:

- How many students and teachers were involved?
- If students were divided into treatment groups, what were the group sizes?
- What was the instructional context?
- What was the language/writing level of the students?

Peer Feedback Procedures:

- Was any modeling or training given prior to peer review sessions?
- How were the peer review sessions structured?
- How were peer groups/dyads formed?
- How consistently was peer review utilized?
- What did students do after receiving peer feedback?

Research Design Issues:

- What specific research questions were being explored (e.g., nature of interactions, student attitudes, effects on revision, etc.)?
- How were effects measured?
- Were multiple raters or coders used, and were interrater reliabilities calculated and reported?

FIG. 4.2.   Evaluation questions for peer response studies.

Peer Feedback Procedures

One generalization that emerges from the L2 peer response literature is that the nature of peer response sessions is critically important to understanding their (in)effectiveness. As observed by Bell (1991), the unstructured, student-directed peer feedback activities suggested in Elbow's landmark 1973 book, *Writing Without Teachers*, may be especially inappropriate for ESL writers, who have linguistic and rhetorical differences not only in constructing their own texts but in reading and evaluating those of other students, and who because of differing cultural expectations may need a teacher-directed structure for the activity in order to feel most comfortable with it. Specific issues that arise include whether students were prepared for the peer response activity prior to participating in it (via discussion, modeling, or formal training), whether the teacher structured the sessions by giving guiding questions, suggesting time frames, and so on, how the peer groups or dyads were formed, whether peer review was a consistent part of the course, and what students were expected to do after receiving peer feedback.

Research Design Issues

As I discuss in more detail, peer response studies have investigated a variety of questions, including the nature of peer feedback interactions, attitudes of students toward peer feedback, and the effects of peer response on revision and/or on improvement in writing quality. Obviously, the specific questions being asked will determine the research designs. If the goal of the study is to describe the characteristics of the peer interactions, we would expect to see analysis of audiotaped or videotaped peer response sessions (or researcher observation notes and perhaps written student feedback forms), a coding scheme operationalized to describe and measure these characteristics, and the use of multiple raters or coders to analyze transcripts or notes on the peer review sessions. However, if the purpose of the study is to focus on what students do with peer feedback after receiving it, we would expect to see extensive text analysis—comparison of original and revised drafts with the suggestions received by peers—similar to studies on the effects of teacher commentary and error correction reviewed in chapters 2 and 3 (e.g., Chaney, 1999; Conrad & Goldstein, 1999; Ferris, 1997, 2001a; Ferris et al., 2000; Ferris & Roberts, 2001; Komura, 1999; Roberts, 1999).

In either case, if multiple raters or coders are involved in data analyses, we need to ask whether interrater reliabilities have been calculated and clearly reported. A summary of all of the empirical studies reviewed in this chapter and their characteristics with regard to the three parameters outlined in Fig. 4.2 is provided in Appendix 4A.

STUDIES OF PEER RESPONSE

As shown in Appendix 4A, studies of peer response have examined a variety of research questions, but they generally fall into three major categories: (a) studies describing the nature of the interactions taking place during peer feedback sessions; (b) research investigating the effects of peer response, usually on student revisions, but sometimes on overall writing quality; and (c) examinations of student attitudes toward peer response. Studies in the third category are discussed in detail in chapter 5 (Student Views About Response), so the discussion in this chapter focuses on research on the nature and effects of peer feedback. Although many of the studies focus on one area but not the other, there are several that focus simultaneously on the description of peer interactions and trace their influence on students' subsequent drafts. Finally, several studies employ experimental designs to investigate specific questions related to peer feedback (such as the effects of prior training on the peer review process).

Studies Describing the Nature of Peer Response

The first group of studies to be discussed looks at the characteristics of L2 peer response sessions. These studies are summarized in Fig. 4.3. The prototype study along these lines is a 1992 study by Mangelsdorf and Schlumberger. Though the particular study itself has its limitations in that it is decontextualized, it is important because it opened a line of investigation that has been carried on by several other researchers. In this study, the authors asked 60 ESL students in university freshman writing classes to provide written comments about a student essay from a previous semester. The researchers then categorized the student comments according to the

Study	Research Questions	Major Findings
Mangelsdorf & Schlumberger (1992)	(1) What stances do students take in responding to a sample student essay? (2) On what writing issues do they focus? (3) How do their stances relate to final course grades?	1. Three stance types identified: Prescriptive, Interpretive, and Collaborative. 2. Students who assumed the collaborative stance got higher course grades.
Nelson & Murphy (1992)	(1) How do students approach the task of peer review? (2) What roles are assumed by individual members of peer response groups?	1. Students largely stayed on task. 2. Students assumed predictable roles that may have been counterproductive to the health and functioning of the group.
Lockhart & Ng (1995a, 1995b)	What stances do students take in peer review dyads, and how do they relate to language functions used and writing topics discussed?	1. Four stances identified: Authoritative, Interpretive, Probing, and Collaborative. 2. Probing and Collaborative stances most beneficial to the peer review/writing process.
Villamil & de Guerrero (1996)	How do stances (collaborative vs. noncollaborative) relate to activities, linguistic functions, and social behavior during peer response?	They found a complex interaction of the various behaviors.

FIG. 4.3.   Overview of studies on peer feedback characteristics.

types of stances the students took in response to their hypothetical peer. They identified three general personae that the student respondents took as they approached the task: the Prescriptive stance (45%), the Collaborative stance (32%), and the Interpretive stance (23%). Mangelsdorf and Schlumberger further linked these stances to the types of issues students commented on (content, thesis, organization, and diction) and to the final grades (on a 1–4 scale) that the students ultimately received in the class. As to student outcomes, they found significant differences between students who adopted the Collaborative stance (who received the highest course grades) and those who took the Interpretive stance (who received the lowest). The researchers concluded that the "collaborative reviewers displayed a sophistication in reading and writing that teachers not only need to impart, but to emulate themselves" (p. 248).

Two later studies by Lockhart and Ng (1995a, 1995b) also investigated peer reviewers' stances, but this time in the context of students' actual responses to each other's papers. These two studies, focusing on 54 and 32 students respectively, involved the analyses of transcripts of audiotaped peer feedback interactions between dyads (pairs) of student writers. As in Mangelsdorf and Schlumberger's earlier study, Lockhart and Ng linked reviewer stances (authoritative, interpretive, probing, and collaborative) across different language functions (summarize essay, express intention, give suggestion, give opinion, and give information) and topics discussed (writing process, ideas, audience, and purpose). They concluded that the collaborative and probing stances are the most beneficial for student writers and that they "engage students in a fuller understanding of the writing process" (1995a, p. 606). A summary of the categories utilized in these three studies is provided in Fig. 4.4.

In a 1996 study, Villamil and de Guerrero examined similar types of issues, adopting somewhat different terminology. For instance, rather than identifying three or four different stances as in the previous studies, they classified all interactions as collaborative or noncollaborative. Using transcripts of taped interactions between 27 pairs ($N = 54$) of ESL student writers in a Puerto Rico university, they also look at the types of activities taking place during peer response (reading, assessing, dealing with trouble sources, composing, writing comments, copying, and discussing task procedures), specific linguistic strategies (employing symbols and external resources, using the L1, providing scaffolding, resorting to interlanguage knowledge, and vocalizing private speech), and social behavior (management of authorial control, collaboration, affectivity, and adopting reader/writer roles). They concluded that peer response is "a complex process involving a myriad of recursive behaviors" (p. 66).

Finally, in a smaller case study analysis, Nelson and Murphy (1992) studied one writing group of four students that met weekly over a 6-week period. This group's meetings were videotaped. Using transcripts, the researchers looked both at how the group members approached the task and at the social dynamics within the group. They used Fanselow's (1987) classroom observation instrument, Foci for Observing Communications Used in Settings (FOCUS) to assess whether or not the group was on task, concluding that, by and large, it was. As to social dynamics, the authors noted that "This group was not an ideal community of writers helping writers. Perhaps the more apt metaphor for describing the group interactions is a duel" (p. 181). Group roles, defined as "a set of 'common perceptions shared by the members [of the group] about the behavior of an individual in ... group interaction'" (Bormann, 1975, p. 201, cited in Nelson & Murphy, 1992, p. 182) included "the attacker," "the weakest writer," "the best writer," and "the facilitator." It is important to note that the students' TWE scores were not consistent with the group's own perceptions of who the strongest and weakest writers were! The authors concluded that although the writing group was successful in accomplishing its task, its social dynamics hindered its effectiveness and certainly influenced students' attitudes about the peer response process. They suggested a number of procedural modifications (including the teacher in the group, periodically changing group membership, and training) that could lead to more beneficial and positive experiences in peer review sessions.

These five studies, considered together, underscore the complexity of social interactions underlying peer response activities in the L2 writing class. They further suggest how important social dynamics and reader stances may be in predicting the success or failure, in both practical and affective terms, of peer response activities. The researchers in these studies have done a valuable service in identifying specific issues and behaviors to consider, yet in none of these studies are peer response be-

haviors specifically linked to outcomes—student revision, writing quality, or attitudes. It is to studies that link these issues that we turn next.

Mangelsdorf & Schlumberger (1992, Table 7, p. 247)	Lockhart & Ng (1995a, pp. 616–632; 1995b)
Interpretive Stance • Interested in creation of personal meaning. • Puzzles out text. • "Rewrites" for own understanding. • Distances self from author. • Reacts to perceived inaccuracies in content. • Uses text as prompt for personal elaboration. **Prescriptive Stance** • Prescriptive. • Tends to put form before meaning. • Has preconceived idea of what essay should be. • Functions as an editor. • Sticks close to the text, no "conversation" with it. • Identifies faults and/or fixes them. • Certitude of tone. **Collaborative Stance** • Positions self with author of prompt text. • Tries to see text through author's eyes. • Does not try to change author's focus or argument. • Points out problems the hypothesized reader will have. • Makes suggestions to the author. • Does not impose form.	**Interpretive Stance** • "Use peer response as a forum for presenting their personal reactions to the writer's text." • Includes both positive and negative reactions. • Use reactions as criteria for evaluation and give suggestions based on personal preferences. **Authoritative Stance** • Have preconceived ideas of what an essay should be like. • Trouble shooting, "fixing" problems. • Impose their own ideas on the text. **Collaborative Stance** • Negotiate with the writer. • Sees role as facilitating the writer. • Helps writer to articulate new ideas. **Probing Stance** • Puzzle out the meaning in the text and ask writer for clarification. • Focus on areas they find confusing and elicit explanations. • Check the writer's intentions and allow writer time to express their ideas.

FIG. 4.4. Reviewer "stance."

Studies Linking Peer Response Characteristics With Outcomes

Another group of studies attempted to link peer response behaviors with revision activities. A summary of these studies is shown in Fig. 4.5. In an often-cited study, Mendonça and Johnson (1994) looked simultaneously at types of interactions during peer reviews, the use of peers' comments during revision, and students' perceptions about the usefulness of peer reviews. The subjects in their study were 12 international graduate students in an EAP writing course at a U.S. university. For this study, the students worked in pairs, with four of the pairs composed of students in the same major field as their partners and two of the pairs being mixed as to fields of study. Their analysis of the tapes and transcripts of the peer review sessions identified five major types of negotiation: questions (22%), explanations (36%), restate-

Study	Research Questions	Major Findings
Mendonça & Johnson (1994)	(1) What types of interactions do student have during peer review? (2) Do they use peer suggestions in revision?	1. There were five major negotiation types, divided among writer/reader initiated 2. 53% of peer suggestions were incorporated in revision.
Nelson & Murphy (1993)	1. Did students use peers' suggestions in revision? 2. Was there any observed connection between the peer dynamics and use of peer feedback during revision?	1. On a 1 to 5 scale of using peer feedback in revision, the mean score was 3.2. 2. The majority of revisions that used peer suggestions came from peer feedback sessions that were interactive and collaborative. The revisions in which peer suggestions were not utilized followed from peer review that was either noninteractive and/or defensive in nature.
Schmid (1999)	See Mendonça & Johnson (1994); also: Do changes made during revision improve essay quality?	1. Students implemented 70% of peers' suggestions in revision. 2. Suggestions derived from peer feedback had generally positive effects on revision.
Stanley (1992)	Were there differences between coached and noncoached students in response behaviors and in revision?	1. Students who received coaching had more conversation, gave more specific suggestions, and were more engaged and committed to the task. 2. Coached students utilized peer suggestions more frequently during revision.

FIG. 4.5.   Studies linking peer response characteristics to revision outcomes.

ments (28%), suggestions (11%), and grammar correction (1%). They also subdivided the negotiation types as to whether they were writer- or reader-generated, finding that in all categories except one (explanations of content), the reviewer initiated more of the topics (Table 2, p. 757). They also found differences in negotiation patterns depending on whether the partners were in the same or different fields of study.

In looking at revisions, the researchers classified all changes in the students' texts as (a) revised and discussed in the peer review (53% of revisions); (b) not revised and discussed in the peer review (10%); and (c) revised but not discussed in the peer review (37%). Perhaps because of the relatively high percentage of changes made without having been suggested by peer reviewers, the authors suggested that "future studies might investigate if peer reviews develop the students' ability to revise their own writing without receiving input from their peers or teachers" (p. 767).[13]

Mendonça and Johnson (1994) noted in the conclusion to their study that the implications of their findings are limited not only because of the relatively small sample size, but also because their students were so advanced academically. Though the authors did not say this, another important point is the fact that students were writing on topics related to their own major fields of study and that two thirds of them were interacting with partners ostensibly quite knowledgeable about the content of their papers. This latter condition, of course, is less likely to be present in more general purposes freshman composition courses (represented by most of the studies discussed in this chapter).

These caveats make it particularly interesting to consider the findings from a replication study completed as a master's thesis project in 1999 by Schmid. She also examined peer reviews and their effects on revision with 12 student subjects, but in this case, her subjects were undergraduates (mostly freshmen and sophomores) enrolled in a pre-freshman composition university ESL writing course. All of the students were writing in response to the same assigned topic, and the dyads were created based on gender (each pair had a male and a female student) rather than similar academic interests.

Schmid utilized Mendonça and Johnson's methodology in classifying peer review negotiations and their effects on revisions. She took the analysis a step further by also assessing the effects of the revisions on the overall quality of the students' texts, following the analysis model used for teacher commentary by Ferris (1997). The findings of the three studies are compared and contrasted in Fig. 4.5.

The comparison data shown in Fig. 4.6 indicates that there were differences in negotiation patterns between Schmid's undergraduate subjects and the graduate students studied by Mendonça and Johnson. Most notable, however, is the fact that the undergraduate students were far more likely to incorporate peer feedback suggestions (70%) in revision than were the graduate students (53%), and that the changes made by Schmid's subjects after receiving peer feedback were more helpful to essay quality than those made by the students in Ferris' study who got feedback from their teacher. Al-

---

[13]There are a number of other papers, not technically survey studies, in which student views on peer feedback are discussed, at least in passing. These include papers by Belcher, 1988; Bell, 1991; Carson and Nelson, 1996; Davies and Omberg, 1987; Hvitfeldt, 1986; Linden-Martin (1997); McGroarty and Zhu, 1997; Nelson and Carson, 1998.

Study Characteristics & Findings	Mendonça & Johnson (1994)	Schmid (1999)	Ferris (1997)
Subjects	Twelve international graduate students, mostly paired by major field of study	Twelve undergraduate students, paired by gender	Forty-seven students receiving 1,526 comments from teacher
Types of Negotiations:			
• Questions	24%	41%	not applicable
• Explanations	36%	32%	
• Restatements	28%	18%	
• Suggestions	11%	8%	
• Grammar Correction	1%	1%	
Effects on Revision:			
• Revised/Peer Review	53%	70%	not applicable
• Not Revised/ Peer Review	10%	19%	
• Revised/Not in Peer Review	37%	11%	
Effects of Revisions on Essay Quality			
• Not Revised	Not applicable	19%	23%
• Negative Effects		8%	5%
• Mixed Effects		14%	36%
• Positive Effects		57%	38%

FIG. 4.6.   A comparison of studies. (Data taken from Schmid, 1999, Table 3, p. 40; Table 6, p. 49; Table 11, p. 61. See also Mendonça and Johnson, 1994, and Ferris, 1997.)

though Schmid's study, dealing with only one set of peer interactions with 12 students, should not be overgeneralized either, it seems fair to say that both her study and the predecessor that inspired it provide strong evidence that peer feedback can have a substantial impact on revision. Further, as discussed in chapter 5, the students in both studies expressed strongly positive reactions to the peer review sessions they had experienced.

In a case study analysis by Nelson and Murphy (1993), four students in a single writing group were videotaped during their once-weekly meetings over a 6-week period (see also Nelson & Murphy, 1992, discussed previously). Student revisions produced after peer group meetings were analyzed on a 1 to 5 scale (1 = students used none of their peers' suggestions in revision; 5 = students implemented all or nearly all of the comments they received). They then studied papers rated 4 to 5 and papers scored 1 to 2 to see if they could determine from transcripts of the peer review sessions why in some cases peer review suggestions were incorporated whereas in other instances they were not. Based on this analysis, the transcripts related to these papers were coded as being either "interactive" or "noninteractive" (meaning that the writers did/did not interact frequently with other group members during discussions) and "cooperative" or "defensive" (whether the writers listened to others' comments and asked for clarification or whether they seemed more concerned about justifying the choices they had made in their writing) (p. 138).

As to the first issue, whether writers used their peers' comments in constructing revisions, the mean score for all students across all six sessions was 3.2 (on the 1–5 scale), but the authors noted that scores were not consistent across all papers for each student. For the second question, whether the nature of the peer group meetings affected revision outcomes, it was found in the majority of revisions scored 4 to 5 (meaning that peer comments were incorporated), the transcripts were scored as interactive and cooperative. All eight of the revisions scored 1 to 2 had corresponding transcripts that were rated as being either defensive or noninteractive. Nelson and Murphy cautioned that "writers may actually weaken their drafts by incorporating peer comments" (p. 140), reminding readers that their study does not address whether student revisions *improved* after peer review sessions.

In a study that emphasized the effects of training students for peer review, Stanley (1992) considered students' actual behaviors in writing groups and in composing revisions across the trained/untrained conditions. Thirty students were divided into two treatment groups. The experimental group received 7 hours of peer response training whereas the control group was given only 1 hour. Stanley found that the "coached" (experimental) group "produced far more conversation than did the groups who had not received coaching" and their responses "offered their partners substantially more specific responses to their writing," and showed "increased engagement" and "commitment to the task" (pp. 226–227). Stanley also found that students in the coached group utilized peer commentary in their revisions more than did the students in the control group. She concluded that training students to engage in peer response yields benefits both in the quality of the responses and their effects on revision.

Studies Linking Peer Response to Revision

Several other studies, rather than describing peer interactions or explicitly linking them to outcomes, focus exclusively on student revision after they receive feedback from peers (Fig. 4.7). Three studies focusing on revision after peer review utilized the same revision taxonomy (Faigley & Witte, 1981) to classify students' changes during revision (Berg, 1999; Connor & Asenavage, 1994; Paulus, 1999). In the ear-

Study	Research Questions	Major Findings
Connor & Asenavage (1994)	1. What types of revisions Wdo students make after feedback? 2. Are there differences between teacher and peer feedback in influence on revision?	1. Students made both meaning and surface changes. 2. The impact of peer feedback on revision was extremely limited (5%).
Paulus (1999)	See Connor and Asenavage (1994); also, what were the effects of feedback and revision on essay quality?	1. Students made both meaning and surface changes. 2. Impact of peer feedback was much greater than in Connor and Asenavage. 3. Students' paper scores significantly improved from first to third draft.
Berg (1999)	Does training prior to peer feedback affect types of revisions made and overall writing quality?	1. Students who were trained made more meaning-type revisions. 2. Students who were trained wrote higher quality revisions.

FIG. 4.7.   Studies on revision after peer feedback.

liest, Connor and Asenavage (1994) studied eight ESL freshman composition students in two writing groups. Three peer review sessions were audiotaped and transcribed and the students' paper drafts were copied and examined. The focus of this study was not only to classify the revisions made but also to compare whether the source of feedback (teacher or peers) influenced the effects that response had on revision. It was found that, generally speaking, the students made both text-based and surface revisions in healthy proportions (see discussion in chapter 2 about the limitations of the Faigley and Witte model), but that very few of the changes made (5%) could be traced to comments made during peer review, and about 35% of the revisions appeared to derive from teacher suggestions. The authors described their results as to the effects of peer response as "disappointing" and suggested that L2 writing teachers "may expect too much from peer response groups without understanding how effective collaboration works among ESL writers" (p. 267). They suggested that students may need more explicit instruction on revision, better peer response training, and hard copies of peers' papers rather than having them read aloud in the groups. (It is also worth noting that the effects of the *teacher* feedback in this study were substantially less pronounced than in studies that have connected teacher feedback to revision, discussed in detail in chapter 2).

Paulus' 1999 study similarly looks at the effects of feedback on revision using the Faigley and Witte taxonomy and compares findings across teacher and peer response rounds. This study was analogous to Connor and Asenavage's (1994) study in that the 11 student subjects revised their papers once after peer feedback and again after teacher feedback. Two significant differences in design were (a) that students recorded think-aloud protocols as they revised each time; and (b) that first and third drafts of student essays were scored, using a 10-point holistic rating scale, to see whether between-draft changes had affected the overall essay quality. Paulus found that peer feedback influenced 32% of the revisions between first and second drafts and teacher feedback led to 57% of the revisions between second and third drafts, but that the source of the majority of revisions overall was "self/other" (52%). She also found differences between drafts and feedback sources in the types of revisions made, finding more meaning changes as a result of teacher feedback (43%) than peer feedback (33%). There were statistically significant differences in holistic scores from first to third drafts, indicating that the feedback and revision cycles had resulted in improved essay quality. Compared with Connor and Asenavage's study, Paulus' results show that feedback, whether from peers or teacher, had much more influence on student revisions, and it can be speculated that the feedback had positive effects on student writing, though it is difficult to isolate the benefits of different types of feedback and the mere act of rewriting. In fact, the finding in both studies that "self/other" was the major source of revision changes argues that the mere act of rereading and rewriting, even without feedback from peers or teacher, may lead not only to substantive changes but improved writing quality (see also Fathman & Whalley, 1999; Russikoff & Kogan, 1996; both discussed in chap. 2).

Finally, Berg (1999) looked at the effects of training for peer feedback on the types of revisions made by ESL writers. In this study, 46 students were divided into two treatment groups (trained and untrained). Revisions made after peer review were measured using both the Faigley and Witte scheme as well as the Test of Written English (TWE) rubric to assess quality changes between first and third drafts. Berg found that the "training" group, which not only went through an 11-step training sequence but also had the benefit of a peer feedback form, wrote higher quality revisions than the control group students did and that they made more "meaning" changes (as opposed to "surface" changes), which she attributed to the effects of the training sequence. She suggested that her results "imply that appropriate training can lead to more meaning-type revisions, which in turn may result in better quality writing in a second draft" (p. 230).

Other Experimental Studies on the Effects of Peer Feedback

In addition to the body of studies already reviewed, which focus on the characteristics of peer feedback and/or its effects on students' revisions, several studies of peer response have utilized experimental designs to investigate other questions related to the effectiveness of peer feedback. Two studies (Rothschild & Klingenberg,

1990; Stanley, 1992) have, like Berg's study, focused on the effects of training on peer review processes. In Rothschild and Klingenberg's study, 56 students divided into two treatment groups scored 14 sample student essays using a rating scale (the analytic scale by Jacobs, Zingraf, Wormuth, Hartfiel, & Hughey, 1981). One group ($N = 32$) was given training in the use of the scale prior to scoring the essays whereas the other group was not. The ratings given by the two groups of students were compared with those given by instructors. It was found that there was "a slight trend" in favor of the experimental group as to matching the ratings given by the instructors, that the two groups of students used different sets of criteria to judge essays, and that the experimental group students expressed more positive attitudes toward writing on a 10-item survey.

Finally, an experimental study by Hedgcock and Lefkowitz (1992) compared the effects of peer and teacher feedback on the quality of students' final drafts. The subjects, 30 French FL (L1 = English) students, were divided into two groups. Each group wrote three drafts of a composition. The control group received teacher feedback after each draft, and the experimental group worked in peer feedback groups, guided by a written protocol. An analytic scoring scale was used to compare the final drafts between the two groups. Hedgcock and Lefkowitz found a statistically significant advantage for the students who worked collaboratively over the ones who revised alone with the help of teacher feedback. However, they stopped short of claiming that peer feedback is "necessarily superior" to teacher feedback, but rather that their findings suggest "that peer assessment constitutes a satisfactory way of managing revision in the FL classroom" (p. 266).

Other Peer Response Issues

Two other issues arise at various points in the literature and seem important enough to be mentioned here, even though in neither case is there empirical evidence to support a particular viewpoint. One issue that seems especially important in considering the merits of peer review particularly for L2 writers is the impact of cultural differences and attendant expectations on the peer response process and on student attitudes toward it. Allaei and Connor (1990) observed that culturally mixed groups might experience problems in working together because of differing expectations and intercultural communication patterns. In a series of related pieces, Carson (1992) and Carson and Nelson (1994, 1996) suggested that students who come from collectivist cultures (e.g., Chinese, Japanese) may value a "positive group climate" more than helping individual writers with their papers (Carson & Nelson, 1994, p. 23). This value, of course, could lead to peer commentary that is overly positive or even dishonest, to the potential detriment of a student writer expecting to receive constructive criticism if it is warranted. In a case study of three Chinese students interacting with Spanish speakers in peer writing groups, Carson and Nelson (1996) observed that "the Chinese speakers were reluctant to initiate comments, and when they did, monitored themselves carefully so as not to precipitate conflict within the group" (p. 1); a follow-up study with the same students (Nelson & Carson, 1998) showed that the students' perceptions of the peer interactions were not especially positive. Other than these two qualitative case studies with the same subjects, there is as yet no empirical evidence that the cultural backgrounds of students have an impact on the nature and effects of peer feedback sessions in either homogeneous or mixed L2 groups. However, given the evidence discussed earlier about the range of stances taken by peer reviewers (Lockhart & Ng, 1995a, 1995b; Mangelsdorf & Schlumberger, 1992; Villamil & de Guerrero, 1996), it seems plausible both that such stances could be culturally, not just individually, based and that the personae expressed by students during peer review could have substantially positive or negative effects on their outcomes and on student attitudes about the value of peer response (Nelson & Murphy, 1992, 1993).

Second, it has been directly or implicitly suggested by several scholars and researchers that peer review is most effective when students work with peers who share knowledge about the topic or task, either because they are in the same major field of study (Belcher, 1988; Jones, 1995; Mendonça & Johnson, 1994) or because they are working collaboratively on the same writing task (Arndt, 1993). Belcher (1988) argued persuasively that pairing students in the same field (or fields as close as possible to one another) helps to resolve the thorny problem in EAP writing classes of the writing teacher not having enough content knowledge to give helpful feedback to the students (Spack, 1988). As previously noted, Mendonça and Johnson (1994) found that students had more favorable reactions to peer review when they were paired with other students in the same discipline than when their partner came from a different field of study. Though in both cases the authors asked students for their reactions to peer response, there is as yet no research evidence that intentional pairings of students according to shared content knowledge makes a difference in the effectiveness of peer review. Still, it seems likely that such matching would indeed facilitate peer response, in the same way that linguistics professors do peer review work not only for linguistics journals (as opposed to chemistry, e.g.) but typically within their own areas of specialization in the field. It also should be noted that in typical college-level ESL writing classes, student writers usually do bring shared knowledge about task and content to peer feedback sessions, given that they are often responding to a task set by the teacher on a topic they have been discussing and/or reading about as a class. In any case, these two issues—the impact of cultural differences and of shared content knowledge on the peer review dynamic and its outcomes—should be the focus of future investigations.

SUMMARY

The review presented in this chapter demonstrates that there are a number of issues to consider when evaluating the effects of peer feedback. These include the characteristics of peer review, including what writing issues students talk about and what linguistic choices students make or stances they take in relating to peers about their writing, as well as the roles that individuals take on within dyads or writing groups. They also include the effects of peer review on student revision, on improvement in writing quality, and on student attitudes.

Here we come to an unfortunate dilemma as we examine the existing research base. The set of studies examining the characteristics of peer feedback is detailed and thorough and considers respectable numbers of subjects. Unfortunately, none of them links the stances taken to what students do next with the feedback they have received. Similarly, studies of student revision after peer feedback use elaborate coding schemes (most commonly, Faigley & Witte's taxonomy) to describe student actions during revision, but do not make a causal link to the peer feedback dynamics to explain the effects (or lack thereof) of peer response sessions on students' subsequent writing.

The only exceptions are the studies by Mendonça and Johnson (1994), Nelson and Murphy (1993), and Schmid (1999), which do attempt to make this connection. However, compared with the two previous sets of studies, the researchers in these studies use far less detailed and precise descriptions of what students do during peer feedback and the nature of their revisions. The reason for these gaps in the literature is no doubt practical—the transcribing and coding of peer review tapes and the coding of student revisions are all extremely labor-intensive endeavors. (It is notable that in all of the studies that examine revision, with the exception of Berg, 1999, there are 12 subjects or fewer involved in the study!)

Still, we are left with a lot of information about what goes on during and after peer review and very little that demonstrates or even posits cause and effect. Thus, the most critical need for future peer feedback research is for multifeatured, triangulated projects that simultaneously consider peer feedback characteristics and outcomes. Though there definitely is a gap that needs to be closed, such projects do not need to begin at square one, as a number of promising insights and analytic models have been identified through the projects completed thus far:

- Peer reviewers assume a range of stances or personae toward their partners and the responding task ranging from authoritative or prescriptive to collaborative. If groups of writers meet together regularly, they may also assume consistent roles within the group.
- These stances are realized through a number of linguistic forms and communicative functions such as questioning, explaining, restating, and so on.
- In their revisions, students may exhibit a range of responses to peer review, which include incorporating some of their peers' suggestions and ignoring others. These peer-motivated changes may further have either positive or negative effects on the overall quality of student writing.
- As has been demonstrated in other studies of ESL writers' revision processes, revision that takes place following peer review may be more or less effective as to making meaning or surface changes and as to improving essay quality from early to final drafts.
- Training students to take part in peer review seems to have a beneficial effect both on students' behaviors during peer response and on their attitudes toward it.
- Feedback from both teachers and peers may impact the revision process and writing quality, but possibly in different ways.
- Differing cultural expectations among L2 writers may impact the peer review process.

- Content knowledge shared by writer and reviewer may cause peer feedback
  to be more effective and satisfying.

Research issues aside, the news on peer response for L2 writers seems to be quite good. With the exception of one fairly small study (Connor & Asenavage, 1994), the evidence is fairly consistent that ESL writers are able to give one another feedback that is then utilized in revision and that is often helpful to them. The odds of peer feedback being beneficial appear to improve even more if students are carefully trained in advance of the peer response task. Even more heartening, the evidence is strong that L2 student writers enjoy peer feedback and find it valuable (with the exception of small-scale case studies in which there were group dynamics problems). This evidence is discussed in detail in chapter 5.

Thus, teachers who believe in peer feedback and want their L2 writers to experience the benefits discussed at the beginning of this chapter can proceed with confidence that, as our L1 colleagues have suggested, this is an instructional procedure that has the potential to have great value. Specific ideas for how to implement peer review successfully in ESL writing classes are presented in chapter 8.

APPENDIX 4A: OVERVIEW OF PEER RESPONSE STUDIES

Study	Subjects and Setting	Peer Feedback Procedures	Research Design Issues
Rothschild & Klingenberg (1990)	• Fifty-six students in two treatment groups (N = 32; N = 24). • Intermediate-level students in integrated skills ESL course at Canadian community college.	• Not applicable—decontextualized experimental design.	• Focus was effects of training students in use of a rating scale on evaluation of 14 sample essays. • Analytic scoring scale (Jacobs et al., 1981) used. • No interrater reliabilities reported.
Hedgcock & Lefkowitz (1992)	• Thirty French FL (L1 = English) students divided into two treatment groups (N = 16; N = 14). • First-year students at Michigan State University.	• Experimental group was given a "written protocol" for peer revision; control group received only teacher feedback. • Both groups wrote three drafts each of essays and got peer or teacher feedback between drafts.	• Focus was comparing effects of peer revision to teacher feedback. • Analytic scale used to rate quality of both groups' final drafts. • Four raters participated; interrater reliabilities reported.
Margelsdorf & Schlumberger (1992)	• Sixty students. • ESL freshman composition classes at U.S. university.	• Not applicable—decontextualized study.	• Focus was on stances students took in responding to one student essay. • Students made written comments about the (same) essay. • Researchers categorized student comments; coding procedures and reliabilities reported.

(continued on next page)

87

OVERVIEW OF PEER RESPONSE STUDIES *(continued)*

Study	Subjects and Setting	Peer Feedback Procedures	Research Design Issues
Nelson & Murphy (1992)	• Four students in one writing group. • Intermediate ESL writing class at U.S. University. • Peer feedback used regularly.	• Students had discussing, training, and modeling before beginning peer review. • Teacher gave "guiding questions" and guidelines for group sessions. • Groups of four assigned by the teacher.	• Focus was to describe group interactions using case study methodology. • Data included videotapes, transcripts, interviews, and student texts. • Intercoder reliabilities reported.
Stanley (1992)	• Thirty students in two intact classes (N = 12; N = 18). • ESL freshman composition class at U.S. university. • Peer response used throughout the course.	• One class received 7 hours of "extensive training"; the other group received 1 hour of training. • Not specified whether students received a feedback form. • Students revised drafts after peer feedback.	• Focus was effects of training on whether peer response led to revisions. • Transcripts of peer review sessions taped and transcripts coded as to response types; revisions coded as to effects of peer responses. • Independent raters/coders used and reliabilities reported.
Nelson & Murphy (1993)	• See Nelson & Murphy (1992).	• See Nelson & Murphy (1992).	• Focus was effects of peer response on revision. • Transcripts of peer reviews and student drafts read and coded by researchers; 1 to 5 scale used to judge effects of peer suggestions on revision. • Intercoder reliabilities reported.

Study	Participants/Setting	Procedures	Analysis
Connor & Asenavage (1994)	• Eight students in two groups of four. • ESL freshman composition class at U.S. university.	• Peer response modeled and practiced before first session. • Teacher provided peer review sheet. • Peer review used consistently throughout course. • Students revised papers for final portfolio after receiving teacher and peer comments.	• Focus on revisions made based on peer and teacher comments. • Three peer review sessions audiotaped; paper drafts copied. • Faigley & Witte (1981) scheme used to classify revisions. • Coding done by the two authors after achieving agreement on a subsample.
Mendonça & Johnson (1994)	• Twelve international graduate students arranged in dyads. • EAP course at U.S. university.	• No prior training mentioned. • Students given four "guided questions" (p. 749). • Not specified whether peer review was used consistently. • Four pairs of students were in the same academic field as their partners; the other two pairs were not. • Students revised papers after receiving peer and teacher feedback.	• Three research questions: (a) types of interactions during peer reviews; (b) use of peers' comments in revisions; (c) students' perceptions of usefulness of peer reviews. • Peer review sessions taped and transcribed; student drafts (before and after peer feedback) collected; postinterviews with students taped and transcribed. • Authors analyzed transcripts of peer reviews and interviews; one additional rater checked reliability on one transcript with 89% agreement; analysis procedures for student texts not specified.
Lockhart & Ng (1995a)	• Fifty-four students arranged in dyads. • Freshman writers in Hong Kong university. • Peer response used throughout course.	• Discussion and training provided before first peer response sessions. • Teacher provided guiding questions. • Students revised drafts after peer feedback.	• Focus was on "stances" taken by peer reviewers. • Peer feedback sessions audiotaped and transcribed. • Categories determined by researchers based on analysis of transcripts. • Rating/coding procedures discussed.

(continued on next page)

OVERVIEW OF PEER RESPONSE STUDIES *(continued)*

Study	Subjects and Setting	Peer Feedback Procedures	Research Design Issues
Lockhart & Ng (1995b)	• Thirty-two students arranged in dyads. • See Lockhart & Ng (1995a).	• See Lockhart & Ng (1995a).	• See Lockhart & Ng (1995a).
Villamil & de Guerrero (1996)	• Fifty-four students arranged in pairs. • Intermediate college-level ESL writing course in Puerto Rico. • Peer review used at regular intervals during course.	• Students introduced to peer review and given model essays to examine. • Peer review fairly unstructured (see p. 55) • Pairs randomly formed. • Students revised at home after peer review.	• Focus of study was to describe characteristics (activities, strategies, social behaviors) during peer review. • Recordings of peer review sessions transcribed and analyzed. • Researchers created categories for analysis from the transcripts; no reliabilities reported.
Berg (1999)	• Forty-six students in two treatment groups (24 and 22). • Intermediate ESL classes in Intensive English Program at U.S. university. • Peer response used for each of five writing assignments.	• Experimental group students trained using 11-step. • Experimental group used peer feedback form; control group did not. • All students revised after peer reviews.	• Focus of study was effects of trained versus untrained peer reviews on revision quality. • Faigley and Witte (1981) taxonomy used to classify revisions; TWE scores used to compare quality of first drafts and revisions. • Coding/rating/reliability procedures described.

Paulus (1999)	• Eleven students working in pairs for peer review. • Pre-freshman composition course at U.S. university. • Not specified whether peer response used consistently.	• Teacher provided modeling and discussion of peer review at beginning of course. • Students given peer review form. • Students paired based on oral language proficiency and different L1s. • Students wrote second drafts after peer review and third drafts after teacher feedback.	• Focus was on effects of peer and teacher feedback on revision and on overall writing quality. • Faigley and Witte (1981) taxonomy used to classify revisions; 10-point holistic scoring scale used to measure essay quality. • Independent raters used for both analyses; reliability procedures reported.
Schmid (1999)	• Twelve students arranged in dyads. • Pre-freshman composition class at U.S. university. • Peer response used consistently.	• Students had discussion and modeling with teacher before first peer review session. • Teacher provided peer feedback forms. • Students divided into male/female pairs. • Students revised after getting teacher and peer feedback.	• See Mendonça and Johnson (1994). • Quality of students' revisions was also assessed using scale from Ferris (1997). • Independent raters used; interrater reliabilities reported.

<table>
<tr>
<td>

CHAPTER

5

</td>
<td>

Student Views
on
Response

</td>
</tr>
</table>

One substantial area of research on response to student writing is student surveys of their opinions about different types of feedback on their writing. This line of inquiry, beginning with a 1987 study by Cohen, appears to follow directly from similar investigations in L1 composition (see Straub, 1997, for a review). Besides investigating issues similar to those that concern L1 researchers, L2 writing researchers have asked additional questions about the appropriateness and efficacy of various response practices (error correction, peer feedback, teacher-student conferences) for L2 writers, and have noted differences across student populations (most broadly between L1 and L2 students) in their affective responses to different feedback techniques.

As Joy Reid has noted for years in various conference presentations, it is important on a number of levels for teachers and researchers to ask students about their preferences and to respect them as much as possible. In the conclusion of her survey of 100 ESL writers about their teachers' error correction practices, Leki (1991) argued that "Ignoring their request for error correction works against their motivation.... It seems at best counter-productive, at worst, high-handed and disrespectful of our students, to simply insist that they trust our preferences" (p. 210). Though teachers and reviewers must always take care to consider the larger context in which survey data are gathered and to assess its generalizability to other settings, such research helps us to be aware of what our students may think and how they may react to our pedagogical practices. This awareness in turn may cause us to listen more carefully to students and to explain our own decisions to them, leading to a more collegial classroom community and to improved student motivation and confidence in their instructors.

Student survey research, in addition to helping us understand what students want and how they feel about what we do, can assist us in perceiving ways in which our philosophies and practices and even our specific feedback techniques may be misunderstood by the students. For example, one consistent finding in surveys on teacher commentary and error correction is that students may struggle with symbols and codes that teachers use to provide various types of feedback. Other results have indicated that students in some settings do not understand the common teacher practice of providing different types of feedback on different drafts (e.g., content feedback on first drafts and grammar feedback on penultimate drafts) or why teachers may use selective rather than comprehensive error correction. Again, being aware of what students do not understand may help us to communicate with them and explain ourselves better, rather than assume that everyone (both instructor and students) is operating under the same philosophies and assumptions.

Clearly, improved student motivation, better instructor understanding, and heightened communication between teacher and students are all valuable benefits of asking students for their views on responding practices. However, it is important to state from the outset that this research has some key limitations. First, as already noted, student characteristics, experience, and motivations may vary dramatically from one setting to another. It can be dangerous to overgeneralize the responses of one group of survey subjects to a markedly different setting. Second, with only a few case study exceptions, the research discussed in this chapter merely reports on student observations and claims about feedback they have received and its effects on their writing development. There have rarely been any attempts to link student reactions to actual teacher or peer feedback or to student revision; further, attempts to ask the teachers to provide their perspectives on feedback given have been few and far between. This is only problematic if the authors of research studies do not appropriately hedge or qualify their findings with the constant awareness that they are dealing only with student report data, and not proven fact. For instance, in my own survey research on student reactions to teacher feedback (Ferris, 1995b), I noted that 79% of the students reported that they received "a lot" or "some" grammar feedback on their first drafts, despite the fact that the teachers were ostensibly only giving content-focused commentary on first drafts, per program policy. The teachers whose students completed this survey strongly disputed their students' responses to this question, and I noted that "the students may have been confused as to what their teachers actually did on the various drafts because they were relying on their memories to complete the survey" (p. 42). Third, survey research itself (like any other methodology) is limited in its design and scope—the questions that are asked and the ways in which they are framed can greatly affect the results; further, interpretation of survey results can be challenging and conditioned by the assumptions and biases of the researcher(s).

With both benefits and caveats in mind, this chapter includes reviews of student survey research on teacher commentary, on error correction, and on peer feedback. It also covers several studies that compare a combination of feedback treatments such as teacher versus peer feedback. The chapter concludes with a critical analysis of the previous research to date and its implications for future studies and for response strategies.

SURVEY RESEARCH ON TEACHER COMMENTARY

Researchers who have examined student views on teachers' written commentary have typically investigated one or more of the following questions: (a) According to students, what types of feedback do teachers give them and what aspects of writing does teacher feedback address? (b) What are student preferences about the types of teacher feedback they would like to receive? (c) What are student reactions to teacher feedback they have received? (d) What types of problems do students have with teacher feedback? (e) How seriously do students take teacher commentary? (f) What strategies do students use to process and apply teacher feedback, particularly if they have trouble comprehending it? and (g) What do students think is the impact or effect of teacher commentary on their (students') development as writers? A summary of the studies covering these issues is provided in Fig. 5.1; a summary of the findings related to these questions is given in Fig. 5.2.

The earliest study along these lines (Cohen, 1987) has served as a prototype for several subsequent survey research projects (Cohen & Cavalcanti, 1990; Ferris, 1995b; McCurdy, 1992). Cohen surveyed 217 college students at a U.S. university, asking questions about the topics covered about teacher feedback and about student strategies for processing teacher feedback. The student respondents claimed that their teachers' commentary focused mainly on grammar. Although they also reported that they read and attended to teacher feedback, they identified only "a limited repertoire of strategies for processing teacher feedback" (pp. 64–65). The student subjects also noted that they had trouble understanding or using teacher comments when they were cryptic (single words or brief phrases) such as "confusing" or "not clear." Cohen concluded from his data that "the activity of teacher feedback as currently constituted and realized may have more limited impact on the learners than teachers would desire" (p. 66). Though Cohen's study on this topic broke new ground and posed important questions, it was limited in several important ways. First, his subjects were drawn from ESL writers, English-speaking students in foreign language classes, and native-English-speaking writers in freshman composition classes. There is no discussion of the possible impact of the differing subject characteristics and writing contexts on the results (Ferris, 1999b; Hedgcock & Lefkowitz, 1994). Second, it appears that most or all of the subjects were operating in single-draft contexts. As discussed in chapters 1, 2, and 6, it seems clear that teacher commentary is most efficacious when it is provided on intermediate rather than final drafts of student texts. Third, Cohen's comment about the "limited impact" of "the activity of teacher feedback as currently constituted and re-

FIG. 5.1.　Survey studies on teacher commentary.

Study	Research Questions	Subjects
Cohen (1987)	(1) What does teacher feedback deal with? (2) How much of teacher feedback do students process? (3) What strategies do students use to cope with teacher feedback? (4) What problems do they have interpreting teacher feedback?(see p. 60)	Two hundred seventeen college students (NES in freshman comp., ESL writers, FL writers)
Radecki & Swales (1988)	What are student attitudes toward teacher commentary—its scope, its usefulness, on Tee versus Ess responsibility, and Tee expectations of utilization of feedback? (see p. 357)	Fifty nine students in four ESL-oriented writing courses at University of Michigan (four different levels)
Cohen & Cavalcanti (1990)	See Cohen (1987); see p. 156	
McCurdy (1992)	See Cohen (1987)	
Arndt (1993)	(a) What are students' and teachers' perspectives on feedback in process writing classes? (b) What are the major areas of match and mismatch between students' and teachers' perspectives on various types of feedback given and the ways and means of giving it? (p. 95)	Seventy-five EFL students and 8 teachers in a Hong Kong Polytechnic college
Enginarlar (1993)	Follows Radecki & Swales (1988), see p. 195.	Forty-seven EFL college students in Turkey
Hedgcock & Lefkowitz (1994)	(1) How do L2 students react when they receive teacher feedback? (2) How do these responses affect the evolution of students' perception of text quality and their composing processes? (3) Do ESL and FL learners differ systematically in terms of self-appraisal patterns and responses to feedback? (see pp. 141 & 146)	Two hundred forty-seven college L2 writers—ESL & FL students

(continued on next page)

(FIG 5.1 continued)

Saito (1994)	(1) What kinds of feedback do teachers give? (2) What are students' preferences? (3) How do students handle the feedback they receive? (4) What are students' attitudes toward- different types of correction prompts (see p. 48)	Three teachers and 39 ESL students at a Canadian university
Brice (1995)	(1) What kinds of teacher-written feedback do students understand and what kinds do they have trouble understanding? (2) What kinds of teacher-written feedback do students like best and least on their drafts? (3) What kinds of teacher-written feedback do students find most and least useful in helping them to revise drafts and write future essays? (p. 3)	Case study with interviews of three ESL students at a U.S. university
Ferris (1995b)	See Cohen (1987) & McCurdy (1992)	One hundred fifty-five ESL students at a U.S. university (multiple-draft setting)
Hedgcock & Lefkowitz (1996)	See Hedgcock & Lefkowitz (1994)	Three hundred sixteen L2 university writers (both ESL & FL)— factor analysis of 1994 survey results; interviews with 21 student subjects about how they incorporate feedback

alized" is not adequately hedged to reflect the fact that his study shows us nothing about what the activity of teacher feedback consists of, but merely the degree to which students say they consider it and utilize it in their writing.

Cohen's survey, in slightly modified forms, has been used in at least three subsequent studies. Cohen and Cavalcanti (1990) studied nine EFL college students in Brazil. Unlike most other studies of student views on teacher feedback, this study actually examined teacher commentary itself in addition to the student survey responses. As in Cohen's earlier U.S.-based study, the students reported that teacher

FIG. 5.2. Summary of survey findings on teacher commentary.

Study	Student Preferences of Reactions About Feedback	Student Reports of What Teacher Feedback Covers	Student Problems with Feedback	Student Strategies for Teacher Feedback	Other Findings
Cohen (1987)	Students read and attended to feedback	Mostly grammar	Single words or short phrases like "Confusing"	A "limited repertoire" —mostly "made a mental note"	
Radecki & Swales (1988)	Positive, appreciative reactions; students divided into "Receptors," "Semi-Resistors" and "Resistors"	Substantive comments on content + error correction	Students wanted direct teacher correction of all errors		
Cohen & Cavalcanti (1990)	Students generally pleased with teacher feedback; wanted feedback on all areas of writing	Mostly grammar and mechanics		A range of strategies (see Table 4, p. 169)	Authors report a "poor fit" between student reports about teacher feedback and actual teacher commentary
McCurdy (1992)	Students happy with teacher feedback and found it valuable	A range of writing issues		A range of strategies (see Cohen and Cavalcanti, 1990)	

(continued on next page)

(FIG. 5.2 continued)

Study	Student Preferences of Reactions About Feedback	Student Reports of What Teacher Feedback Covers	Student Problems with Feedback	Student Strategies for Teacher Feedback	Other Findings
Arndt (1993)	(1) Macro concerns should precede micro concerns; (2) Clues are better than corrections	All areas of writing	Students sometimes misunderstood teachers' written comments and did not always function well in conferences		(1) Students preferred written comments to be in-text rather than on a separate form; teacher preferred a separate sheet (2) Students preferred both written feedback and conferencing; teachers preferred conferencing
Enginarlar (1993)	"Positive" feelings toward teacher feedback; student responses similar to Radecki and Swales (1988)	Aattention to linguistic errors, guidance on composition skills, evaluative comments on content and quality of writing		Revision is a collaborative effort between teacher and students	A problem-solving approach to revision and error correction is preferred and most useful
Hedgcock & Lefkowitz (1994)	Written feedback combined with conferences	ESL writers: feedback on both content and form; FL writers: grammar and vocabulary	Students disliked the red pen and were moderately favorable toward correction symbols		Very different attitudes found between ESL and FL student populations in motivations for writing and attitudes toward feedback

Study					
Saito (1994)	Students prefer teacher feedback to focus on grammatical errors; clues and better than corrections	Teacher commentary in margins, direct and indirect error correction	Students found "rule" pr4ompts more helpful than "La/L2 comparison" prompts	(1) Read paper again; (2) Made a mental note; (3) Corrected errors or rewrote paper	Students preferred teacher feedback (written and conferences) to nonteacher feedback
Brice (1995)	Students "quite invested" in reading and acting on teacher commentary		Students disliked error coding system		Two of three students utilized error codes successfully in revisions, even though they disliked them
Ferris (1995b)	Students very appreciative of teacher feedback and find it helpful	All areas of writing on both preliminary and final drafts	Correction symbols and teacher questions sometimes confusing	A range of strategies (see Cohen and Cavalcanti, 1990)	First study to separate reactions to feedback on preliminary drafts versus final drafts
Hedgcock & Lefkowitz (1996)	FL students preferred feedback on form; ESL students preferred content and form feedback	See Hedgcock and Lefkowitz (1994)	Students sometimes confused with teacher markings and error corrections	Revision = error correction	FL students: The purpose of writing is for language practice; teacher feedback should reflect this

feedback mainly consisted of comments about grammar and mechanics, but that they would like to receive feedback on all areas of writing (including content and organization). The students in this study also noted that they valued positive feedback (praise). The students in this study reported a broader range of strategies for dealing with teacher feedback than in Cohen's 1987 study. The authors noted that their findings suggest a need for "a clear agreement between teacher and student as to what will be commented on and how such comments will be categorized" (p. 175). Though the authors are to be commended for better contextualizing the student survey responses, this study is limited in that there was a small number of subjects and they were drawn from three distinct institutions or programs and had different teachers.

In a 1992 study, Pamela McCurdy used Cohen's questionnaire to survey 155 college ESL students at a U.S. university. She found that students reported being happy with the feedback received from their teachers and that they felt it valuable to their development as writers. They reported that their teachers' comments covered a broad range of writing issues and that they used a variety of strategies to address it. In short, the findings were far more positive about teacher feedback strategies and student engagement with teacher commentary than in Cohen's original study.

None of the previous three studies were conducted in settings in which students routinely wrote multiple drafts of their papers and received feedback on preliminary drafts. However, a study by Ferris (1995b) specifically addressed this issue by adapting Cohen's survey for multiple-draft settings. As in McCurdy's study, 155 ESL writers in a U.S. university completed the survey, again reporting that they reread their papers, attended to teacher feedback, and used a range of strategies for processing teacher feedback. They claimed to pay more attention to teacher comments on preliminary drafts than on final drafts, but they seemed to feel that feedback was helpful even at the end of the process. Like McCurdy's subjects, students reported that their teachers gave them feedback on the whole range of writing issues, but like the respondents in earlier studies, they also felt that feedback on grammar was the most important to them. The students claimed to experience few problems in comprehending teacher feedback, but when problems occurred, they included confusion over error codes and correction symbols as well as teacher questioning strategies (see chapters 2 and 6 for further discussion of teacher questions in written feedback). Finally, although the students seemed to appreciate and remember positive comments of praise, they expressed a strong preference for a mixture of praise and constructive criticism. The two studies by McCurdy and by Ferris avoided some of the pitfalls of Cohen's original study by surveying homogeneous groups of ESL college students and (in the case of Ferris) considering the effects of multiple-draft settings, but they are similarly limited in that they rely on student report data and are not further triangulated with teacher survey or interview data or text analysis of teacher commentary and student revisions.

Another earlier study that has been replicated is that of Radecki and Swales (1988). They questioned 59 ESL writers at the University of Michigan about their attitudes toward teacher feedback (its scope and its usefulness) and the relative responsibilities of teachers and students to make changes and corrections in student texts. Radecki and Swales divided their respondents (based on preliminary analyses of their answers) into three groups: Receptors (46%), Semi-Resistors (41%), and Resistors (13%), finding that the students' attitudes differed across these group lines (see Fig. 5.3 for an overview). It was found that students generally appreciated teacher feedback in the form of substantive comments about their ideas, but that they also "expect the instructor to correct all their surface errors" (p. 362). The authors concluded that "Clearly, teachers must intervene and change student attitudes" (p. 362) about error correction.

In a 1993 study, Enginarlar replicated Radecki and Swales' (1988) design with 47 EFL college students in Turkey. Again, the students reported positive feelings toward teacher feedback and that they valued "shared responsibility between teacher and students" for student progress. He also found that the students' orientations toward feedback mirrored the divisions reported by Radecki and Swales. He summarized by saying that "What students perceive as effective instructor feedback encompasses: (1) attention to linguistic errors; (2) guidance on compositional skills; and (3) overall evaluative comments on content and quality of writing.... When feedback in these areas is provided in a problem-solving manner, students seem to regard revision work as a collaborative type of learning where responsibility is shared by the two parties" (p. 203).

Two other studies connected to each other were completed by Hedgcock and Lefkowitz (1994, 1996). Unlike nearly all of the other studies discussed in this section, Hedgcock and Lefkowitz addressed the critical issue of differences in writing contexts and learner motivation by comparing and contrasting survey responses between ESL writers and writers in foreign language (FL) classes at a U.S. university. Using an extensive questionnaire that covered a wide range of issues, they surveyed 247 subjects about their reactions to teacher feedback and how teacher response affected their views of text quality and their writing processes. They reported the following major findings: (a) Students' preferred mode of receiving feedback was

Group	Marking Preferences	Error Correction	Rewriting	Perception of Teacher's Views
Receptors	(1) Substantive content-specific comments (2) All errors marked	Joint responsibility of teacher and student	"Would gladly rewrite essays if teacher asked them to do so"	Felt obligated to pay attention to teacher feedback or teacher would be disappointed
Semi-Resistors	Same as Receptors	Varied by class context	Reluctance or hostility	Same as Receptors
Resistors	Grade alone or grade with short evaluative comment preferred	Teacher's job to correct errors	Same as Semi-Resistors: rewriting is punishment	Don't know (don't care?)

FIG. 5.3.   Receptors, semi-resistors, and resistors (Radecki & Swales, 1988; Enginarlar, 1993).

written feedback combined with one-to-one writing conferences with the teacher; (b) the students in general were most concerned with issues of grammatical and lexical accuracy, but the ESL students were more favorably disposed toward content feedback than were the FL writers; and (c) students had a moderate preference for the use of correction symbols but disliked the use of the red pen. The authors noted that "the two student populations expressed very distinct attitudes toward teacher intervention" (p. 155).

In a follow-up study, Hedgcock and Lefkowitz (1996) factor-analyzed their questionnaire responses and supplemented them with interviews of 21 student subjects. This more finely grained quantitative and qualitative analysis clearly identified the differences in views of writing and response between ESL and FL writers. As in the previous study, it was found that the FL writers clearly valued form-focused feedback over content feedback, whereas the ESL students valued both types. The authors noted that for FL writers, composing and revision in L2 writing are seen as providing grammar practice, not for trying out new ideas or for demonstrating creativity. Most FL writers and some ESL writers explicitly equated "revision" with "error correction." Both groups of writers expressed at least occasional confusion about interpreting teachers' marks and corrections. Hedgcock and Lefkowitz concluded that "Instructors' reported response habits may exert a strong influence on the views of L2 writers about the priority of formal accuracy over the transmission of meaning, and vice versa" (p. 299).

Three other individual studies have examined a range of questions and issues related to feedback. Arndt (1993) is somewhat unusual in that she surveyed both teachers and EFL college writing students in Hong Kong, comparing teacher and student attitudes on several issues. There appeared to be agreement between teachers and students that "macro concerns" (e.g., comments on content and organization) should precede "micro concerns" (i.e., feedback on linguistic issues). Students and instructors also agreed that students learned better from "clues" than from "corrections" (see discussion in chapters 3 and 7 on indirect vs. direction error correction). On the other hand, students preferred to receive written comments embedded in their texts, next to the point in question, whereas teachers preferred the use of separate feedback sheets. Arndt recommended that the parties reach a "negotiated compromise" on this point. In addition, although students expressed a preference for *both* written commentary *and* teacher–student conferences, the teachers said that they felt conferences were more beneficial and that, in fact, certain aspects of texts could only be adequately addressed in face-to-face conferences: "… minor points of language or style could be cleared up by means of a written comment, but major points relating to meaning and organization needed to be clarified, explained, and negotiated through discussion and dialogue" (p. 100). Arndt further observed that the potential for misunderstanding and confusion between teachers and students exists for both written feedback and conferencing and notes that "the art of conferencing" does not come naturally to all students (cf. Goldstein & Conrad, 1990; Newkirk, 1995; Patthey-Chavez & Ferris, 1997; and chapter 2 of this volume). (It is worth observing that the "art of conferencing" probably does not come naturally to all teachers, either!)

In a 1994 study, Saito looked not only at the reactions of 39 college-level ESL students, but also examined their texts and their teachers' comments and corrections. She found variation across the three teachers and classes she studied, but generally all three teachers provided feedback on both ideas and errors, though in different ways and at different stages of the composing process. As to student preferences, she found that students were equally favorable to indirect error correction (error identification or "feedback with prompts") compared with direct correction by the teacher. The students reported in varying proportions that they would read their compositions again after receiving feedback, make a mental note of corrections, or correct errors and/or rewrite their papers (see also Cohen & Cavalcanti, 1990). Saito noted that "students' strategies for handling feedback may differ depending upon the way their teacher provides feedback" (p. 61). Finally, the students were asked for their reactions to five different types of thinking prompt:

1. *Word:* Is this the right word or expression? Possible words are …
2. *L1/L2:* How do I say it in my language? Does it make sense in English?
3. *Goals:* Will people understand this? What do I want to tell my reader?
4. *Fit:* Does this part fit with the other parts?
5. *Rules:* Do I know a grammar or spelling rule for this? The rule is….
   (Saito, 1994, Appendix A, p. 68).

Students generally had favorable reactions to all five prompt types, but the highest mean (most preferred) was the "Rule" prompt, and the lowest was the "L1/L2" prompt, which Saito noted may have been less useful because the teachers and tutors in the study were not always sure when to invoke it in their feedback.

Finally, Brice (1995) undertook a case study of three university ESL writers. Unlike the other studies discussed in this section, which relied primarily on written questionnaires, Brice used videotaped think-aloud protocols "in which they reacted to comments their teacher wrote on their second and final drafts" (p. 4). Brice found considerable variation across her three subjects (see also Conrad & Goldstein, 1999), but did find that all three students seemed to be "quite invested" in reading and responding to their teacher's commentary. The students also were unanimous in expressing dislike for their teacher's coding system for error marking, saying that they would have preferred more explicit verbal cues. (Nonetheless, Brice noted that two of her three subjects were able to utilize the coded error feedback quite successfully in their revisions.)

To summarize the 11 studies on student views of teacher commentary reviewed in this section, several generalizations can be made:

• Students value and appreciate teacher feedback in almost any form. The exceptions were the "Resistors" in the studies by Radecki and Swales (1988) and Enginarlar (1993), but they were clearly in the minority (comprising about 13% of the subjects studied).

• Students in nearly all of the studies expressed strong preferences for teacher feedback on language issues. In no case did any student subjects say that they resented teacher feedback on their errors or found it unnecessary.

- In some of the studies, student writers also expressed appreciation for feedback on their ideas and composing strategies.
- When asked about specific types of error feedback, students seemed open to the idea of indirect error correction rather than insisting that only the teacher could correct errors, and they felt that they would learn more if they collaborated with the teacher in the revision and correction processes.
- As to strategies for dealing with teacher feedback, they seemed to vary according to both the nature of the feedback received and the teachers' expectations or requirements after giving feedback. In other words, if the teachers expected rewriting or revision and gave the students substantial responsibility for utilizing teacher feedback in such revisions, the students would attempt various strategies to do so successfully. However, if the teacher merely returned papers with feedback and grades and did not require or expect students to do anything specific with the comments, the students were unlikely to take initiative to rewrite or correct their papers or to resolve any difficulties or misunderstandings.
- In the studies in which students were asked about the relative merits of written teacher commentary versus face-to-face conferences with their teachers, the students said they preferred both. (It is not surprising that, given the option, students would select to receive the most feedback possible in several different modes of delivery. It is also not shocking, from a simple workload perspective, that the teachers in Arndt's [1993] study did *not* prefer the "both/and" option!)

STUDIES ON ERROR CORRECTION

Whereas a number of the studies already reviewed looked at error/language feedback in conjunction with studying various questions about teacher commentary, several other researchers have looked specifically at student views about error correction. These studies are summarized in Fig. 5.4.

The first study of this type focusing on ESL writers and their views on error correction was published by Ilona Leki (1991). She surveyed 100 university ESL writers to investigate two major issues: (a) How concerned are ESL students with errors in their writing, and (b) What are the best ways (in the students' opinion) for teachers to give error feedback? The students perceived that accuracy in writing (as few errors as possible) was very important to them, although a significant minority (38%) said that their content instructors ignored ESL errors. As to error correction mechanisms, students preferred comprehensive (all errors marked) over selective error correction, and 67% wanted their teachers to locate errors and give them a clue about how to correct them.

In a 1999 survey of 65 university ESL writers, supplemented with interview data from 25 of the subjects, Komura investigated several questions similar to those examined by Leki as well as other issues. Like Leki, Komura found that students preferred correction to be comprehensive rather than selective and that they felt they learned more from indirect correction (errors underlined with error codes attached) than from direct correction by the teacher. Komura also looked at whether students were satisfied with the error feedback they received from their teachers (three

Study	Research Questions	Subjects	Major Findings
Leki (1991)	(1) How concerned are ESL students with errors in their writing? (2) What are the best ways for teachers to give error feedback?	One hundred college-level ESL writers in the U.S.	(1) Students felt that accuracy in writing (as few errors as possible) was very important. (2) 70% favored comprehensive correction (all errors marked). (3) 67% preferred teachers to locate errors and give correction clues compared with direct correction.
Ferris & Roberts (2001)	(1) How do students self-rate their grammar problems? (2) What kinds of grammar feedback do they prefer to receive from teachers?	Sixty-three ESL writers at a U.S. university	(1) The majority of students felt that their grammar errors were serious and affected their writing. (2) Students preferred indirect correction with codes over other choices. (3) Students' self-reported most frequent errors matched well with independent error analysis of their texts (verbs, sentence structure, and word choice were biggest problems).
Komura (1999)	(1) Do ESL writers find teachers' error feedback helpful? (2) Do they find maintaining a log of their errors helpful?	Sixty-five ESL writers at a U.S. university	(1) 92% of respondents expressed satisfaction with their teachers' feedback; 85% said they understood it. (2) Students preferred indirect correction with error codes and felt they learned more from it than from direct correction. (3) 65% of respondents preferred comprehensive correction (all errors) to selective correction (only most frequent errors marked). (4) Students felt that their biggest grammar weaknesses with verbs (tense, form, agreement) and word choice. (5) Students generally felt that the grammar log was beneficial.
Rennie (2000)	(1) Do ESL students want grammar feedback and instruction, and do they find it effective and helpful? (2) What kinds of grammar feedback do students want?	Three hundred thirty-two ESL students at a U.S. university; 15 ESL writing instructors	(1) Students found error correction very helpful and beneficial. (2) Students preferred comprehensive to selective error correction. (3) Students preferred indirect feedback (with or without error codes) to direct feedback. (4) Students did not find error feedback demoralizing or offensive.

FIG. 5.4.   Studies of student views on error correction

teachers were represented in the study), finding that 92% of respondents expressed satisfaction with their teacher's error feedback and 85% said they always understood it. Komura further asked students what they felt their specific weaknesses in grammar were, finding that the major categories of student concern related to verbs (tense, form, subject–verb agreement, word choice) and word choice. Finally, students were asked about the effectiveness of a grammar log requirement in their writing classes (in which they charted the errors they made on successive essay drafts throughout the semester); though students expressed some concerns about the mechanics of the error logs (see also Roberts, 1999), they generally felt it was a good idea and beneficial for their writing and learning.

The largest study to date of this type was a master's thesis project by Rennie (2000), who included 332 university ESL students and 15 ESL writing teachers in her survey project. Her research questions and findings corroborated the earlier ones by Leki and Komura (as to students finding error correction valuable and preferring comprehensive, indirect error feedback). One additional issue she looked at was whether her subjects found error feedback from their teachers offensive or demoralizing (as some scholars have suggested). Rennie found that even when her subjects were given the opportunity to express negative views about teacher error correction, they did not do so, but rather articulated overwhelmingly positive feelings about receiving feedback on their errors.

A final study in this line (Ferris & Roberts, 2001) again investigated similar questions and reported results analogous to those of the previous three studies. Surveys completed by 63 university ESL writers indicated that they felt their grammar errors were serious and negatively affected their writing; they also preferred indirect correction with error codes attached to other types of feedback. One difference in the design of this study was that students' texts and errors were also examined, making it possible to assess the "fit" between their survey responses and their text production. This led to two interesting observations. First, though the students expressed a strong preference for indirect error correction with codes attached, they did equally well in self-correcting when errors were merely underlined but not labeled. Second, the students' views about their primary areas of weakness (verbs, sentence structure, and word choice) matched up identically with the error patterns identified in their texts. Thus, though they had good self-awareness of what their particular language problems were, they were better able to respond to inexplicit error feedback than they had expected.

To summarize, the four studies outlined in Fig. 5.4 present a consistent picture of what students surveyed about their reactions to and preferences regarding error feedback think:

- Linguistic accuracy in writing is important to their overall effectiveness as second language writers.
- Teacher feedback on errors is a vital ingredient for students to improve the accuracy of their writing.
- Comprehensive error feedback is preferable to selective error feedback.
- Indirect correction (errors marked and labeled by error types) is more valuable than direct correction (teachers making the corrections for students).

These error correction studies, together with findings of the more generalized research on teacher feedback discussed earlier in this chapter, lead to an inescapable conclusion: L2 student writers feel that teacher feedback on their errors is extremely important to their progress. Truscott (1996), who argued for the abolishment of error feedback in L2 writing classes, acknowledged that students want error correction but says that this preference is no argument for giving it to them. It is certainly true that students should not be the sole judges of what is best for them. As noted, in the study by Ferris and Roberts (2001), though students greatly preferred more explicit feedback (i.e., errors coded vs. simply underlined), results of an experimental study on students' ability to self-edit after receiving different feedback treatments showed no significant differences in editing success ratios between the group that received error codes and the group that only had errors underlined. Similarly, there are sound arguments in the literature for selective error correction (focusing on a few patterns of frequent, serious error rather than marking every single error in a paper); though the students in these four studies all preferred comprehensive error correction, teachers should not necessarily provide it for them. (Experienced teachers will note with some irony that, in the body of studies discussed so far in this chapter that, when given the opportunity to state a preference, students will, not surprisingly, opt for getting the *most* feedback possible—written commentary *plus* one-to-one conferences, coded feedback rather than just underlining, comprehensive rather than selective correction. Teachers must, of course, balance these stated student preferences with their own time and energy limitations.)

On the other hand, simply dismissing the students' desire for error feedback, as Truscott recommended, is probably not the optimal strategy, either. As Leki noted, so doing may work against students' motivation and cause us as teachers to appear "high-handed and disrespectful" (1991, p. 210). Although Truscott argued that the teacher's job, rather than complying with students' wishes for error feedback, is to get them accustomed to its absence, most experienced teachers would respond that this is easier said than done. In fact, in a study designed to investigate Truscott's claim about the affective disadvantages of withholding error feedback, Brice and Newman (2000) concluded that student desire for error correction was a strongly held position that could not be changed, even though the teacher carefully explained why she was not correcting errors and the students clearly liked and respected the instructor. In short, the body of student survey research on grammar feedback clearly suggests that if we neglect error feedback and issues of accuracy in our L2 writing classes, we most likely do so at peril of alienating and frustrating our students.

STUDIES ON PEER FEEDBACK

As discussed in chapters 4 and 8, peer feedback has emerged as a popular instructional option in L2 writing classes, both in response to the recommendations of L1 composition theorists and because interaction of all types is recommended for the purposes of facilitating second language acquisition. However, though many ESL writing teachers have jumped on the peer response bandwagon over the past 15 years, some have quickly jumped back off, fearing not only that peer feedback was ineffective for L2 writers ("the blind leading the blind") but that students were uncomfortable with it for a variety of reasons. In response to these concerns, several researchers have investigated ESL writers' reactions to peer response. The studies are summarized in Fig. 5.5.

Studies of ESL writers' reactions to peer feedback have typically addressed one or more of the following questions:

- Do ESL writers enjoy peer feedback sessions?
- Do they find peers' comments beneficial when they are revising?
- Do they value peer feedback as much as teacher feedback?

The earliest published ESL paper along these lines is by Leki (1990b). Twenty students, at the end of an ESL writing class in which between-draft peer response sessions occurred throughout the course for all assignments, were asked to respond in writing to two questions: (a) How useful was it to you to read other students' papers? and (b) How useful was it to you to read/hear other students' comments on your papers (pp. 6–7). In response to the first question, 16 of 17 comments were positive. Responses to the second question were more mixed, with 15 positive comments and 5 negative comments (two students gave both positive and negative reactions in the same response). Based on these student comments and her own observations, Leki went on to identify a number of possible problems with peer response sessions in ESL writing classes, including ineffective responding behaviors (confusing revision with editing, making vague, rubber-stamped comments such as "Give some examples"), comments that are overly directive, blunt, or even unkind, and lack of face validity (ESL writers do not trust their peers' expertise). Despite these concerns, Leki concluded that although novice L2 writers' ability to truly help each other progress may indeed be limited, these students do "gain experience in reading, in recognizing academic writing patterns, and most importantly in manipulating text to respond to a reader's needs" (p. 17). She suggested that peer responding may be made more effective if the task is modeled for and discussed with students, if peer feedback sessions are structured with "response guide questions" (p. 16), and if the teacher monitors peer response and lets both authors and responders know that she or he is holding them accountable for taking the activity seriously (see chapter 8 for specific suggestions along these lines).

Mangelsdorf (1992) asked 40 ESL students enrolled in five university freshman composition courses to respond in writing to the following questions:

- Do you find it useful to have your classmates read your papers and give suggestions for revision?
- What kinds of suggestions do you often receive from your classmates?
- What kinds of suggestions are most helpful to you?
- In general, do you find the peer-review process valuable? (pp. 275–276)

Mangelsdorf categorized students' overall responses to peer review as positive (55%), mixed (30%), or negative (15%). She further categorized specific positive

Study	Subjects	Major Findings
Leki (1990b)	Twenty college-level ESL writing students	1. Sixteen of 17 students made positive comments about the helpfulness of reading peers' papers. 2. As to whether peers' comments were helpful to them: 15 positive reactions, 5 negative reactions, and two comments that included both positive and negative remarks.
Mangelsdorf (1992)	Forty ESL writing students at a U.S. university	Many respondents said that peer reviews had helped them in revision; some commented that peers were not able to give helpful advice.
Arndt (1993)	Seventy-five EFL students and eight teachers at a Hong Kong college	Students liked peer feedback in the context of collaborative or team writing but appreciated it less when someone outside the team context gave feedback.
Mendonça & Johnson (1994)	Twelve international graduate students at a U.S. university	1. All subjects found peer feedback helpful. 2. Students found peer feedback more helpful when peers were in the same field of study (and could offer content expertise).
Zhang (1995)	Eighty-one ESL students at two U.S. colleges	Students preferred teacher feedback over peer feedback but chose peer feedback over self-evaluation.
Jacobs, Curtis, Braine, & Huang (1998)	One hundred twenty-one college EFL writers in Hong Kong and Taiwan	Ninety-three percent of the respondents said they wanted peer feedback to be one of their feedback options.
Schmid (1999)	Twelve undergraduate students at a U.S. university	1. Ten of 12 students liked the peer review activity and found it beneficial. 2. Seven of 12 said they utilized peer comments in their revisions. 3. Seven of 12 said they preferred both peer and teacher feedback; four said they preferred teacher feedback only.

FIG. 5.5.   Student views on peer response.

and negative comments into subcategories (1992, Tables 2 & 3, p. 277). Of the positive responses, 68% said that peer review helped them with various content issues, including clarifying ideas, giving different views on the topic, and developing ideas. Sixteen percent of the positive comments dealt with issues of organization and style (including errors). Negative comments focused on two general areas: (a) The "limitations of students as critics" (77%) and (b) the "limitations of peer-review task" (23%). Examples of students' limitations cited included "student criticism can't be trusted" (because students are not expert enough in writing or in English) and "student critics are apathetic." As to limitations of the task, three students suggested that there was not enough time given to peer response in class.

Mangelsdorf also asked the five teachers represented in the study to respond to the questions. The teachers' concerns about the limitations of peer review paralleled those of the students, but they also pointed out additional benefits of peer response: that it "exposed students to a diversity of thought," encouraged them to become more active readers and writers, and that it promoted a sense of writing as a shared social activity. Like Leki, Mangelsdorf moved from her findings to suggestions about improving the effectiveness of peer review activities, discussing the need for modeling the technique, giving students awareness of the purpose for the activity, having students work in groups rather than pairs, conferencing with students after the peer review exercise, and basing a percentage of the course grade on peer reviews. She concluded that peer review takes patience on the part of both students and teachers but that the process can be valuable and enjoyable for students if it is carefully presented.

Arndt (1993) used written questionnaires from 75 EFL students and eight teachers in a Hong Kong college and follow-up interviews with 10 students and all of the teachers to investigate a number of questions related to feedback (see also Figs. 5.1 and 5.2 and accompanying discussion). In this context, students often wrote their papers in a "team writing" environment, with either a partner or a small group. In the "team writing" scenario, the student respondents felt that peer feedback was natural, authentic, and helpful. However, they were less appreciative of feedback from individuals or groups outside of their team, noting problems such as lack of time to get a grip on the other team's topic and lack of knowledge of or interest in these topics—both of which resulted in giving and receiving feedback to peers that was superficial or focused only on errors in grammar or spelling. Based on her findings, Arndt suggested that teachers utilize team writing more often and perhaps de-emphasize "traditional" peer feedback activities in which students who are not invested or engaged in each other's topics are expected to respond substantively to them nonetheless. This is an intriguing argument that makes some intuitive sense when one thinks about the role of peer review in professional or academic settings. Scholars are rarely, if ever, asked to review papers by peers outside of their areas of interest and expertise and might indeed feel both resentful and ill-equipped if asked to do so. It should not be surprising to find that students might have similar reactions.

Another angle on the issue of shared knowledge or expertise and its effects on peer feedback in the writing class is taken by Mendonça and Johnson (1994). In this study, 12 international graduate students at a U.S. university participated in peer review sessions in pairs and then revised their papers after receiving both peer and teacher feedback. Student texts (originals and revisions) and peer commentary were examined to see the effects of peer suggestions on student revisions, and the student writers themselves were interviewed about their reactions. Of the six pairs, four were composed of students in the same field of study, whereas the other two pairs had students in different fields. In their interviews, all students indicated that they had found the peer review activity beneficial, saying that it had "helped them see points that were clear in their essays and points that needed revision" (p. 764). They also noted that they had enjoyed reading their peers' papers. Interestingly, though two of the four students with partners outside their major field said that they did not find the peer review process helpful, the authors noted that "both of these students used their peers' comments in their revisions and were able to give feedback on their partners' essays. The remaining 10 students, however, reported that even though peers in the same field of study can offer more ideas, peers who are in different fields are better able to pinpoint parts that are not clear in their drafts" (p. 765). In short, the graduate students in this study seemed very favorably impressed with peer response, and analysis of their texts demonstrated that they had indeed incorporated many of their partners' suggestions into their revisions (see chapter 4 for further discussion of this study).

A study by Zhang (1995) set out to reexamine "the affective advantage of peer feedback in the ESL writing class." Like Leki (1990b), Zhang pointed out that many L1 composition scholars have encouraged, even urged the use of peer feedback, arguing that it is just as helpful as teacher commentary, that it saves teachers time, that it provides an authentic audience (and one less prone to the dangerous excesses of appropriation discussed in chapter 1), and, most importantly, that student writers like peer feedback better and resent constructive criticism less if it comes from classmates rather than an overbearing teacher. To examine this last point, Zhang asked 81 ESL students in U.S. academic settings to respond to two questions:

1. Given a choice between teacher feedback and nonteacher feedback—that is, feedback by your peers or yourself—before you write your final version, which will you choose?
2. Given a choice between peer feedback and self-directed feedback before you write your final version, which will you choose? (p. 215)

The students, who had all had previous exposure to all three forms of feedback, were asked to simply check off boxes in response to the two questions. Zhang found that his subjects overwhelmingly (94%) preferred teacher feedback to nonteacher feedback, but that the majority (61%) preferred peer feedback over self-directed feedback. Zhang cautioned that because his study was designed to assess the "relative appeal" of teacher, peer, and self feedback, the results "should not be misinterpreted to mean that peer feedback is detrimental to ESL writing or resented among ESL learners. It may well be that all three types of feedback are beneficial, although with varying degrees of appeal" (p. 219).

After Zhang's study was published in 1995, a team of researchers (Jacobs, Curtis, Braine, & Huang, 1998) expressed concern that because of the way the choices were presented to the student subjects in Zhang's study, it did not provide a sufficiently precise examination of students' affective responses to peer feedback. To address this issue, they asked 121 EFL writers in Hong Kong and Taiwan to read the following statements and respond by choosing between the two options and writing a brief explanation:

1. I prefer to have feedback from other students as one type of feedback on my writing.
2. I prefer not to have feedback from other students on my writing (p. 311).

The important distinction between this design and Zhang's is that respondents were not forced to choose between teacher and peer feedback but rather to focus exclusively on whether they liked or disliked peer response. When the choice was framed in this way, 93% of the subjects said that they would like to have peer feedback as one of their feedback options. In written comments, the two most important reasons given for including peer feedback were that "peers provided more ideas and were able to spot problems they had missed" (p. 312). In addition, though they had not been asked about this, 25 students wrote comments about the benefits they received from reading other students' writing. The authors also noted that none of the respondents rejected the need for teacher feedback in their comments (again, of course, teacher commentary was not the focus of the investigation). They concluded by arguing for "a middle path" in which teacher, peer, and self feedback are "judiciously combined" (p. 314). It should be noted that though the design and focus of this study was intended to rectify problems the authors had noted in Zhang's (1995) study, in both cases the researchers arrived at the conclusion that, at least according to student perceptions, there was probably room for several different types of feedback in the L2 writing class.

In a response to the concerns raised and findings presented by Jacobs et al. (1998), Zhang (1999) pointed out this considerable convergence of results and conclusions. However, he also noted that the focus of his study was to reexamine the alleged affective *advantage* of peer feedback, especially in comparison with teacher feedback, put forth by L1 composition researchers. He argued that in neither study is there any evidence that students *prefer* peer feedback over other forms of response, but rather that they would rather have peer feedback than not have it. A careful reading of the two studies and of Zhang's response leads to the clear conclusion that Zhang is correct that the L2 writers in these studies did not claim to prefer peer feedback over teacher response but that they also declined to reject it as a feedback option, even when given the chance to do so (in Question 2 of Zhang's 1995 study and in the Jacobs et al. 1998 study). As is discussed further later, this dialogue suggests that, as to student preferences, it is not advisable either to use peer feedback exclusively or to abolish it altogether.

The most recent study dealing with student views about peer response is a master's thesis by Schmid (1999). Schmid replicated the earlier study by Mendonça and Johnson (1994), looking at the types of peer interactions in six dyads (12 students), the effects of peer commentary on student revision, and student reactions to the peer review process (this study is discussed in more detail in chapter 4). An important distinction between the two studies was that Mendonça and Johnson were examining graduate students writing papers about their major fields of study whereas

Schmid's subjects were undergraduates in a general purposes composition class, all responding to the same assignment. In interviews conducted after students had participated in peer review and revised their papers, Schmid found that 10 of the 12 students said they had enjoyed the peer review session, and 7 of 12 said they had utilized peer comments in constructing their revisions, and that they preferred to receive both teacher and peer feedback. Four of the 12 students, however, said they would rather receive feedback from the teacher only. Students who either did not like the activity or said they did not find it particularly helpful cited a lack of specificity in their partner's feedback as the main problem, despite the fact that the teacher had given students fairly detailed instructions about what to look for and how to go about giving feedback (see pp. 23–24 and p. 86).

The group of studies that specifically examines ESL/EFL student reactions to peer feedback is, again, quite consistent as to results. Despite the fact that concerns have been raised about the effectiveness and appropriateness of peer review activities in L2 writing classes (see, e.g., Connor & Asenavage, 1994; Leki, 1990b; Nelson & Carson, 1998), there is no evidence in any of these studies that L2 writers dislike peer review. On the contrary, in several of the studies, students were overwhelmingly positive in their evaluation of such activities; in the remaining studies, a clear majority favored its use. Although there are definitely limitations as to what teachers can expect from peer feedback and clear suggestions about what is needed to make the activity beneficial (see chapter 8), based on the existing research base, teachers can consider including peer review in their catalogue of feedback strategies without fear of an "affective disadvantage" for L2 student writers.

COMBINATION OR COMPARISON STUDIES

The foregoing discussion has suggested that, in students' minds, a combination of feedback techniques might be most optimal and pleasing for them. Several studies of student opinion have been designed to compare feedback alternatives. One already discussed is the study by Zhang (1995), in which he found that students preferred teacher, peer, and self feedback, respectively. In the study by Arndt (1993), she found that students highly valued both written teacher commentary and face-to-face writing conferences with teachers, but that they only appreciated peer feedback under certain circumstances (in the "team writing" context). Mendonça and Johnson (1994) and Schmid (1999) both found that students appreciated receiving both teacher and peer feedback; one third of Schmid's subjects said that they would prefer to get feedback only from the teacher. Findings of Saito's (1994) study indicated that students preferred all forms of teacher feedback (including conferencing) over either peer or self feedback. However, Saito's findings are a bit hard to interpret because she considered students in more than one context and classroom—in two of the three classes she looked at, the students were relatively less positive about peer feedback, but the third group was more favorable toward it. Finally, Berger (1990) compared the perceptions of 54 ESL students in California community colleges regarding peer feedback versus self evaluation. She found that students in both treatment groups found the feedback process helpful but that nearly half of the students in the self-feedback group wished they had received peer feedback.

SUMMARY OF STUDIES REVIEWED

As noted throughout this chapter, student views about various forms of feedback (teacher commentary, error correction, and peer response) appear to be remarkably consistent, despite differences across studies in context and research design. The clear picture that emerges is that L2 writing students find feedback of all types important and helpful and that they have specific ideas about the benefits and drawbacks of the various forms of feedback about which they were asked. Three significant generalizations emerge from these various research projects:

1. Although L2 writers appreciate response on all aspects of their writing, they feel very strongly about receiving feedback about their language errors.
2. If they had to choose between forms of feedback, they clearly prefer teacher feedback, whether written or oral.
3. Students feel that a combination of feedback sources (teacher, peer, self) can also be beneficial to them.

CAVEATS AND LIMITATIONS

As already noted, students cannot and should not be the sole judges of what is best for them. Several researchers who have compared student views with actual text production (Brice, 1995; Ferris & Roberts, 2001; Mendonça & Johnson, 1994) have found that what students say they like or need does not always match up well with what happens in their writing processes. This is why findings from surveys of student reactions need to be carefully weighed against teacher opinions and intuitions as well as results of studies using other research paradigms (e.g., text analysis, experimental designs). In particular, it seems apparent that studies that assess both student reactions (using written surveys and/or interviews) and their written texts and revision behaviors have the potential to be more valuable than studies that utilize only survey data.

It is also important, in survey research, to rely not only on students as informants but also on the teachers involved. It is noted in Ferris (1995b) that some of the teachers represented by the students surveyed were dismayed by their students' characterizations of their feedback, and that one teacher even refused to submit her students' surveys after they were completed, feeling strongly that they were inaccurate. (However, it may well be that it was the student respondents who more accurately represented what the teachers were doing. As this was a survey study and not a text analysis, it is impossible to know for certain.) As I have noted elsewhere (Ferris, 1998), an informant or group of informants is limited by their own knowledge and perspective on a particular situation or interactions.

Even with these limitations in mind, it is hard not to be impressed with the clear picture of student views toward response that emerges from reviewing the studies discussed in this chapter. Unlike studies of error correction (see chapter 3) or of the nature and effects of peer response (see chapter 4), from research on student preferences, we have a consistent set of findings on which to build future research efforts and instructional practices.

APPENDIX 5A: STUDENT SURVEY
ON TEACHER FEEDBACK

Source: Ferris (1995b, pp. 52–53); see also Cohen (1987).

1. How much of each composition do you read over again when your instructor returns it to you?

   1st/2nd drafts

   All of it ___ Most of it ___ Some of it ___ None of it

   Final drafts (the one that receives a grade/score)

   All of it ___ Most of it ___ Some of it ___ None of it

2. How many of the instructor's comments and corrections do you think about carefully?

   1st/2nd drafts

   All of them ___ Most of them ___ Some of them ___ None of them

   Final drafts

   All of them ___ Most of them ___ Some of them ___ None of them

3. How many of the comments and corrections involve:

1st/2nd drafts	A lot	Some	A little	None
Organization				
Content/Ideas				
Grammar				
Vocabulary				
Mechanics				
(Punctuation, Spelling, etc.)				

Final drafts	A lot	Some	A little	None
Organization				
Content/Ideas				
Grammar				
Vocabulary				
Mechanics				
(Punctuation, Spelling, etc.)				

4. If you pay attention to what your instructor wrote, how much attention do you pay to the comments and corrections involving:

1st/2nd drafts	A lot	Some	A little	None
Not Applicable				
Organization				
Content/Ideas				
Grammar				
Vocabulary				
Mechanics				

Final drafts	A lot	Some	A little	None	Not Applicable
Organization					
Content/Ideas					
Grammar					
Vocabulary					
Mechanics					
(Punctuation, Spelling, etc.)					

5. Describe what you do after you read your instructor's comments and corrections (e.g., Do you look up the corrections in a grammar book? See a tutor? Rewrite your paper?)

   1st/2nd drafts

   Final drafts

6. Are there ever any comments or corrections that you do not understand? If so, can you give any examples?

7. What do you do about those comments or corrections that you do not understand?

8. Are any of your instructor's comments positive? If so, can you give an example?

9. Do you feel that your instructor's comments and corrections help you to improve your composition writing skills?

10. How would you rate yourself as a learner?
    Excellent ___ Good ___ Fair ___ Poor

11. How would you rate your skills in writing compositions?
    Excellent ___ Good ___ Fair ___ Poor

PART

II

PRACTICE

<table>
<tr><td>

CHAPTER

6

</td><td>

Preparing Teachers
to Respond
to Student Writing

</td></tr>
</table>

Novice and experienced teachers alike are typically intimidated by the prospect of responding to student writing. New writing instructors worry about how to identify and prioritize issues in student writing and how to construct responses that are clear and helpful. Veteran teachers, on the other hand, are continually frustrated by the amount of time it takes to comment on student writing and wonder whether anyone is paying attention or being helped by all the effort they put forth.

As discussed in chapters 2 and 5, the available research evidence is fairly compelling that teacher feedback does indeed influence student writers: They value and appreciate it, attend to it, and utilize it to write revisions and make progress in their writing. Also, as discussed in chapters 2 and 4, though alternate forms of delivering feedback—from teacher–student writing conferences to computerized feedback to peer response—are touted by writing experts, for practical reasons, it is likely that written feedback will continue to be the prevailing method of teacher response.

The focus of this chapter, therefore, is to help both new and experienced L2 writing teachers develop and refine their responding practices so that they are optimally helpful for student writers, in whatever context instructors find themselves. Though the focus is primarily on the teacher—on how to decide *what* to say and *how* to say it—techniques for helping the students to take responsibility for their own progress and develop self-evaluation skills are also discussed. Finally, some guidelines for conducting effective teacher–student writing conferences are presented.

DEVELOPING SOUND RESPONDING PRACTICES

To learn or to refine one's commenting strategies, teachers can work through several important steps. These are outlined in Fig. 6.1.

Identifying Sound Principles for Response to Student Writing

Before tackling actual student texts and constructing feedback, it is important for teachers to articulate specific philosophies or principles for response to student writing. One principle, for instance, to which many teachers adhere is "Do not give form-based feedback on a student's first draft." Another is "Take care not to 'take over' or 'appropriate' the students' papers by being too directive in written feedback." Whereas these two sample principles are not uncontroversial, they illustrate the point that writing teachers engage in the process of responding with certain principles in mind (whether consciously or not, reflected on or not).

Figure 6.2 presents some guiding principles that may be helpful to teachers in developing their own approach to response.

In brief, these guidelines remind teachers to prioritize, to treat students as individuals, to be encouraging, to be clear and helpful, and to avoid imposing their own ideas on student writers, leaving final decisions in the hands of the writer. As we see later, there is a range of options by which these principles can be acted out, but keeping these guidelines in mind will help teachers focus on the big picture of how and why they should provide comments to students.

Examining Student Texts and Identifying Major Feedback Points

It should be admitted at the outset that this second step of the process is easier said than done. As I have trained and prepared groups of writing teachers over the years, one of the biggest questions they struggle with is knowing "what to look for" and "where to start" in responding to a student paper. Further, even experienced teach-

---

1. Identify sound principles for response to student writing.

2. Examine student texts and identify major feedback points.

3. Prioritize issues on various essay drafts.

4. Construct feedback that is clear and helpful.

5. Explain your feedback philosophies and strategies to your students and be consistent.

6. Hold students accountable for considering and utilizing feedback.

FIG. 6.1.　The process of teacher response.

- Do not feel that you, as the teacher, need to respond in writing to every draft of every student paper. Decide at which point(s) of the drafting process you will intervene.
- Do not feel that you must address every issue and problem you see in a student paper. Be selective and prioritize.
- Tailor written responses to the needs of individual students and their texts. Do not attempt to give the same amount and type of feedback to every student, and do not adhere to rigid prescriptions (e.g., "content feedback only on the first draft"; "use questions rather than statements etc.").
- Give personalized feedback that includes encouragement: Consider using the student's name, signing your own, making comments of praise in the margins and in endnotes, and referring to previous drafts or assignments to show the student that you are aware of his or her progress. Show interest in the student's ideas, writing progress, and in the student him/herself.
- If you have to choose between clarity and brevity or efficiency, choose clarity. Feedback that the student does not understand cannot help him or her to improve.
- Strike a careful balance between giving clear, helpful, specific feedback and appropriating the student's text.

FIG. 6.2. Guiding principles.

ers will have different opinions about the major issues and feedback points on which to focus in the same student paper.

Though "knowing what to look for" is a skill that develops with repeated practice, there are several general pieces of advice that I share with pre-service and in-service teachers on this issue:

- **Use the course grading criteria as a starting point for assessment and feedback.** Most, if not all writing programs have entry and exit criteria or grading rubrics to guide teachers at various levels of the program. For instance, at the beginning levels of an L2 writing sequence, students may simply be aiming for production of one well-structured paragraph by the end of the course, whereas in college-level (freshman composition or higher), students will be expected to write well-developed, clearly organized essays of five or more pages that effectively incorporate ideas from other authors' texts. Clearly the grading criteria, teacher expectations, and the nature of feedback will be very different in these two settings. If a formal rubric or set of grading criteria does not exist, the teacher may wish to design one for the purposes of assessment and ongoing feedback. Figure 6.3 shows an essay feedback check list that I designed for a class that was derived directly from the exit examination grading criteria. (Appendix 6A shows a student paper with a completed feedback form for illustrative purposes). I used this every time I gave feedback to the students and for peer response sessions as well. This not only helped me to focus on the most salient issues that would help students pass the course, but it also served to regularly remind students of the standards they were aiming for (see White, 1999). (It could also be useful to give the checklist to the students and discuss it with

I. Response to Prompt/Assignment

____ The paper responds clearly and completely to the specific instructions in the prompt or assignment.

____ The essay stays clearly focused on the topic throughout.

II. Content (Ideas)

____ The essay has a clear main idea or thesis.

____ The thesis is well supported with several major points or arguments.

____ The supporting points are developed with ideas from the readings, facts, or other examples from the writer's own experiences or observations.

____ The arguments or examples are clear and logical.

____ Opposing viewpoints have been considered and responded to clearly and effectively.

III. Use of Readings

____ The writer has incorporated other texts into his/her essay.

____ The ideas in the readings have been reported accurately.

____ The writer has used summary, paraphrase, and quotations from the readings to strengthen his or her paper.

____ The writer has mastered the mechanics of incorporating ideas from other texts, including accurate use of quotation marks and other punctuation, accurate verb tenses, appropriate identification of the author & title, and effective integration of quotations into the writer's own text.

IV. Organization

____ There is a clear beginning (introduction), middle (body), and end (conclusion) to the essay.

____ The beginning introduces the topic and clearly expresses the main idea.

____ The body paragraphs include topic sentences that are directly tied to the main idea (thesis).

____ Each body paragraph is well organized and includes a topic sentence, supporting details, and a summary of the ideas.

____ Coherence devices (transitions, repetition, synonyms, pronoun reference, etc.) are used effectively within and between paragraphs.

____ The conclusion ties the ideas in the body back to the thesis and summarizes why the issue is interesting or important.

V. Language and Mechanics

____ The paper is spell-checked (typed essays only).

____ The paper is proofread and does not have serious and frequent errors in grammar, spelling, typing, or punctuation.

____ The paper is double-spaced and has appropriate margins all around.

____ The paper is legible (handwritten papers).

Additional Comments:

FIG. 6.3.   Sample essay feedback checklist.

them at the beginning of the course, even before the first writing/feedback cycle.) I would read through a student's paper and put checkmarks indicating which parts the student had done well. Any issue that did not have a checkmark was a starting point for identifying and prioritizing major feedback points.

• **Use the specific writing assignment or task to identify possible points for specific feedback.** Generalized course grading criteria, as discussed earlier, can offer an excellent starting point for analyzing student writing and identifying possible issues for feedback. In addition, the specifications of the particular assignment or task can give a teacher guidance about ways to look at student writing in order to provide helpful commentary. For instance, a first assignment I have given frequently in an ESL freshman composition class at my institution is the following:

> Write an essay in which you draw from your own experience to express a personal viewpoint. Describe in detail an event or experience that has led you to learn, believe, or understand something. Your purpose in writing this essay will be to reveal to your classmates and your instructor the significance of what you have learned. (Spack, 1990, p. 37.)

In reading student papers responding to this prompt, I found that in many cases, I need to address one or both of the following issues: (a) the need for the student to "describe in detail a [specific] event or experience" (students may either fail to identify a specific experience or to provide adequate detail); or (b) the need for analysis of the experience: "… the significance of what you have learned." (See Fig. 7.7, especially Draft 1 feedback, for sample teacher commentary related to this particular prompt.) The sample student paper shown with teacher feedback in Appendix 7A was responding to the following prompt:

> You have read Lucille K. Forer's article, "How Birth Order Influences Your Life Adjustment" (Smalzer, 1996, pp. 5–7) and have thought about how birth order has influenced your own life and family experiences.

> Now write an essay in which you respond to the following question:
> *Does birth order have an important influence on people's lives?*
>
> In supporting your opinion, be sure to consider the ideas in Forer's article as well as your own experience or examples from the lives of people that you know.

As can be observed both from the student essay and the teacher feedback, "Aya" did not respond completely to the instructions in the prompt. She did not utilize the ideas in the article she had read (it was not even mentioned in her essay), and she included only one example from her own family life. The teacher feedback on the form in the endnote reminds Aya to include references to the reading and to develop more than one subpoint in response to the prompt.

• **Get to know the students' abilities as writers as quickly as possible so that you can construct feedback appropriate to their individual needs.** Given the principles outlined in Fig. 6.2, it is also important to consider individual student strengths and weaknesses in providing written responses. If a student, for instance, has recurring problems with focus, you may want to suggest using a working thesis statement and outline as she or he drafts essays. On the other hand, if a student has relative strengths in idea development and organization but glaring weaknesses in proofreading and self-editing, you may wish to call this to his or her attention consistently. Whereas feedback needs first and foremost to be responsive to the text at hand, getting to know the student and his or her writing can also help the teacher know what issues to select and prioritize in written feedback. Personalities of individual students may factor into this equation as well. For example, if you know that a student has failed the class before, lacks confidence, and is extremely anxious about his or her writing, you may wish to be as encouraging and positive as possible. This point implies that one of the first orders of business for a writing instructor is to get to know the students and their writing. I do this by obtaining a diagnostic writing sample during the first week of class and analyzing it in great detail for both rhetorical and grammatical problems. I also have students either write a homework journal entry or in-class freewrite that helps me get to know them and how they feel about writing in general and about being in this course in particular. Finally, I schedule various in-class discussions so that I can get to know them in person and observe their attitudes and interactions with me and with peers (important for forming peer response groups; see chapter 8).

Prioritizing Issues on Various Essay Drafts

The first two principles outlined in Fig. 6.2 suggest that the teacher not only needs to *identify* problem areas and possible feedback points in student texts, but also to make some decisions about *which* issues to address (or even whether to address them at all in that particular writing cycle). The first principle reminds teachers that they should not feel that they need to write comments on every draft of every student paper. Many instructors, myself included, like to use a judicious combination of peer feedback, teacher–student conferences, written commentary, and self-evaluation as students move through various drafts of an essay assignment. It is also important to explain one's feedback philosophies and strategies to the students so that their expectations are reasonable and they are not frustrated. For example, in the course description for an ESL freshman composition class that I taught a few years ago, I outlined the following procedures to the students:

Each assignment will progress as follows:

First Drafts: You will receive in-class peer response with both written and oral comments from your writing group. You will also meet with me in my office for a brief conference to discuss the content (ideas) in your draft.

Second Drafts: You will submit these to me. I will return them with extensive written comments.

Third Drafts: You will bring these to class for a focused editing workshop. Then you will make final changes/corrections.

Final Drafts: These should be carefully edited and proofread. They will receive a grade and final comments.

The second principle of teacher feedback in Fig. 6.2 is that teachers should not necessarily attempt to address all writing problems they see in every draft of a student paper. The primary reason behind this, of course, is that trying to do so could overwhelm both the teacher and the student writer. In addition, however, different assignments and various stages of the process may call for an emphasis on distinct aspects of the writing. For example, in the early phases of the writing process, the teacher may wish to focus primarily on whether the evolving draft addresses the specifications of the task and whether the writer's ideas need more development. On the next draft, the instructor and writer may want to fine-tune elements of the essay's rhetorical structure—well-focused body paragraphs, transitions between paragraphs, an adequate conclusion—an emphasis that might have been premature if the main content of the essay was still developing in a previous draft. Finally, once the ideas and essay structure have settled into place, the teacher may wish to call particular editing issues to the writer's attention (e.g., repeated errors in verb tense, punctuation problems, omitted noun plural endings, etc.—see chap. 7 for specific suggestions).

As also discussed in chapters 2 and 7, this suggestion should not be misinterpreted as a rigid prescription about providing certain types of feedback on specific essay drafts (e.g., content only on first drafts, grammar only on penultimate drafts). A teacher may wish to give feedback on several different writing issues on a student paper but emphasize one issue in particular, as shown in Fig. 7.7. Prioritizing issues and being selective about feedback is an important priority, yet it does not negate the guidelines discussed about responding to individual students and their texts at their points of greatest need.

Constructing Feedback That Is Clear and Helpful

This guideline is obviously the most important and challenging of all. Teachers, after all, provide feedback in an effort to help their students to develop and improve their writing abilities. If the student fails to understand the teacher's comment or if the teacher's responses are not ultimately helpful to the student, the purpose of providing feedback is defeated. Before launching into specific suggestions, from previous research on this topic and from my own observations, I want to offer some general thoughts. First, teachers need to remember that written commentary, rather than being a tedious burden, is a critical instructional opportunity for both teacher and student. Reading a student paper and giving feedback that meets the student's needs allows the instructor to make a personal investment in each student's progress and to provide or reinforce instruction given in class. Bearing this in mind, the instructor needs to see the process of reading the paper, identifying and selecting key feedback points, and constructing comments in ways that communicate clearly and helpfully to the student as a dynamic, creative, cognitively demanding process. It cannot be rushed or done at the last minute. I find that doing the work of feedback effectively takes me so much time and mental energy that I must plan ahead—give myself adequate turn-around time to respond to a set of student papers (ideally 5 to 7 days), and divide the job over several days so that I don't get tired and start shortchanging student papers near the bottom of the stack. I put student paper due dates on my own calendar so that I can plan for enough time to do the job well.

A second, and related observation, is that writing instructors should not make "responding to student papers as quickly and efficiently as possible" their primary goal. Studies have suggested that it can take a teacher 20 to 40 minutes to provide written feedback on each individual paper. I have found that thoughtful selection of feedback points can indeed shorten the process (especially if a feedback check list like the one shown in Fig. 6.3 is used); this is a fortuitous by-product of decision making that I believe is pedagogically sound rather than the primary reason for it. The danger with making "speed" or "efficiency" a primary goal is that the teacher may use responding shorthand that is either incomprehensible to the student (using jargon or symbols unfamiliar to them) or that is too cryptic to be helpful.

Third, writing instructors need to think of written feedback as part of dynamic two-way communication between the teacher and the student. As with any other form of interpersonal communication, the needs and knowledge of the target audience must be considered, and the pragmatic demands of the situation (as to formality, directness, quantity, and relevance) must be kept in mind. When I write comments in response to a student paper, I try to keep two key questions in mind: (a) Does this student have enough background knowledge to understand my intent in this comment? and (b) If the student acts on this comment, will it improve this paper and will it inform his or her writing development? Although asking myself these questions does not of course forestall all communication problems (see point 5, following)—any form of human communication can and does misfire at times—it helps me to focus on the primary goal of interacting with the student in a clear and straightforward way.

With these points in mind, I offer some concrete suggestions about how to construct written comments that will be helpful to student writers. These are summarized in Fig. 6.4 and discussed further in the following.

The first three suggestions in Fig. 6.4 follow naturally from the earlier discussion about being selective and prioritizing feedback issues. It should go without saying that a teacher cannot possibly identify the major problems in a student paper until she or he has read the entire paper. Then, keeping the course grading criteria, the specifications of the assignment, the needs of the individual student, and the phase of the writing cycle in mind, the teacher can identify several major issues—I have found that 2 to 4 feedback points is about the right range—to discuss in a summary endnote. The teacher endnotes shown in Appendix 6A and Fig. 7.7 provide illustrations. In both cases, the teacher addresses the student by name, begins with an encouraging comment that refers specifically to the student's text, and then provides several questions, comments, or suggestions for the writer to address on the next draft. In both examples, the student writer is also made aware of 1 or 2 specific language-related problems to which she or he should pay attention during the revision process.

I have also found it extremely helpful as a discipline not to write any in-text (marginal) notes until I have read the entire paper and written the summary endnote. If I simply annotate the text as I go along in a first reading, I may write comments or questions that are not relevant to the overall direction of the text (because I have not finished reading it yet) or which may distract the student from addressing the major feedback points I have outlined in the endnote (because I have not yet selected the

1. Read the paper through once without making any marks or other comments on it.

2. Write an endnote (either at the end of the paper itself or on a separate feedback form if you are using one) that both provides encouragement and summarizes several specific suggestions for improvement.

3. Add marginal comments, if desired, that provide specific examples of the general points you have raised in the endnote.

4. Check both your endnotes and your marginal notes for instances of rhetorical or grammatical jargon or formal terminology (thesis, subject–verb agreement) that may be unfamiliar to the student.

5. If you write comments in the form of questions, check them carefully to make sure that the intent of the question is clear, that the answer to the question, if provided, would actually improve the quality of the paper, and that the student will know how to incorporate the ideas suggested by the questions into their existing text.

6. Whenever feasible, pair questions and other comments with explicit suggestions for revision.

7. Use words or phrases whenever possible instead of codes or symbols.

8. Design or adapt a standard feedback form (like the one shown in Fig. 6.2) that is appropriate to the goals and grading criteria for your course.

9. Do not overwhelm the student writer with an excessive amount of commentary.

10. Be sure that your feedback is written legibly.

FIG. 6.4.   Suggestions for writing clear and helpful comments.

most important issues to write about in the endnote). If I make the decision to only add marginal comments if they will help the student understand the general points I have raised in my endnote, then these annotations will be relevant and well focused. Appendix 6B shows an example of a student paper annotated with marginal comments that complement the endnote.

Suggestions 4 to 6 in Fig. 6.4 address the formal characteristics of the feedback, specifically the use of jargon or technical terminology and the syntactic form of the commentary. As discussed in chapter 2, available research evidence suggests that both the vocabulary and the syntactic/pragmatic form of teacher feedback can be potentially problematic, at least for some students. As to jargon, if you use terms like "thesis," "transition," or "agreement," be sure that the students will understand them. The best ways to make certain of this are either to cover these terms explicitly in class before writing them on student papers or to use more general terminology instead ("main idea sentence" instead of "thesis").

As previous research has shown, teacher questioning strategies can cause confusion and frustration for some students (Ferris, 1995b; Ferris, 1997, 2001a). If teacher questions are straightforward requests for specific information known to the writer, it is likely that the student will be able to process them accurately (e.g.,

"Did you quit school?" or "What is the end of the story?" in Appendix 6B).[14] However, if the questions are really indirect speech acts—comments phrased in the form of a question that are intended to challenge the student's thinking or logic—it is less likely that the student writer will understand the question or be able to address it effectively in revision even if she or he does grasp the intent of the question. For any question, even information questions, it may be helpful to link the question to a specific revision suggestion that shows the student how to incorporate the requested information into the text (e.g., "Maybe you could add 1–2 sentences at the end of this paragraph that give more detail about this experience"). As to questions that are really indirect comments, it may be more effective to make a declarative statement rather than asking a question with which the student cannot cope. Returning to the example discussed in chapter 2, we saw that the teacher's indirect statement *"Is this really a crossroads friendship if you're not in contact?"* misled the student writer and did not lead to an effective revision. A more straightforward and effective approach might have been something like the following:

> *Your description of this friendship does not fit Viorst's definition of a crossroads friendship because you say you "don't know of each other any more." Take a look at Viorst's discussion of crossroads friendships (Spack, 1990, Guidelines, p. 70), and decide if you need to choose either another category for this example or another example for this category. Or you may need to add more detail to explain why this friendship really DOES fit Viorst's definition.*

In addition to examining our questioning strategies to make sure that the intent of the questions are clear and that the student will know how to include the requested information, we also need to ask ourselves if the answers to the questions will really add to the overall effectiveness of the text. Writing teachers seem prone to jotting numerous short questions in the margins, in an effort to appear Socratic and involved, but many of the questions are either too cryptic to be clear ("Why?") or actually irrelevant to the overall focus of the essay. As an example, a student writer composed an essay describing a good friend of hers from high school and explained how this friendship had influenced her life. She noted briefly at one point that even though she and her friend are now at different colleges, this friend's example still impacts her. The teacher wrote in the margin at this point *"What is her major?"*—a completely irrelevant detail that would add nothing to the student's text. Given that our time and energy and our students' attention spans are limited resources, we should not waste them writing questions (or comments in any form) that are not central to the focus of a paper and that will not add to its effectiveness if acted on.

Another issue related to not only to teacher questioning but to other characteristics of written feedback is the risk of "appropriating" student texts. L1 and L2 scholars such as Brannon and Knoblauch (1982), Sommers (1982), and Zamel (1985) have warned teachers against taking over student texts and advancing their own

---

[14]It was pointed out to me that the student's ability to process a teacher's question accurately does not necessarily mean that *answering* the question will improve the overall content of the student's paper!

agendas by being too directive and intrusive in their written commentary. The use of questions, rather than statements or imperatives, is one way in which teachers can avoid appearing too authoritarian. Another set of linguistic devices on which teachers rely in written feedback is hedges (Conrad & Goldstein, 1999; Ferris, 1997; Ferris et al., 1997), including lexical hedges such as "Please" or "Maybe," syntactic hedges such as suggestions phrased indirectly as questions, and the pairing of critical comments with positive "softeners" in the same sentence (*"Nice introduction, BUT...."*).

The issue of teacher appropriation is one that writing instructors need to consider seriously. Survey research findings have demonstrated repeatedly that student writers resent it when their teachers try to impose what they (teachers) want to say onto the student's text (Ferris, 1995b; Straub, 1997). When a teacher is excessively directive, there is also a very real danger that they will misread the student author's intentions. For instance, in "Antonio's" paper (shown in its entirety in Appendix 6B), the classroom teacher attempted to have him change the wording and focus of his third paragraph:

> After all this struggle I think my father was right to bring me to this country because I have more opportunities here than in Mexico, for example know I know two languages, being a minority made me more stronger in the way I think, I understand more about other cultures. For example, some people have a way of dressing, which are only allow to wear certain things and sometimes even only expose certain parts of the body. Also I learned about that some people have *different ideals,* which other people see this unusual and strange but we have to accept and respect other cultures.

Antonio's classroom teacher made the following comments in the margins and in a endnote: *Good topic, but change "stronger" to "weaker"! Para. 3 has a good idea but it does not fit your thesis? Change it to "weaker"!* She was apparently operating on the belief that Antonio's real feelings about being a member of a minority group were expressed in his original thesis in the first paragraph: "Being a member of a minority group has *effected* me negatively because I *being descrimineted* so many times that I lost the count." Her comments were intended to get Antonio to change the third paragraph (in which he begins to talk about the positive effects of living in a new culture) so that it matched the thesis statement (thus the injunction to change "stronger" to "weaker"). However, a more accurate reading of Antonio's essay would suggest that his clear intent was to discuss how being a minority in a new culture has been both a struggle and an adventure for him, and thus that his thesis statement, not paragraph 3, should change to fit the rest of the essay. Unfortunately, this teacher's feedback appeared to lead Antonio to give up altogether, as the offending paragraph was deleted entirely in his next draft, leaving the resulting revision far less interesting and underdeveloped. Another, more minor example of teacher appropriation in the same paragraph was the teacher's striking out of the clauses "I have more opportunities here than in Mexico" and "I know two languages now," with the comment "Omit—off topic." But because Antonio was changing focus to talk about the positive aspects of his new life in the United States, it could well be argued that neither idea was "off-topic." Chapters 1 and 7 provide further discussion of how a teacher's word- or sentence-level feedback can similarly cross the line toward appropriation.

On the other hand, teachers need to take equal care that in their efforts to avoid appropriative responses, they are not so indirect, circuitous, or tentative that they fail to give students the input and assistance they clearly need to progress as writers. Reid (1994) spoke strongly about the "myths of appropriation," arguing that we should not abdicate our responsibilities as teachers to give students the instruction they need, and that there is a very real difference between effective, necessary intervention and excessive appropriation. Patthey-Chavez and Ferris (1997), commenting on their findings about teacher–student writing conferences and their impact on student revisions, noted that "teachers tend to use indirect approaches or hedges to mask or soften the display of power differences. And yet … if the rules of a given game are to be communicated to outsiders effectively, indirectness is not an optimal communication strategy" (p. 87). At one extreme are the overbearing teacher responses that misrepresent student intentions and frustrate their purposes, as in the example of "Antonio" and his teacher discussed previously. At the opposite end is a comment I saw written in the margins of a student paper when the writer had neglected to put a period at the end of a sentence: "Don't you think you need to put a period here?"

Although this discussion of appropriation of student writing could apply equally to L1 or L2 student writers, a further danger of indirectness and hedging in written feedback for L2 writers is that they will either misunderstand the comment (because of linguistic or pragmatic competence gaps) or they will lose respect for the teacher because what the instructor thinks is "collegial" appears to a student from another culture as "wishy-washy" or "lacking in confidence." So, for example, if a teacher writes *"Can you maybe add an example here?"* in the margin of a student paper, an L2 writer might either misinterpret it as a true yes–no question rather than an indirect request ("Sure I can, but I don't really want to") or assume that the teacher wasn't really serious about the suggestion because it is so heavily hedged (*"Can you maybe …"* and phrased as a question rather than a command). The teacher, on reading a revision, might then wonder why the student had "ignored" what appeared to be a fairly straightforward request.

In summary, for all of these reasons, teachers of L2 writers need to take care in using questions to give feedback, being careful that they will not be misinterpreted, that they are helpful enough (as to providing revision strategies), and that they will elicit responses that are truly relevant and consistent with the writer's purposes. Given these constraints, it could well be appropriate for writing teachers to reconsider the entire issue of whether questions in written response are an optimal strategy and perhaps to use them far more sparingly than they might have done previously.

The final four suggestions in Fig. 6.4 focus on the mechanics of feedback, such as using words or phrases rather than codes or symbols, utilizing a feedback form, not writing too many comments or making them too wordy, and making sure that handwritten commentary is legible. Though all of these ideas would seem fairly self-apparent, in working with teachers over the years, I have seen many written responses that are hard to read and crammed into inadequate margins and that use symbolic shorthand that is not as transparent to the receiver as the writer might believe. Perhaps the most difficult idea to evaluate is how much written feedback is adequate and how much is overkill. I have seen teacher endnotes that are actually longer than the student's original text, with numerous additional marginal annotations, corrections, and so on. Although it is important to be clear, specific, and helpful, there may well be a point of diminishing returns at which student writers become simply overloaded with information. This is why the earlier steps of prioritizing and selecting key issues on various drafts is so vital and helpful. Finally, the suggestion to use a standard feedback form is not an uncontroversial one. One argument against it is the issue just discussed, that of teacher appropriation. Using a checklist (like the one in Fig. 6.2) to show what the student has done well definitely communicates the teacher's priorities. However, if the checklist is related to the composition skills that students will have to master in order to succeed in the course, it is a helpful tool or road map showing the student where to go rather than a tyrannical or arbitrary privileging of the teacher's preferences over the student's ownership of the paper as its author. I have found that the use of a feedback checklist is extremely helpful in that it focuses my own feedback efforts, streamlines my workload (I don't have to write the same things over and over on different student papers), and continuously reminds students about and reinforces the course grading criteria. I have also found that students like this feedback tool and find it helpful and user-friendly (especially if I spend time walking them through it with a sample essay or two). It can also be helpful to involve the students themselves in designing the feedback checklist.

The length of this discussion about constructing clear, helpful feedback should make it apparent that, in my opinion, this is the most critical issue for teachers to consider in writing responses for their students. Thinking and working through these process steps takes time and experience, but it is time well spent if the result is written commentary that empowers students and helps them to succeed as writers.

Explaining Your Feedback Philosophies and Strategies to Your Students and Being Consistent

The final two principles for teacher response include the other participant in the communicative exchange, the students themselves. It is important for writing teachers to explain their responding procedures to students at the beginning of the course, and it is probably necessary to provide brief reminders throughout the term. For instance, if a teacher plans to have only peer feedback on first drafts but provide written commentary on second drafts, it can relieve student anxiety to know this throughout the process. Similarly, if an instructor chooses not to address grammar issues on early drafts but will give detailed feedback about them on the second-to-last draft, the teacher should explain this to students (along with the reasons why). If error codes, feedback forms, and the like are being used, the teacher should go over them carefully with students so that they can interpret the feedback they receive.

One counterproductive tendency of many teachers is to return papers to students at the very end of class while they are on their way out. Teachers may do this so that they can get through their lesson plans without students being distracted by looking at teacher comments, or they may simply be taking the coward's way out and avoiding confrontations with disappointed students. However, despite our best efforts to be clear, concrete, and helpful, it is likely that students will not understand or know how to deal with all of our comments. Thus it is a valuable strategy to return papers to students during, not after, a class period and allow them time to read through our feedback and ask us questions about it. Rather than being a waste of time, it is time well spent: Don't we want those comments we spent hours composing to be well understood and effectively utilized by our students? To make the feedback-and-revision cycle even more formative, teachers could have students write a paragraph that summarizes in their own words what they think their teacher is saying about their paper and how it will impact their revision of that paper, even including areas of disagreement that the student writer might have with the teacher's feedback.

Holding Students Accountable for Considering and Utilizing Feedback

Teacher feedback is only helpful to student writers if they read it, think about it, and seriously consider whether or not to act on it. This does not, and should not, mean that the students should slavishly obey every suggestion that their teacher makes, but it does suggest that they should at least be able to articulate why they will or will not act on a particular suggestion. The suggestions about giving students time in class to reread their papers and ask questions about teacher feedback (and perhaps to even respond briefly in writing about what they thought about the teacher's commentary) provide a good start to this process.

There are at least two other ways in which teachers can hold students responsible for utilizing feedback in their revisions. First, teachers can grade revised drafts separately from earlier drafts, assessing the effort students put into reconsidering their own texts and feedback they have received and making changes accordingly. To do this effectively, teachers should require students to submit writing projects in folders that include all drafts to date, feedback forms, and so on, so the teacher can compare drafts and be reminded of his or her own previous comments.

Second, the writing teacher can utilize a procedure required by editors of many academic journals: the "revise-and-resubmit" cover letter. Prospective authors are often asked to revise and resubmit manuscripts after receiving peer reviews prior to a final decision being made about whether or not to publish the paper. Writers are asked to include with their revisions a detailed cover letter that describes how they responded to the reviewers' feedback (including both explicit references to changes that were made and justifications for suggestions not acted on). Besides being an accountability checkpoint for the journal editor (that the writer has treated the reviewers' feedback with the appropriate respect), this is a helpful cognitive exercise for the writer, demanding that she or he think carefully about each feedback point, make changes as appropriate, and explain why she or he feels some of the reviewers' suggestions were not as helpful.

Student writers can similarly be asked to reflect on the feedback they have received (from both teacher and peers) and to construct a cover letter to accompany revised essays, with this cover letter being a required part of their essay grade or counted as a homework assignment. This exercise not only requires them to think critically about their own text and the feedback they have received, but it also underscores the seriousness of their responsibility to consider feedback carefully. In the same way that prospective authors of journal articles should show respect for the review process and for the time and effort expended by the editor and peer reviewers (and not be too arrogant to consider thoughtful feedback), students should be encouraged to respect the energy and effort put forth by their teachers and their peers to read and respond to their writing. An additional benefit of this exercise is that it can help show teachers where their feedback can improve in clarity, specificity, and helpfulness.

The foregoing discussion demonstrates that providing effective written feedback is far from the late-night, hurried, slapdash affair that it often devolves into. Rather, it is an ongoing process that is demanding for teachers and students alike—it demands time, thought, careful decision making, schedule planning, and critical evaluation of whether feedback is accomplishing its purposes. When it is done purposefully and thoughtfully, teacher feedback can be an amazingly powerful and effective pedagogical tool. Not only that, it builds bonds between teachers and students that can be rewarding for teachers and highly motivating for students. After all, every writer wants to know that his or her readers have attended to and appreciated their efforts.

PREPARING TEACHERS TO RESPOND TO STUDENT WRITING: A TRAINING SEQUENCE

Given my own clear biases about the critical importance of teacher feedback, it should not be surprising that in the graduate and undergraduate teacher preparation courses I teach, I spend a fair amount of time helping students to develop philosophies and practical strategies for responding to student writing. Though the specifics vary depending on the nature of the class, in general, my training sequences proceed as follows:

1. *Ask trainees to reflect on feedback they have received about their own writing.* For instance, I ask students to respond in writing and/or in class discussions to some variation of the following questions:

- From your own experiences as a student writer, what specific memories do you have of teacher responses to your texts?
- What types of feedback have you as a writer found most helpful? Most problematic?

(adapted from Ferris & Hedgcock, 1998, p. 123)

2. *Present trainees with principles and guidelines for responding to student writing.* I walk students through similar issues and suggestions to the ones already presented in this chapter, relating them to major findings of relevant empirical research. The lists presented in Figs. 6.2 and 6.4 are illustrative of the points that can be covered. I also present numerous examples of commentary types using actual student writing and real teacher responses.

3. *Have trainees examine models of teacher commentary.* One application activity in Ferris and Hedgcock (1998, p. 150) asks students to look at an unmarked copy of a student paper and then to examine the same paper with comments written by three different novice teachers. The trainees compare their own initial responses to the paper with the three different sets of comments, discussing the strengths and weaknesses of each in light of the principles to which they have been exposed. I have also found that trainees appreciate the opportunity to look at *expert,* well-done written commentary so that they can get a picture of what optimal responses look like.

4. *Walk trainees through the process of constructing their own commentary, using sample student essays.* I have found this works best using a multistage process. First, we examine the course grading criteria and the specific task or prompt and identify some issues that might be important. Second, we look at a student paper together, identify major feedback points, and select which ones are most critical for written feedback. Third, students write endnotes and marginal annotations. Fourth, they compare their responses in small groups. Fifth, I show them my own response to the student paper(s) and we debrief the process as a larger group.

5. *Ask trainees to critically evaluate their own feedback, using an objective analysis system.* For this purpose, I have adapted the analytic model developed for the research project described in Ferris et al. (1997). I model the process on an overhead or handout, using a sample essay with teacher feedback. Teachers are asked to number each comment consecutively and code it as to length, intent of comment and syntactic form, and to indicate whether the comment includes a hedge and whether it is generic or text-specific. They complete a chart for at least three student papers that gives them a visual representation of their own commenting strategies. (Details of this exercise can be found in Ferris and Hedgcock, 1998, pp. 151, 167–168; an updated version is provided in Appendix 6C.)

6. *Ask trainees to reflect on their responding processes.* After asking teachers to respond to student writing and to analyze their responses, I ask them to compose a brief reflective essay that covers the following issues: As you responded to the student papers, what do you focus on? What principles guided you? What struggles did you have? What do you think you still need to learn/practice to respond effectively to student writing? As you think about responding to student writing in your present or future teaching, what questions or concerns come to mind? (Questions from Ferris & Hedgcock, 1998, pp. 123, 151).

Over the past several years, my colleague John Hedgcock and I have walked through versions of this training sequence with nearly 100 graduate students in master's TESOL programs who were pre-service teachers enrolled in classes on teaching ESL writing. In examining our students' work, we have found both that they appreciate the effort and struggle it takes to respond to student writing after walking through the process, but that they also feel better prepared to do so. As a student of mine wrote recently: "Well, I finished responding to the student papers, and I think I still want to be a teacher!"

GUIDELINES FOR CONDUCTING TEACHER–STUDENT WRITING CONFERENCES

In chapter 2, it was noted that although many L1 and L2 researchers have expressed great enthusiasm over the pedagogical potential of teacher–student writing conferences, research on their nature and effects, especially with L2 writers, has been extremely limited thus far. The two published L2 studies (Goldstein & Conrad, 1990; Patthey-Chavez & Ferris, 1997) reported the following findings:

• There were clearly observable relationships between issues discussed during the conferences and changes made by student subjects in their subsequent revisions.

• There were quantitative and qualitative distinctions across case study subjects in the specifics of their conference discourse: Some students were more likely than others to initiate topics, to speak more frequently and at more length, to negotiate meaning, and even to argue with the teacher about the paper.

• It was suggested by Goldstein and Conrad that cross-cultural differences may have played a part in subjects' relative willingness to be active participants in their conferences—differences related to individual students' expectations of teacher–student relationships and differing roles. Patthey-Chavez and Ferris, who included both L1 and L2 subjects in their study, did not find differences that appeared attributable to students' L2 status but rather to subjects' strengths and weaknesses as writers. However, they expressed agreement with Goldstein and Conrad that cultural expectations could indeed be an issue for some L2 writers.

Suggestions for teacher–student writing conferences in L2 settings that emerge from these research findings include the following:

1. Before conducting conferences with students, teachers should discuss purpose and possible participant roles with the whole class. They should not assume that students will understand why they are meeting with the teacher or how they are supposed to behave in that setting. In fact, where teachers may anticipate a two-way collegial interaction, students' default assumption may well be that the teacher will deliver a monologue of comments and corrections—that a conference is merely the same as written feedback, only presented orally.

2. Teachers should consider individual students' possible discomfort with the conferencing situation and either make conferences optional or three-way (two students with the teacher for a longer period of time).

3. Teachers should, if at all possible, read the student's paper to be discussed in advance of the conference so that they can provide carefully thought-out suggestions during the conference. (This is analogous to the suggestion earlier in the chapter to read through a student paper and identify and select key feedback points before making any written comments).

4. Students should also be encouraged to prepare for conferences by reading through their papers and making a list of strengths, weaknesses, and questions to bring up during the conference. The teacher should model and structure this preparation step for students in class.

5. During conferences, teachers should encourage student participation by asking them to begin with a self-evaluation of their own papers and by asking any questions they might have. Teachers should strive throughout the interaction to ask questions of the students to draw them out, acknowledge student viewpoints, and so on.

6. Considering that conferences place additional stress on L2 students' aural/oral skills, teachers should encourage students to summarize orally at the end of a conference what has been discussed and what the "next steps" are for the paper, to take notes and/or audiotape during the conference, and to write a cover memo to submit with the next draft explaining how the conference influenced the revision process.

7. At the beginning of a writing course, teachers might consider writing comments on one set of student papers and conducting conferences for the next set.

Then the teacher can ask the students which they prefer and tailor future feedback to individual student preferences.

8.   Finally, the teacher needs to plan adequate time and appropriate space for conferences and be willing and able to accommodate students' schedules. For some students, an online interaction may be more convenient, and may even offer the best of both worlds—the opportunity to negotiate and ask clarification questions but the slower paced, more concrete nature of written feedback.

CONCLUSION

Providing feedback to student writers, whether written or oral, can be a daunting endeavor to both new and experienced teachers. The suggestions given in this chapter provide the tools teachers need to approach this process with more confidence, and, it is hoped, with more enthusiasm. Individualized teacher feedback is a powerful tool and perhaps the greatest gift a writing instructor can give to his or her students. Though giving feedback may seem costly, frustrating, and even fruitless, taking the time to articulate one's philosophies and to construct feedback carefully and thoughtfully can transform what may appear to be a tedious, thankless job into a creative, dynamic, rewarding process.

APPENDIX 6A: SAMPLE STUDENT ESSAY
WITH COMPLETED CHECKLIST

I believe everyone has certain incident which has influence on one's life. After the incident, his/her lifestyle is totally different than before. I also had the very incident when I was eight years old. That was my younger brother's birth. Before my younger brother was born, my family member was father, mother, older brother and me. I was the youngest child in my family and I get the most help and attentions. However, I had to face the reality that I had a younger brother and I have to give up my comfortable position to grow up for my younger brother.

I would say I was the only one who was not happy about my younger brother's birth. Because I felt he took my parents love away from me. I have to give my comfortable position as youngest child in the family which I wanted to stay forever to him. My parents treated me different way as older sister and I felt he is the priority in the family. I did not like that. Also I had to learn endurance and forgiveness which were very difficult for me. When my brother was a child he loved to play with my important stuff such as dolls, pretty boxes, necklaces, etc. and he always broke them. I was told to understand that he was a little so he does not understand how important they were. Then I have to learn how to forgive people. That was very difficult for me and it took me a long time.

As I got older, the birth order or the position of the family did not bother me any longer. I assume that I didn't know how to adjust nor react the new environment and sudden changes in my life (my parents' treatment, etc.). Although I had hard time getting along with my younger brother and adjusting my new position as older sister, I am glad that my younger brother was born. This is not only I have more people to share my life with but also I could mature myself from the lesson and grow up as human beings.

Having discussed above, my younger brother's birth did have influence on my life. Although I had difficult time with him, my parents and the new environment, as a result, these helped me to grow up and mature myself. I needed this change in my life. Thus I would say birth order have an important influence on people's life.

ESSAY RESPONSE FORM

Student Name: _Aya_

Essay # _1, Draft 1_

Score: _3+ (based on six-point rubric; 4 is minimal passing level)_

I. Response to Prompt/Assignment

_x (3)_ The paper responds clearly and completely to the specific instructions in the prompt or assignment.

✓ The essay stays clearly focused on the topic throughout.

II. Content (Ideas)

_x (1)_ The essay has a clear main idea or thesis.

_x (2)_ The thesis is well supported with several points or arguments.

✓ The supporting points are developed with ideas from the readings, facts, or other examples from the writer's experiences or observations.

✓ The arguments or examples are clear and logical.

_x_ Opposing viewpoints have been considered and responded to clearly and effectively.

III. Organization

✓ There is a clear beginning (introduction), middle (body), and end (conclusion) to the essay.

x (1) The beginning introduces the topic and clearly expresses the main idea.

✓ The body paragraphs include topic sentences which are directly tied to the main idea/thesis.

✓ Each body paragraph is well organized and includes a topic sentence, supporting details, and a summary of the ideas.

✓ Coherence devices (transitions, repetition, synonyms, pronoun reference, etc.) are used effectively within and between paragraphs.

✓ The conclusion ties the ideas in the body back to the thesis and summarizes why the issue is interesting or important.

IV. Language & Mechanics

_x (4)_ The paper is proofread and does not have serious and frequent errors in grammar, spelling, typing, or punctuation.

✓ The paper is double-spaced and has appropriate margins all around.

✓ The paper is legible.

✓ = done well or adequately; x = needs work

(1)–(4): refers to specific comments, below

Aya—Very nice discussion of your own family—thoughtful and interesting. Also, an excellent conclusion. Some specific suggestions for revision:

(1) You could add a thesis that states your opinion on the question in the introduction.

(2) Your one point (your own experience) is excellent. But can you add other examples of birth order effects?

135

(3) Don't forget to include ideas from the article you read!

(4) You'll need to edit carefully for verb tense errors and noun plural errors.

Nice essay—I enjoyed it!

APPENDIX 6B: STUDENT PAPER WITH TEACHER ENDNOTE AND MARGINAL COMMENTS

Background: *Antonio was a freshman student originally from Mexico. He was enrolled in a high-intermediate level university ESL class two semesters before the freshman composition level. This was an early draft of an essay written at the beginning of the semester on the topic of "the effects of being a member of a minority group (or a different culture)."*

"Going to another country will be perfect for you," my father told me that right before we moved to California. He told me that because *none* of my two sisters *didn't go* to college, so he *taught* that I was going to do the same thing as they did. I lived in Mexico for fourteen years, I came to the United States *with out* knowing a single word of English. At the *begining* I was afraid because I didn't know *nobody,* I didn't know the language and the culture was so different. Being a member of a minority group has *effected* me negatively because I *being descrimineted* so many times that I lost the count. **Good job writing a clear thesis statement here—but not all of your experiences in a new culture have been negative, have they?**

Being a member of a minority family is so hard, that when I came to the U.S.
Nice specific   I never imagine that this would happen to me. For example
example here!   the first day I went to school, in my English class most of the students were making fun of me just by the fact that I didn't know English. In my country I never passed by this situation before, so this situation really desmotivated me to go to school. **What is the end of the story, Antonio?**

After all this struggle I think my father was right to bring me to this country because I have more opportunities here than in Mexico, for example know I know two languages, being a minority made me more stronger in the way I think, I understand more about other cultures. For example, some people have a way of dressing, which are only allow to wear certain things and sometimes even only expose certain parts of the body. Also I learned about that some people have *different ideals,* which other people see this unusual and strange but we have to accept and respect other cultures. **Can you give an example of the "different ideas" you have seen? Why do you think it's important to respect differences in other cultures?**

I understand both of my cultures and this mekes me feel good about my self because I know what my identity is and I feel proud of who I am. Being a
I like the "journey"   minority is like journey, is like a adventure, like story that
and "adventure"   at the begining you passed by a lot of obstacles but at the
images here   end there is a happy ending. Each one of my cultures have special things that I like and enjoy very much. For example the language that is spoken, traditions that each one has, believes, customs, and ideals. I wouldn't change any of this for nothing and I'm very happy with who I am. Can you tie your conclusion back to the opening quote from your father? You could say that his hopes for you came true—since here you are in college!

Antonio—You did a great job discussing both the good and bad experiences you've had since coming from Mexico to the U.S. You have an especially strong conclusion, and I also liked the way you began the essay with the quote from your father.

On your next draft, please consider the following issues:

(1) Your thesis (main idea) statement at the end of the first paragraph does not really cover all of the ideas in your essay. You say that "being a member of a minority group has affected you negatively." The second paragraph gives an example of this, but the rest of the essay talks about the positive effects of being part of two cultures. I'd suggest you rewrite your thesis to "match" the rest of the essay—that even though being a minority has been hard sometimes, you have also had many valuable learning experiences.

(2) The story in the 2nd paragraph about other kids at school teasing you because you didn't know English is good, but it doesn't provide enough detail. When you say that "this situation really demotivated [you] to go to school," does that mean that you quit school, felt sad at school, or what? You might add a couple of sentences at the end of this paragraph to explain this more clearly.

(3) I really like the 3rd paragraph, in which you talk about what you have learned about different cultures by living in the U.S. I think it would be a stronger paragraph if you rewrote the first sentence to make it clearer that even though you've had struggles in the U.S., you have learned some new and valuable things as well.

You also have a number of errors in spelling, word choice, and grammar. I've underlined some examples in your first paragraph. As you revise, be sure to spell-check, proofread to make sure you're using the right words, and look carefully at your verbs to make sure they have the right endings. We'll work more on this in class after your next draft.

Excellent start to this essay, Antonio! I'll look forward to reading your next draft!

APPENDIX 6C: PROCEDURES FOR ANALYZING TEACHER COMMENTARY

1. After completing endnotes and marginal commentary on a student paper, go through your comments and number them consecutively. For comments that are lengthy or which cover more than one issue, use your own best judgment as to whether to count them as one long comment or several shorter ones.

2. For each numbered comment, complete the attached chart, indicating the comment's length, intent, the presence/absence of hedges, and the relative text-specificity of the comment. Explanations with examples for each coding category are provided below.

Analytic Model & Codes for Teacher Commentary

A. Comment Length (Number of Words)

1 = Short (1–5 words)

2 = Average (6–15 words)

3 = Long (16–25 words)

4 = Very Long (26+ words)

B. Comment Types

1 = Ask for Information/Question

EXAMPLE: Did you work out this problem with your roommates?

2 = Direction/Question

EXAMPLE: Can you provide a thesis statement here—What did you learn from this?

3 = Direction/Statement

EXAMPLE: This paragraph might be better earlier in the essay.

4 = Direction/Imperative

EXAMPLE: Mention what Zinsser says about parental pressure.

5 = Give Information/Question

EXAMPLE: Most states do allow a waiting period before an adoption is final—Do you feel that all such laws are wrong?

6 = Give Information/Statement

EXAMPLE: Iowa law favors parental rights. Michigan and California consider the best interests of the child.

7 = Positive Comment/Statement or Exclamation

EXAMPLE: A very nice start to your essay! You've done an impressive job of finding facts and quotes to support your arguments.

8 = Grammar/Mechanics Comment/Question, Statement, or Imperative

EXAMPLES:

*Past or present tense?
*Your verb tenses are confusing me in this paragraph.
*Don't forget to spell-check!

C. Hedges

0 = No hedge

1 = Hedge included:

*Lexical hedges: "Maybe," "Please," "might," etc.
*Syntactic hedges: e.g., "<u>Can you</u> add an example here?"
*"Positive Softeners": "<u>You've raised some good points</u>, but ..."

D. Text-Specific Comment

0 = Generic comment (could have been written on any paper)

EXAMPLE: Nice Intro

1 = Text-Specific Comment

EXAMPLE: Why is the American system better for children, in your opinion?

Comment #	Length	Type	Hedge	Text-Specific

Note: The form below summarizes the commenting patterns of four different teachers responding to the same student paper (see Ferris & Hedgcock, 1998, Application Activities 5.4 & 5.5, p. 150).

Teacher				
	1	**2**	**3**	**4**
Total Comments	18	22	16	15
Short	1	8	3	3
Average	15	12	12	10
Long	2	2	1	2
Ask for Info.	8	8	3	2
Request/Question	1	0	2	2
Request/Statement	1	5	6	4
Give Info.	1	3	2	4
Positive	6	5	1	1
Grammar	1	1	2	2
# of Hedges	2	0	2	2
# of Textbased	14	12	11	7

<table>
<tr><td>CHAPTER

7</td><td></td></tr>
</table>

CHAPTER 7

Suggestions for Error Correction

As discussed in chapter 3 (Research on Error Correction) and chapter 5 (Student Views), there are good arguments to be made for teachers providing error feedback to their student writers. Though the analysis of existing research in Chapter 3 did not demonstrate conclusively that error correction "works" to help students improve their writing over time, it was noted that in most studies in which error feedback was provided and improvement was measured, students showed clear, measurable improvement in overall accuracy (see Fig. 3.3 and accompanying discussion). If the body of studies reviewed consistently showed no student improvement or even regression in linguistic accuracy, an argument could be advanced for suspending error correction until/unless further research conclusively showed its benefits. However, this is not the case—despite design inconsistencies and the lack of a true control group in most instances, the majority of studies suggest that error feedback is beneficial to student writers. Thus, although further research is clearly needed, as discussed at length in chapter 3, in my view there is more evidence to support the ongoing provision of feedback than there is to eliminate it altogether.

A perhaps more compelling reason to continue providing error feedback is found in the body of studies reviewed in chapter 5. Without exception, L2 writers asked about teacher response make it clear that they expect, value, and benefit from language-related feedback from their instructors, and particularly information about their written errors. Truscott (1996), in his article arguing against the continued use of grammar correction in L2 writing classes, acknowledged this student preference, but asserted that just because students want error correction does not mean that teachers should provide it, and that it is the teachers' job to help their students adjust to the absence of error feedback. However, many L2 writing researchers and certainly most teachers would likely take issue with Truscott's dismissal of student desires and preferences, arguing that ignoring students' wishes about error feedback may lead to frustration (due either to expectations from prior educational experiences or to learning style needs), anxiety, decreased motivation, and a corresponding loss of confidence in their writing instructors (Bates, Lane, & Lange, 1993; Brice & Newman, 2000; Ferris, 1999b; Ferris & Hedgcock, 1998; James, 1998; Leki, 1992; Reid, 1998b). Indeed, some scholars feel that in various aspects of SLA and of L2 instruction, student desires and preferences ought to be taken into account far *more* than they are presently (see Reid, 1998b, for discussion).

Because both of these strands of evidence—existing empirical research on error correction and survey research on student views—argue in favor of teacher provision of error feedback, this chapter proceeds on the assumption that such response is useful, and focuses on the various ways in which teachers can and should provide error correction in order to utilize most effectively for the benefit of their students' writing development over time. To do this, I synthesize the research findings discussed at length in chapters 3 and 5 and use them as a springboard to provide specific suggestions for L2 writing teachers.

ERROR CORRECTION: ISSUES AND OPTIONS

A number of L2 scholars and teachers have published lists of questions, issues, or suggestions for writing instructors to consider when constructing error feedback for their student writers. Following several early influential pieces by Hendrickson (1978, 1980), they sometimes take the form of "Who?" "What?" "When?" "How?" questions (e.g., "*When* should a teacher give error feedback?—on all drafts, on the penultimate draft, on the final draft …") (see, e.g., Ferris, 1995a, 1995c; Ferris & Hedgcock, 1998; Reid, 1998b). Others provide straightforward imperative lists (see Bates, Lane, & Lange, 1993, p. 33; James, 1998, pp. 249–256; Reid, 1998b, Table 7.1, p. 125). Though all of these individual frameworks are extremely helpful, in the interests of attempting to link pedagogy directly to empirical research, I have chosen to structure the discussion in this chapter around the last five questions found in Fig. 3.3, which were derived from a review of existing error correction studies. These are summarized, together with the major research findings available on each specific question, in Fig. 7.1.

Part A: Options for Error Correction

Issue 1: Direct Versus Indirect Feedback. Studies reviewed in chapter 3 generally demonstrated that indirect feedback helps students' development more over time when compared with direct feedback. Indirect feedback, after all, forces students to think about their own errors and try to self-edit them, rather than merely copying the teacher's corrections from one draft to the next. This conclusion validates the suggestions of both SLA and L2 writing researchers (e.g., Bates, Lane, & Lange, 1993; Ferris, 1995c; Ferris & Hedgcock, 1998; Hendrickson, 1980; James, 1998; Reid, 1998b). Both James (1998) and Reid (1998b) referred to error feedback

Research Question	Summary of Previous Findings (see also chap. 3)
Part A: Error Correction Options	
1. Do direct and indirect feedback have different effects on accuracy?	Four studies reviewed found differences between direct and indirect feedback in effects on accuracy. In all cases, indirect feedback seemed to benefit student writers more over time. Two studies found no differences in student accuracy between varying feedback treatments.
2. Do students respond better to feedback on certain types or categories of error?	Few studies on written error correction have examined this issue, but those that have done so reported clear findings that various error types do respond differently to error treatment.
3. Is there a difference in outcome depending on whether indirect feedback is coded or uncoded?	There is little clear evidence on this question, but the existing research thus far suggests that uncoded indirect feedback may help students nearly as much as coded feedback.
Part B: Supplementing Error Feedback	
4. Does revision after correction help student accuracy?	No studies separated "revision versus no revision" from other variables—feedback, instruction, and so on. However, in most cases in which students were required to revise after receiving feedback, their written accuracy improved over time. The only clear counter-evidence is that reported by Polio et al. (1998), which was of relatively brief duration.
5. Does maintenance of error logs lead to improvement in accuracy over time?	Four studies have examined this question, and two of them clearly contrast the "log versus no log" condition (Ferris & Helt, 2000; Roberts, 1999). In three of four cases, maintenance of error logs (combined with other treatments) led to improved accuracy over time.[1]
6. Does supplemental grammar instruction (along with error correction) make a difference in student accuracy?	The evidence is extremely unclear on this point, as "grammar instruction" as a variable can be hard to operationalize and measure. Any suggestions on this issue should be regarded as purely speculative as to written error correction, although there is evidence from SLA research on spoken language that "form-focused" instruction can speed up acquisition processes (Doughty & Williams, 1998; Ellis, 1998; James, 1998).

FIG. 7.1.   Questions to consider in giving error feedback.

[1]The fourth study (Roberts, 1999) reports that in a case study of eight student writers, maintenance of error logs appeared to make no difference in accuracy or editing ability over time. However, the larger study by Ferris and Helt (2000) considered a much larger sample (N = 55) from the same database, and they found a clear advantage for error log students in reduction of errors over time.

that leads to student awareness and problem solving as "remediation," and both argued that remediation is the most valuable form of error feedback. Reid argued that leading students to revise their own work for correction "goes well beyond making a piece of *writing better.* It can make a student a *better writer* by expanding her knowledge and skills with written English" (1998, p. 131).

However, this conclusion—that indirect feedback is more valuable to student writers than is direct feedback—must be qualified on at least one count. Indirect feedback, depending on its form, assumes a relatively advanced level of formal knowledge and/or acquired competence in the L2 student writer. In other words, if the student is not sufficiently proficient in the L2, she or he may not benefit from indirect correction, simply because she or he does not possess adequate knowledge to self-correct even if errors are pointed out (Brown, 1994; Ferris & Hedgcock, 1998). In such instances, direct feedback, even if it only leads the student to recopy the correct forms, may be preferable, simply because it provides input for further acquisition and it gives students negative evidence about their written production (Doughty & Williams, 1998; Ellis, 1998; James, 1998; Schwartz, 1993).

Options for Direct and Indirect Feedback. Direct feedback as a pedagogical "option" is relatively straightforward: The teacher uses substitution, insertion, deletion, or reformulation to provide the correct form or structure to the student writer (see Fig. 7.2).

However, it should be noted that it is not always as easy as it might appear to directly correct a student's error, either because it is unclear what the writer intended to say and/or because there are multiple errors in a sentence, clause, or phrase that could be corrected in a variety of ways. In such cases, the teacher has several distinct options for giving feedback, including suggesting several different possible word-level rewrites (depending on alternate interpretations of the text) or actually reformulating the entire sentence so that it is clearer (see Fig. 7.3).

An even more serious problem with direct feedback is that the instructor may inappropriately cross the line between giving feedback to help the student rewrite and rewriting the student's text such that the writer's intended ideas are misunderstood,

---

Example 1: Deletion

This is not the life they ~~have~~ imagined before they came.

Example 2: Insertion

              to find   an

Immigrants should expect ^ true happiness in America because of ^ unbeatable economy, better education, and freedom.

Example 3: Substitution

                                 better

To them, this country is the place to seek a ~~more appropriate~~ future.

Example 4: Reformulation

    , in spite of their new life,

But ~~with all of this modern conveniences~~ can an immigrant be truly happy in America?

FIG. 7.2.   Examples of direct feedback. (Source of examples: Ferris et al., 2000, research corpus. Used with permission.)

Problem A: Unclear Word Choice

Example 1:

"How to get along with people?"

It is an **hot** problem existing between people.

Possible direct connections:

a difficult

...it is ~~an hot~~ problem

a controversial

...it is ~~an hot~~ problem

Example 2:

(That advice) reminded me of my bad experience which I cannot count.

Possible Direct Connections:

which I cannot recount.

Reminded me of my bad experience ~~which I can not count~~

so many bad experiences that I cannot count them.

Reminded me of ~~my bad experience which I can not count~~

Problem B: Multiple Errors in the Sentence

Example:

Even though in a strange situation that you don't know anyone, if a^ individual possesses a cheer smile, he should be welcomed and gain others concerns.

Possible Direct Connections:

where/in which   **n**

Even ~~though~~ in a strange situation ~~that~~ you don't know anyone, if a^ individual

ful   **receive concern/consideration from others**

possesses a cheer^ smile, he should be welcomed and ~~gain other's concerns~~.

Even in a strange situation in which an individual doesn't know anyone, if s/he has a cheerful smile, s/he will be welcomed and others will care about their concerns
~~Even though in a strange situation that you don't know anyone, if a individual possesses a cheer smile, eh should be welcomed and gain other's concerns.~~

FIG. 7.3.   Direct feedback options for problematic constructions. (Sources of examples: Ferris & Roberts, 2001, research corpus.)

changed, or subverted. This again raises the issue of "appropriation" discussed in chapters 1 and 6. Teachers who wish to avoid "taking over" a student's text need to take extreme care when providing direct feedback that their suggestions are in line (as far as can be reasonably determined) with the student writer's intentions and/or that they explicitly give the student choices about whether or not to take the text in the direction suggested by the teacher.

Although the range of direct feedback choices is somewhat limited, indirect correction as an option raises a number of questions. Even though the definition of indirect error feedback remains constant—the teacher lets the student know that there is a problem and the student is left with the responsibility of solving it (i.e., providing the correct form)—the instructor has choices to make about the location, the form, and the level of explicitness of the feedback.

As to location of feedback, options range from marking errors at the specific point in the text at which the error occurs to making a note or check mark in the margin to making more general verbal observations in an endnote. Options about feedback forms including underlining, circling, highlighting, or striking out errors, drawing an arrow to show that a word or morpheme needs to be inserted, using a correction code, and using words or sentences to call attention to a problem or explain the nature of the problem. Error feedback may range from very explicit (such as a verbal direction to "use past tense here") to moderately informative (a code of "vt" or "tense" to indicate that a verb tense error has been made) to vague (underlining the erroneous form or putting a check mark in the margin without indicating what type of error has occurred or how to solve the problem). Examples of these options are provided in Fig. 7.4.

Sample Student Sentence (errors in bold):

I sometimesd get so jealous about somebody's success, but I try be calm and praise him as much as I could.

Correction Options (from more- to less-explicit):

                ww   **ss**

1. I sometimes get so jealous **about** somebody's success, but **I try**^ **be** calm

                            vt

   and praise him as much as I **could**.

[Note: **ww** = wrong word; **ss** = sentence structure error (missing word); **vt** = verb tense error. Sample codes & definitions taken from Ferris et al. (2002)]

2. *I sometimes get so jealous <u>about</u> somebody's success, but I* try^ *be calm and*

   preaise hi m as much as I <u>could</u>.

3.   ✓✓   *I sometimes get so jealous about somebody's success,*

      ✓   *but I try be calm and preaise him as much as I could.*

(Note: Each check mark indicates a separate error in that line.)

4. **Verbal Endnote:** As you revise your paper, be sure to check for word choice errors (especially with prepositions), and errors with verb tense. Also, try reading your paper aloud to see if you can find any missing or unnecessary words in your sentences. I have marked a few examples of these errors in your paper so you can see what I mean, but you will need to find the others!

FIG. 7.4.   Indirect feedback options. (Sources of examples: Ferris & Roberts, 2001, research corpus.)

To select the "right" indirect feedback option for students, teachers should consider a variety of issues, including their students' prior experience with revision and self-editing strategies, their level of L2 competence and especially their formal knowledge of English grammar terms and rules, and teachers' own goals for providing error feedback. If teachers have as an objective helping students to develop self-editing skills, they might consider deliberately moving from more- to less-explicit feedback as the writing course progresses (perhaps varying the progression according to the abilities and preferences of individual students). For instance, they might begin the semester by circling or underlining all in-text errors, reducing the marking to underlining the first few examples of a particular error type and adding a verbal marginal or endnote about the error pattern, to requiring students to make passes through their texts for specific problematic constructions (such as verb tenses or noun plurals) without any feedback from the teacher (see also Ferris, 1995c, and Ferris & Hedgcock, 1998, for further discussion). It is also important that the teacher carefully consider students' level of formal linguistic knowledge in providing indirect feedback. If students have acquired English primarily through informal exposure to the language rather than through formal teaching of grammar, marking errors with codes or words intended to elicit learned rules may be not only fruitless but actually confusing to the students (Ferris, 1999a; Ferris & Hedgcock, 1998; Reid, 1998b). On the other hand, if the teacher pairs error feedback codes with in-class grammar mini-lessons on the constructions to which the codes refer, the feedback may become increasingly meaningful and helpful to the students and very efficient for the instructor (see Ferris, 1995c, and Reid, 1994).

Issue 2: Varying Feedback According to Error Type.   As already noted, previous studies of error correction have consistently found that students' progress in accuracy varies across different types and categories of error. For instance, in a study by Ferris (1995a), five major categories of error were targeted for feedback and instruction and subsequently used for analysis of student progress over five essay assignments in a semester. Students reduced their error percentages significantly in four of the five categories, but the reductions were far more substantial in one category (nouns), moderately impressive in two categories (verbs and miscellaneous), and relatively small in the fourth category (sentence structure).[15]

Similarly, Ferris and Helt (2000) analyzed students' progress in accuracy in five major error categories (verbs, noun endings, articles, word choice, and sentence structure) between the first and last essay assignments of the semester. Although students' reductions in total number of errors were statistically significant, of the individual error types, only the "verb" category showed significant positive change (the "word choice" category approached significance

---

[15]A follow-up study with new data by Ferris and Roberts (2001) utilized the five error categories shown in Fig. 7.6 for both feedback and analysis. For pedagogical purposes, it was recommended that the "word choice" category be separated into "wrong word" and "wrong form" feedback, as merging the two appeared to confuse the students at times.

at $p = .07$), and students actually made slightly *more* errors in articles and sentence structure in the final essay assignment.

In considering the effects of different error types on feedback, revision, and student progress in accuracy, an important issue is whether certain error types are better treated with direct feedback because they are idiosyncratic, idiomatic, and not rule governed. Most lexical errors would fall into this category. For instance, if a student writer inserts the wrong preposition into a sentence (an extremely common occurrence in ESL writing!), if the teacher underlines the error, marks it "wc" (word choice) or "prep" (preposition), in most cases the student will not be able to consult a learned rule, a grammar book, or even a dictionary to correct the error. If the student is able to self-correct, it will be because she or he is able to access some acquired knowledge of the target structure from prior exposure to linguistic input, not because the teacher feedback was informative, except to the extent that it let the student know that a problem existed. In such cases, many teachers might feel that crossing out the incorrect form and writing in the correct one could be more helpful to the student writer (see Hendrickson, 1980, for further discussion of blending direct and indirect feedback).

Though this position—that certain types of errors are inherently "untreatable" because they are not rule governed (Ferris, 1999b) and thus should either be ignored or simply corrected by the teacher—is intuitively appealing, it is important to note that the scant research evidence that exists on this point suggests that it makes little difference whether such errors are treated by direct or indirect feedback. For instance, in Robb et al.'s study (1986), which looked at four different types of correction, ranging from "most salient" (direct feedback) to "least salient" (very vague indirect feedback), no significant differences were found among treatment groups. Two recent studies are even more on-point with regard to this issue. In the first, data examined by Chaney (1999), Ferris et al. (2000), and Ferris and Helt (2000) indicated that for "nontreatable errors" (lexical errors and sentence structure errors exclusive of run-ons and fragments), students edited their errors successfully 73% of the time when they received indirect feedback and in 86% of the cases when they received direct feedback (the numbers were similar for "treatable" errors). In a second, follow-up study, Ferris and Roberts (2001) found no significant differences in students' ability to self-correct lexical (word choice) errors and "treatable" errors (verbs, noun endings, and articles) after receiving exclusively indirect feedback. However, there were significant differences between students' ability to self-correct "untreatable" sentence structure errors and treatable errors. In other words, the available evidence at the time of writing suggests that certain errors (such as complex, multilayered problems with sentence structure) may be less successfully treated by indirect feedback than other, more discrete errors in morphology or single-word choice. Further, because "untreatable" errors may comprise a substantial portion of the errors made by ESL student writers (Ferris, 1999b; Ferris et al., 2000), it may be unwise for the teacher to ignore such problems because they are "untreatable."

Besides considering *how* to mark errors, teachers need to consider *which* errors to address. A number of researchers over the years have identified "common" ESL writing errors and/or created lists of errors for teachers to mark. For instance, Ferris et al. (2000) categorized over 5,700 errors marked by three ESL writing teachers on 146 texts written by 92 college-level ESL composition students. The marks provided by the teachers and subsequently analyzed by five researchers were classified into 15 different categories, with a "miscellaneous" category, added during the analysis phase, accounting for all errors found that did not fit into the other categories (less than 1% of all errors marked). This list is shown in Fig. 7.5.

Although this list should only be considered comprehensive for the particular student population studied by Ferris et al. (2000) (i.e., intermediate-to-advanced mostly immigrant ESL students at a U.S. university), it is illustrative of the types of errors often found in ESL student writing and the lists of errors covered in other texts (e.g., Bates, Lane, & Lange, 1993; Raimes, 1992). However, because the types of errors L2 writers will make vary according to their first language, level of English proficiency, and prior educational background, instructors who plan to give er-

Error Type	Frequency	Percent of Total
Sentence structure	1,287	22.5
Word choice	654	11.5
Verb tense	624	10.9
Noun endings (singular/plural)	506	8.9
Verb form	443	7.8
Punctuation	391	6.8
Articles/determiners	376	6.6
Word form	371	6.5
Spelling	335	5.9
Run-ons	168	2.9
Pronouns	167	2.9
Subject–verb agreement	165	2.9
Fragments	102	1.8
Miscellaneous	51	.9
Idiom	48	.8
Informal	19	.3
Total	5707	100.0

FIG. 7.5.   ESL writing error categories. (Source: Chaney, 1999, p. 20; see also Ferris et al., 2000, Appendix A.)

ror feedback systematically should take time to conduct a class error analysis at the beginning of a writing course. This will give the teacher information about whole-class needs, which may help in planning in-class mini-lessons or selecting resources for at-home study, and about individual student needs to be addressed throughout the course. Results of diagnostic error analyses can also be shared with students for their own information and self-monitoring. Lists of possible error types such as the one in Fig. 7.5 can help teachers know what to look for in these preliminary analyses (see also Appendix 7A for a sample class error analysis form).

Many teachers and their students may find lists of 15 to 20 error types daunting to address in feedback, in-class instruction, and revision. Some experts have suggested that giving error feedback in larger categories that combine several smaller, related types may be more "user-friendly" both for teachers and for students (Ascher, 1993; Ferris, 1995c; Fox, 1992). For instance, following the study described earlier by Ferris et al. (2000), a secondary analysis by Chaney (1999) resulted in a suggestion that the 15 error types shown in Fig. 9.6 could be collapsed into five larger categories without losing much information about student errors. This reanalysis is shown in Fig. 7.6.

Qualitative data (open-ended survey responses and interviews) gathered from the three teachers and 25 of the students in the Ferris et al. study also suggested that

Verb errors	All errors in verb tense or form, including relevant subject–verb agreement errors.
Noun ending errors	Plural or possessive ending incorrect, omitted, or unnecessary; includes relevant subject–verb agreement errors.
Article errors	Article or other determiner incorrect, omitted, or unnecessary.
Word choice errors	All specific lexical errors in word choice or word form, including preposition and pronoun errors. Spelling errors only included if the (apparent) misspelling resulted in an actual English word.
Sentence structure errors	Errors in sentence/clause boundaries (run-ons, fragments, comma splices), word order, omitted words or phrases, unnecessary words or phrases, other unidiomatic sentence construction.

FIG. 7.6.   Larger error categories. Note: The five categories listed here resulted from the merging of several categories in Fig. 7.5 (e.g., verb tense and verb form) and dropping of others that occurred relatively rarely in the larger corpus (5,707 errors marked and analyzed). These five categories represent approximately 83% of all of the errors marked by the teachers. (The two largest categories from Fig. 7.5 not included in the figure were spelling [other than "wrong word" examples] and punctuation [other than run-ons, fragments, comma splices, or noun ending errors otherwise accounted for.])

the use of fewer categories for error feedback would be a welcome change for both instructors and student writers.

To summarize, in constructing error feedback, teachers should consider how they want to treat specific error types, rather than assuming that all errors—lexical, syntactic, morphological, and mechanical (i.e., capitalization, punctuation, spelling) fall into the same domain of linguistic knowledge (Truscott, 1996). Specific considerations include whether the error is treatable or untreatable and therefore whether direct or indirect feedback may be most helpful to the student in that instance, which error types are most frequent and serious for a particular class or individual student writer, and whether to mark errors of many small, discrete types or in fewer large, combined categories. Though research has been scarce on the relationship between error type and teacher feedback, the existing evidence suggests that:

1.   Indirect feedback may be effective for all error types except for complex sentence structure errors (Ferris et al., 2000; Ferris & Helt, 2000; Ferris & Roberts, 2001).

2.   There is considerable variation across individual student writers as to the types of errors they make and their ability to edit various types of errors (Ferris, 1995c; Ferris & Helt, 2000; Ferris & Roberts, 2001), and therefore diagnostic error analysis and individualized feedback may be necessary and appropriate in many instances.

3.   Larger categories of errors efficiently capture most of the information provided by breaking errors into smaller, more discrete error types, and feedback that covers fewer, larger categories may be just as effective and certainly less intimidating to teachers and students (Ferris et al., 2000; Ferris & Roberts, 2001).

Issue 3: Coded Versus Uncoded Error Feedback.   As discussed earlier, one of the specific options for teachers to consider when providing indirect error feedback is whether to simply *locate* the presence of an error or whether to *label* the error by its type. There are arguments to be made for either type of feedback. It could be claimed that error location gives students maximum responsibility and opportunity to reflect on and attempt to solve the problem indicated by the error marking. Student writers not only have to come up with the correct form, but think about what type of error it is, what rule(s), if any, may apply to the construction, and perhaps consult an appropriate source (grammar book, dictionary) for help. Such reflection is argued to promote long-term language acquisition because students are actively engaged in the process of problem solving (James, 1998; Lalande, 1982; Reid, 1998b). On the practical level, it is much easier, faster, and more accurate for teachers to simply mark an error by highlighting, circling, or underlining it than to decide what error type it is and attach the appropriate code or verbal signal.

On the other hand, it could be argued that coded feedback is more helpful to students than simple error location because it helps them to access metalinguistic information they may have learned (e.g., about verb tense rules or subject–verb agreement), giving them more tools with which to solve problems. In the study by Ferris et al. (2000), when students and teachers were asked during interviews about error location versus error identification, they were in agreement that error location did not provide adequate information for student problem solving and revision. However, the data did not support the subjects' intuitions, as students were able to self-correct errors that were uncoded or that used an unfamiliar code nearly as well as those that were marked with a "standard" code—and students were even able to edit successfully when an error was labeled with an *incorrect* code in over 60% of the cases. Further, in a follow-up study of 72 students in the same context (Ferris & Roberts, 2001), no significant differences in self-editing ability were found between students who received feedback labeled with codes from one of the five error categories in Fig. 7.6 and those who had errors in the same five categories merely underlined. Similarly, in their study of 134 Japanese college students, Robb et al. (1986) found no differences in long-term improvement between students who received coded feedback and those who received uncoded feedback.

Thus, it would seem that existing research does not support the intuition that coded error feedback, because it is more informative, helps students more in either the short- or long-term than uncoded feedback that locates but does not label the error. However, it should be remembered that the evidence on this point comes from the three studies discussed previously (and one of those three, Ferris et al., 2000, explored this issue only in passing). It is certainly possible that in other circumstances coded feedback may be more beneficial to students than simple error location. For instance, students at lower levels of L2 proficiency may need and be helped by an indication of error type, not only to correct an error in a particular text, but also to help process grammatical terminology and rules that they may be learning and to apply them to real-world language use. On the other hand, more advanced students, who by definition have more acquired competence in the L2, may be able to utilize their intuitions about the language to self-edit when problems are pointed out to them, just as native speakers do. These more-proficient students may also benefit from the additional level of autonomy that error location, rather than labeling, requires. It is also possible that if a system of coding is used consistently and is tied explicitly to in-class instruction on major patterns of error and strategies for avoiding them, the error feedback codes would be beneficial because they would elicit and reinforce concepts recently covered in class. However, neither of these latter points—the need for more explicit feedback at lower levels of L2 proficiency or the potential benefits of a coding system paired with instruction—has been examined empirically. In summary, it may be safe for teachers of students similar to those examined by Ferris et al., Ferris and Roberts (2001), and Robb et al. (1986) to assume that error location may be adequate and even most beneficial to their students. However, teachers in other contexts (particularly those with students not as proficient) may wish to experiment with different error feedback systems (include codes or verbal cues that indicate error type) to determine which are most effective *and* efficient.[16]

A practical issue that arises with respect to locating or labeling errors is *how* teachers should mark errors. Survey research has indicated that students are

---

[16]It is also important to consider the possible psychological effects on students of receiving uncoded error feedback, as student survey research indicates that most student respondents feel such feedback is inadequate to help them improve their written accuracy (e.g., Ferris et al., 2000; Komura, 1999; Leki, 1991; Rennie, 2000).

sometimes confused, frustrated, or even irritated with teachers' use of mysterious and cryptic symbols and codes on their texts (Ferris, 1995b; Straub, 1997; see chapter 5 for further discussion). Concerns range from legibility (students complain about their teachers' handwriting) to lack of understanding about what various circles, arrows, question marks, check marks, and codes represent. Whereas a symbolic approach to error marking may well be more efficient for teachers than providing verbal cues, instructors should take care to keep such systems simple, use them consistently, and explain them clearly to students, perhaps even appending a sheet with a key to the teacher's symbols and codes to each paper that is returned to students.

Part B: Supplementing Error Feedback

Issue 4: Revision After Correction.   Another decision teachers need to make with respect to error correction is *when* to give such feedback. Most early studies of error correction in both L1 and L2 writing considered the long-term effects of feedback given on final, graded drafts of student papers. To the extent feedback was considered by teachers as formative (helping them improve their writing in the future) as opposed to summative (justifying a grade on a particular paper), it was assumed that students would think about and apply feedback to future papers rather than rewriting or reconsidering a text that had already received error correction. With the advent of the process approach in L1 and L2 composition teaching (see chapter 1), teachers began to encourage and even require students to complete multiple drafts of the same paper, revising and editing the paper throughout the drafting process. Paired with a multiple-draft feedback orientation was a new commitment to providing feedback at intermediate stages of the writing process, through written teacher commentary, individual writing conferences, and peer response. L1 and L2 researchers encouraged such teacher "coaching" throughout the writing process (e.g., Brannon & Knoblauch, 1982; Krashen, 1984; Leki, 1990a; Sommers, 1982; Zamel, 1985), and student writers themselves have indicated that they pay more attention to between-draft feedback than to corrections on a final, graded product (Ferris, 1995b; Hedgcock & Lefkowitz, 1994).

Although the benefits of multiple-drafting and between-draft feedback are hard to dispute, several practical questions and decisions do remain. One question is whether all error feedback should be saved for the very end of the writing process, as suggested by some experts (Krashen, 1984; Sommers, 1982; Zamel, 1985). The argument for this position is that premature attention to form distracts students from more substantive efforts at revising the content of their texts. Further, it may be inefficient and counterproductive for teachers to spend time marking errors on early drafts when the marked sections of the text may ultimately disappear during revision. On the other hand, it has been argued that L2 writers need a lot of help with their errors, and that if teachers ignore form while giving content feedback only, they miss an opportunity to give students important information about their writing problems (Ferris & Hedgcock, 1998). Further, it is important to mention that there is no empirical support for the claim that content- and form-based feedback cannot be simultaneously provided on the same student paper without confusing and overwhelming students and subverting their revision processes. On the contrary, in studies in which feedback on content and form was provided together, students appeared to attend to and benefit from both types of feedback in subsequent revisions (Ashwell, 2000; Fathman & Whalley, 1990; Ferris, 1997). As a result, it has been suggested that feedback on early drafts could emphasize content while making several general suggestions about error patterns to which they should attend, whereas on later drafts more detailed error feedback could be provided, with suggestions about content included as necessary (see Fig. 7.7 and Ferris & Hedgcock, 1998, Fig. 5.6, p. 140, for examples).

As to the specific issue of how to make error feedback most beneficial for students' long-term writing development and second language acquisition, it may be

---

Teacher Endnote on Student First Draft:

Phil—

   This is an interesting story with lots of detail. I would like to see more analysis of your reaction to the guy in your story—explain why you were so suspicious. You also didn't ever tell the end of the story: Did you finally believe he was your old friend? Are you going to see him now?

   You have many verb tense errors. More seriously, you have some word choice/spelling errors, in which you substitute similar-sounding words. I've underlined some examples—be careful!

Teacher Endnote on Student Second Draft:

Phil—

   Excellent revision! You've done a good job of clearing up the questions I had about your story on the last draft. In your analysis in the conclusion, you might try explaining why, in your opinion, you were so suspicious of a stranger claiming to be an old friend.

   As you prepare your final draft, you need to pay attention to the following issues:

(1) verb tenses: You have a number of spots in which you use the present tense form of the verb when it should have been in past tense. I have highlighted examples of this problem throughout the paper. Please go through and try to fix them.

(2) I have also circled examples of word choice problems. You need to both spell-check your paper on the computer (to catch any errors caused by typing or spelling problems) and to double-check words in the dictionary that "sound like" the word you really mean. Be sure to ask me if you have any questions about the words I've circled.

FIG. 7.7.   Sample teacher feedback combining information on content and form. (Source of example: Research corpus from Ferris, 1997; Ferris, 2001a; Ferris, Pezone, Tade, & Tinti, 1997.)

an extremely good investment of class time to allow students to self-edit papers immediately after receiving error feedback from their instructor or from peers. Teachers often return marked papers to students at the end of a class period and expect them to do revision and editing on their own time. However, students might benefit greatly from in-class editing work right after receiving error feedback. Such activities engage students at a "teachable" moment—when they are working on their own writing and interested in the feedback they have received (Lalande, 1982; Lightbown & Spada, 1990)—and thus cause them to engage in meaningful reflection and problem solving that may not only help them to improve the paper on which they are working but also to acquire linguistic knowledge that may enable them to avoid or self-edit similar errors in the future. In addition, they offer the practical benefit of allowing students to process corrections when they can ask their teacher and peers questions about anything they do not understand. Several researchers have examined the effects of in-class editing sessions combined with indirect feedback (Fathman & Whalley, 1990; Ferris & Roberts, 2001; Frantzen & Rissell, 1987; Lalande, 1982). In the first three studies, students had high degrees of success in revising their work during in-class editing sessions. In Lalande's longitudinal study, students who received indirect feedback and revised their papers in class improved significantly in accuracy over the course of a semester. However, no researchers have directly compared students who revised in class and those who did not revise when amount and nature of feedback were held constant.[17] Still, the suggestion to allow in-class editing after feedback appears promising. A sample assignment sheet appears in Fig. 7.8.

Issue 5: Using Error Logs.   As discussed in chapter 3, several researchers have suggested that having students track their success in correcting and/or avoiding errors helps to raise their consciousness about error patterns and encourages them to take responsibility for their progress (Bates, Lane, & Lange, 1993; Ferris, 1995a, 1995c; Lalande, 1982). The limited empirical evidence that exists appears to support the use of error logs, in combination with other feedback, revision, and instructional treatments. The most direct evidence of this comes from a recent study by Ferris and Helt (2000), in which it was found that students who maintained error logs improved in accuracy over the course of a semester more than those who did not. However, though the differences in achievement were apparent, they were not statistically significant, most likely due to relatively small group sizes.

Using the same database as in Ferris et al. (2000) and Ferris and Helt (2000), Roberts (1999) completed a qualitative analysis of the effects of using error logs. She found that instructors and students in that study were frustrated with the large number of categories (15) included in the error logs, that students were not familiar

---

[17]Lalande (1982) compared students who received direct feedback and who did not revise in class with students who received indirect feedback and did revise, finding substantial differences in long-term achievement between the two groups. However, because both the feedback and revision conditions were different, it is not possible to attribute the differences between treatment groups to feedback type alone or to revision alone.

Example 1: Teacher Feedback With Correction Codes

Instructions: Using the codes listed below, I have marked errors in the five categories listed. Please go through your paper and try to make as many corrections as you can, using the codes to help you understand what the error is.

Code	Meaning
V	error in verb tense or form
NE	noun ending (plural or possessive) missing or unnecessary
Art	article or other determiner missing or unnecessary or incorrectly used
WW	wrong word or word form
SS	sentence structure: missing or unnecessary words; wrong word order; run-ons and sentence fragments

Example 2: Teacher Feedback With No Correction Codes

Instructions: Please carefully reread the diagnostic essay you wrote in class and typed in lab (attached). I have marked errors that I have found in five categories (verbs, noun endings, articles, word choice, and sentence structure). Please try to correct them. If you find any other errors that I have not marked, you may correct those as well. You will have 20 minutes to make the changes. Please write changes either above the word(s) or in the margins. Please write as clearly as you can.

FIG. 7.8.   Sample in-class editing assignment. (Source: Ferris & Roberts, 2001.)

with all of the terms and rules included in the logs, and that the logs were not adequately explained and integrated into other classroom work. Given these fairly substantial problems, the positive impact of the logs reported by Ferris and Helt (2000) is striking. It is certainly possible that if these methodological problems were solved, the logs would have an even more substantial impact. Figure 7.9 shows an example of an error log, based on the error categories used in Ferris and Helt (2000) and Ferris and Roberts (2001).

To summarize, like in-class editing sessions, the use of error logs appears to be a potentially valuable supplement to teacher feedback in helping students to improve in accuracy. If instructors elect to use logs, Roberts' findings suggest that teachers should (a) utilize fewer codes; (b) have students maintain them consistently and systematically over the entire writing course; (c) be sure to explain the purpose of and process for completing the logs to the students; and (d) supplement the use of the logs with in-class grammar and strategy instruction that systematically addresses the error categories covered by the logs.

Essay Draft	Verb Errors	Noun Ending Errors	Article Errors	Word Choice Errors	Sentence Structure Errors	Other Errors
1A						
1B						
1C						
2A						
2B						
2C						
3A						
3B						
3C						
4A						
4B						
4C						

FIG. 7.9.   Sample error log.

Issue 6: Supplemental In-Class Grammar Instruction.   It has been suggested by several experts that in addition to feedback, students may benefit from focused, targeted grammar instruction on particular error types that are problematic in their writing (Bates, Lane, & Lange, 1993; Ferris, 1995c; Ferris & Hedgcock, 1998). The thinking behind this suggestion may be traced back to Krashen's (1982) Monitor Hypothesis, which claims, among other things, that for students to be able to use a "monitor," or editor, they must know and be able to apply a rule to their own production. Proponents of supplemental grammar instruction in L2 writing classes would argue that feedback alone may not be enough to help students improve in accuracy—they need knowledge (linguistic information) and tools (strategy training) to help them avoid similar problems in the future. There is virtually no empirical evidence available to help teachers assess whether such instruction is helpful to students. Some of the studies discussed in chapter 3 and summarized in Fig. 7.1 did include grammar instruction as a component, but in no case was the presence or absence of grammar instruction isolated as a variable.[18] Focus-on-Form (FonF) is a somewhat controversial issue in second language acquisition research, as well—although some argue that it is unnecessary and even counterproductive, others argue that form-focused instruction and accompanying feedback to learners can help to accelerate developmental sequences with respect to acquisition of various linguistic structures and prevent fossilization (see Doughty & Williams, 1998; Ellis, 1998; and James, 1998, for detailed discussion of FonF issues in SLA research).

For teachers who wish to incorporate grammar instruction into their L2 writing classes, the following guidelines are suggested (see also Ferris, 1995c; Ferris & Hedgcock, 1998; Weaver, 1996):

1. Mini-lessons should be brief and narrowly focused (e.g., on "simple past vs. present perfect" rather than all verb tenses).
2. Instruction should focus on major areas of student need, rather than minor fine-tuning.
3. Lessons should include (minimally) text-analysis activities so that students can examine the target constructions in authentic contexts and application activities so that they can apply newly covered concepts to their own writing.
4. Instruction should also include strategy training to help students learn to avoid errors and to self-edit their work.

Appendix 7B shows sample mini-lesson materials.

SUMMARY

This chapter has reviewed a number of the options from which teachers can choose in providing error feedback and integrating this feedback (and form-related issues in general) into a process-oriented writing class. The issues and suggestions discussed here are drawn from existing research on the nature and effects of error correction in L2 writing (see chapter 3) and on student views about teacher response (see chapter 5). However, in some cases, very little specific research exists that addresses a particular question head on; in these instances, the lack of relevant empirical evidence has been so noted and my own best guesses about appropriate pedagogical practices are presented. For ease of reference, a summary of the teaching suggestions contained in this chapter is provided in Fig. 7.10.

A careful reading of this chapter should make it apparent that teachers have many choices to make in providing error feedback to their student writers (if indeed they opt to do so at all). Considerations include the knowledge, abilities, needs, and preferences of the students, the types of errors being considered, the stage of development of a particular text, and the time, ability, and willingness of the instructor to incorporate error treatment (including feedback, revision, and instruction) into the overall plan of the writing course. It may seem frustrating to

---

[18]Few if any experts in L2 writing or L2 grammar instruction would argue that grammar instruction should be utilized in isolation in writing classes (i.e., instead of feedback or revision). Most scholars agree that application of grammatical training to real-world language use is vital for student uptake of such instruction. However, a study that compared one group of students who received both feedback and instruction with one that received only feedback could shed some light on the value of supplementary grammar instruction for L2 writers.

1. For intermediate-to-advanced level writers, provide **indirect feedback** in most instances. Possible exceptions may include complex sentence-structure errors (see Fig. 7.3).

2. For writers at lower L2 proficiency levels, provide **direct feedback** paired with required recopying of correct forms—but intentionally move toward indirect feedback as students learn more about the language.

3. Indirect feedback is probably most helpful and student-friendly when it occurs at the specific in-text point of error (as opposed to marginal or terminal comments) (see Fig. 7.4).

4. Uncoded indirect feedback may be just as effective as and more efficient than coded or labeled feedback.

5. If coded or labeled error feedback is used, teachers should take care that students understand the codes or labels and the terms/rules they stand for, and should consider a program of supplemental grammar instruction so that coded feedback elicits information recently covered in class (see Appendix 7B).

6. Teachers should do diagnostic error analyses to discover the most frequent and serious error patterns of a particular writing class and/or group of students (see Appendix 7A).

7. If there is considerable variation across a group of students as to amount, type, and severity of written errors, teachers should consider individualized error feedback plans and individual or small group instruction.

8. For both feedback and instruction, teachers may wish to address errors in larger categories (e.g., "verbs" rather than "verb tense" or "verb form") rather than many different discrete categories (see Figs. 7.6 and 7.7).

9. Students should be allowed or even required to revise their texts after receiving error feedback. Ideally, revision/editing sessions should take place in class immediately after marked papers have been returned (see Fig. 7.8).

10. Teacher or student maintenance of error logs to track student progress in various error categories may be helpful if the logging procedures and categories are kept simple (not too many categories), if logs are used consistently, and if the categories on the log are tied to in-class grammar and strategy instruction and used by teachers for feedback (see Fig. 7.9).

11. In-class grammar instruction may be a helpful supplement to error feedback if such instruction is brief, narrowly focused, explicitly tied to issues covered by teacher feedback, and contextualized (students given opportunities to do analysis of target structures in authentic texts and to apply lessons to their own texts) (see Appendix 7B).

FIG. 7.10.   Summary: Suggestions for teachers.

some instructors to sift through so many different issues and options. Even more frustrating, because research on some questions has been scarce and its results conflicting, there are few clear-cut answers as to the best way(s) for teachers to proceed. However, accuracy in student writing is important in many contexts, and the choices made by teachers about error treatment may have a profound effect on the progress and development of their students' writing. Though it is tempting to select a "one size fits all" approach to error feedback, and perhaps even more so to ignore such issues altogether (Truscott, 1996), the thoughtful teacher will consider these pedagogical questions carefully and select teaching strategies accordingly. As I have noted elsewhere,

> Though it is arguable whether grammar feedback and instruction will be consistently effective for all L2 student writers, it seems clear that the absence of any feedback or strategy training will ensure that many students never take seriously the need to improve their editing skills and that they will not have the knowledge or strategies to edit even when they do perceive its importance. (Ferris, 1999b, p. 8)

APPENDIX 7A: SAMPLE CLASS ERROR ANALYSIS PROCEDURE

Error Analysis Procedures

1. With a highlighter, look carefully through the student essay. Highlight and consecutively number every error you find in the following categories:

- Verbs (tense, form, verb agreement with subject)
- Noun endings (plural and possessive)
- Articles and other determiners
- Word form
- Word choice
- Sentence structure
- Spelling, capitalization, and punctuation (not covered by other categories)
- Other (any errors that do not fit above categories)

2. Use the analysis form to categorize and offer a correction for each error.

3. Use the summary form to total up the types of errors and numbers of each error. Then based upon your reading of the paper and your analysis, identify the three most significant problems and write them in on the bottom of the form. Note: The "most serious problem" is not always the most *frequent* problem.

Error Analysis Sheet

Error #	Type	Possible correction
1		
2		
3		
4		
5		
6		
7		
8		
9		
10		
11		
12		
13		
14		
15		
16		

Error Analysis Summary Form—Diagnostic Essay

Student Name:	
Error Type	Total Number of Errors & Ratio of Total
Verb tense/form	
Noun endings	
Articles/Determiners	
Word Choice or Word Form	
Sentence Structure: Missing or Unnecessary Words, Word Order	
Sentence Structure: Fragments, Run-ons, or Comma Splices	
Spelling, Punctuation, and Capitalization	
Other _____	

Most Serious Errors to Work On:

1.

2.

3.

APPENDIX 7B: SAMPLE MINI-LESSON MATERIALS

Past Perfect Tense

Note: This lesson was the third in a sequence on problematic verb tense contrasts. The practice exercise below reflects material from all three lessons.

1. The focal time of the past perfect is "then" and not "now"; therefore, the past perfect cannot be used in the present time frame. On a time line, the past perfect can be represented in this way:

Example: Before she *enrolled* at CSUS, she *had attended* a community college.

2. As you can see from the example above, the past perfect is used to describe an event that happened **before another past event**.

Examples:

Before she moved to Japan, she *had lived* in Hong Kong for a couple of years.

I didn't go to the movies with them because I *had seen* that movie the night before.

3. The past perfect is formed by using the **past form of the auxiliary have + the past participle of the main verb**: had lived, had sunk, had been, etc.

Examples:

The house *had been* empty for several months before I bought it.

By the time my brother arrived, we *had* already *finished* our dinner.

4. Be careful not to confuse the past perfect with the present perfect. Notice the difference in meaning between the two sentences below:

Present Perfect: I have lived in Vacaville for three years (I moved to Vacaville three years ago, and I still live there).

Past Perfect: I had lived in Vacaville for three years [before I moved to Sacramento] (First I lived in Vacaville, and then I moved to Sacramento).

5. The time signals often used with the past perfect are **before** ("before she moved to Japan") and **by the time** ("by the time my brother arrived").

Examples:

Before she went to the restaurant she *had been* to the movies.

By the time we arrived at the theater, the play *had* already *started*.

Practice Exercise 1

The following paragraph from a student essay contains six errors with verb tenses (in bold). Please examine the text and complete the chart below. Then discuss your answers with your classmates.

1. I still remember when there was no peace in the house. 2. Every day, my brothers and I **have** fights. 3. Sometimes we **fight** over the littlest things. 4. I **remembered** one time when my brother **had borrow** my pen without asking for my permission. 5. I guess I was still very young. 6. When I couldn't find my pen, I

practically **blow** up. 7. We had a great big fight over a stupid little pen. 8. We fought even though my father **has** told us that we should be like a pair of hands, always working together in harmony. 9. We didn't speak to each other for a whole week. 10. That really made my parents mad.

(Text adapted from: Raimes, A. (1990). *How English Works.* NY: St. Martin's Press)

Error	Verb Tense Needed (present, past, present perfect, past perfect)	Suggested Correction
have (sentence 2)		
fight (sentence 3)		
remembered (sentence 4)		
had borrow (sentence 4)		
blow (sentence 6)		
has (sentence 8)		

Practice Exercise 2:

Exchange papers with a partner. Carefully look at each verb phrase in the paper and see if you find any verb tense errors. If you do, *underline them, but do NOT correct them!* When you receive your own paper back, try to (a) correct any errors your partner identified; (b) explain why you disagree with any markings your partner made; and (c) find any other verb tense errors your partner may not have noticed.

CHAPTER	Implementing
8	Peer Response

As discussed in chapters 1, 4, and 5, peer response in the L2 writing classroom has been widely adopted over the past two decades. Research on peer feedback to date has by and large indicated that students find it beneficial and that they consider and utilize peers' suggestions in their revised texts. Some researchers have even presented findings showing that peer feedback suggestions were not only incorporated in student papers but that they helped the quality of the papers and led to student improvement over time.

However, researchers and teachers have also identified a number of questions and issues that may impact the value and effectiveness of peer response. Such issues include the need for training, the need for peer review sessions to be carefully structured and monitored by the instructor, potential problems with social roles and cross-cultural dynamics within pairs or groups of peer reviewers, and the appropriate balance between feedback from teachers, peers, self, and other sources. In this chapter, I proceed on the assumption that peer review can be beneficial to L2 student writers and that the problems that have been identified are not insurmountable, focusing on techniques and strategies for making L2 peer review as successful as possible.

IMPLEMENTING PEER RESPONSE: GENERAL PRINCIPLES

Chapters 4 and 5 present arguments in favor of peer response and research that investigates it. In the literature that exists on L2 peer review (see Fig. 4.1 for an overview), a number of practical issues are raised that in turn lead to suggestions for appropriate utilization of peer response. These suggestions are summarized in Fig. 8.1.

Utilizing Peer Feedback Consistently

Both research and anecdotal evidence make it clear that the ability to critically evaluate writing and to construct helpful feedback emerges over time. (This is true for writing *teachers*, too!) For peer feedback to be a useful tool, teachers must commit to it as an option, communicate from the outset that it will be a regular part of the class, and allow adequate, regular time for it. The decision to implement peer feedback thus has significant implications for syllabus design and lesson planning.

The principle of consistency leads to several specific questions and decisions. First, how often should peer work take place? Some instructors opt to have peer feedback occur at regular points in the multiple-draft writing cycle, for instance, after students have completed the first draft of an essay, with teacher feedback being provided following second drafts. Another possibility is to have collaborative work interspersed throughout the writing process. For instance, students could complete brainstorming or other prewriting exercises together and give feedback about the peers' topic, thesis, introduction, outline, and so on. Several examples of such exercises are shown in Fig. 8.2. Students can also give feedback for revision in response to completed drafts and can participate in peer editing workshops when writers are about to finalize a particular text. Chapter 7 provides specific suggestions for peer editing activities.

Second, how much class time should be allotted to peer response activities? The answer to this will vary depending on how often (and at which stages) peer feedback is utilized. In addition, the amount of class time needed will differ depending on the logistics of the peer response sessions as designed by the instructor. For example, instructors may opt to have students bring completed essay drafts to class, exchange them with group members, and have peers read each

---

1. Utilize peer feedback consistently.
2. Explain the benefits of peer feedback to students.
3. Prepare students carefully for peer response.
4. Form pairs or groups thoughtfully.
5. Provide structure for peer review sessions.
6. Monitor peer review sessions.
7. Hold students responsible for taking peer feedback opportunities seriously.

FIG. 8.1. Guidelines for peer response in L2 writing classes.

1. Listing: For a personal narrative essay, make a list of possible topics (e.g., first day of college, getting a driver's license). Have students in small groups brainstorm a list of at least five topics to be shared with the whole class. Have each group share its list to create a master list on the board. Students should copy the list for future reference.

2. Freewriting: Students can choose a topic from the listing activity (see #1) or a topic of their own. Have them write the topic at the top of a sheet of paper. Explain to them that they should write freely on the topic for five minutes without stopping, and without worrying about spelling, grammar, organization, and so on. After five minutes, have them exchange papers with a partner. Ask the partner to underline the most interesting word, phrase, or sentence in the freewrite. Then have students write that word or phrase (or another of their own choosing) at the top of another page and freewrite on that for five more minutes.

3. Sharing Drafts of Introductions: For an essay in which students are relating an assigned text to personal experience, have them draft an introductory paragraph (after giving them guidance and models about elements of introductions). Then have them share these drafts with their writing group members, who should respond to the following questions:
   - Which essay(s) has your classmate selected to write about?
   - What is the writer's opinion about the essay? How do you know?
   - What ideas or examples do you think the writer might include in his or her own paper? (Can you find hints in the introduction?)
   - What kind of introductory techniques has the writer used (quote, anecdote, moving from general → specific, question, etc.)? Did you find the introduction clear and interesting? Explain.

FIG. 8.2.   Sample peer response exercises for prewriting phase. (Note: See also Ferris & Hedgcock, 1998, Figs. 6.4 & 6.5, pp. 182–183.)

other's papers and complete a written feedback form for homework. This exchange could similarly be accomplished via e-mail. In class, then, time could be allotted for oral discussion of papers and clarification of peers' feedback. On the other hand, if students read and respond to each other's papers on the spot (i.e., the entire process takes place during class), such sessions will take much longer. At the college level, I have found that having groups of three read and respond to each other's papers (completed drafts) takes a minimum of 45 minutes of class time (and could have gone on longer had I permitted it). If, however, students have read and responded in writing to peers' drafts ahead of time, the discussion period can be limited to perhaps 20 minutes. Of course, peer feedback on shorter pieces of text (like introductions) can go more quickly as well. Another alternative is to have students read a number of different peers' texts but give only very limited feedback on each, or even to read just to discuss the ideas in the papers, not to give formal criticism. It is important to mention that in surveys of student opinion about peer feedback (see chapter 5), one of the most often-mentioned complaints was that the time allowed for was inadequate, and the students felt rushed.

Explaining the Benefits of Peer Feedback to Students

Although L2 student views of peer response appear to be generally favorable, there are some consistent concerns that recur in the research. Specifically, students worry that their peers are not competent, either in their grasp of the language or their writing skills, to give them useful feedback. (The corollary anxiety is that they themselves will not be able to help their peers.) Students are also concerned that peers might be unkind or harsh in their criticism and worry both about having their feelings hurt or about losing face. Finally, students fear that instructors will use peer response as a mechanism to avoid giving feedback themselves—and the survey research clearly indicates that, although L2 writers are happy enough with peer feedback, they would never choose peer response over teacher response if they could only have one source of commentary. Finally, some students, because of personality or learning style, simply do not enjoy working in groups with peers. (I have found this to be predictably true among graduate master's TESOL students, as well.)

It is important for teachers to acknowledge and address these concerns from the beginning of the writing course. Depending on the context and audience, students may have had prior experiences with peer feedback in composition classes and need little explanation or "selling" of the idea. However, if the class is primarily composed of students who have recently arrived in the United States from other educational systems (i.e., international visa students), they may have never heard of or considered such an alternative and be bewildered or even horrified by the idea. If the instructor is committed to the consistent use of peer response throughout the writing course, it is time well spent to explore the idea in a class discussion with the students.

I have discovered that this need not be difficult or particularly time consuming, and I have found the following steps to be helpful:

- Ask the students to think of some reasons why having classmates read their papers and give suggestions might be a good idea. Write the ideas elicited on the board and elaborate and add to them as needed. Some of the responses you might look for include: (a) It is easier for others to find mistakes in my papers than it is for me; (b) I can see how other students approach the assignment; (c) It is interesting to read other students' papers; (d) It is fun to get to discuss things with classmates instead of listening to the teacher all the time; (e) My classmates can give me feedback about anything in my paper that isn't clear.
- Then ask the students to think of problems or concerns they might have about peer feedback. They will likely come up with the same list of concerns just outlined. Reassure them that all of these issues will be addressed through careful preparation and structuring of the task (see following).
- It is also helpful to mention research that demonstrates that peer feedback can benefit student writing and that other L2 students have enjoyed peer response (see chapters 4 and 5). Finally, instructors should point out that even very accomplished

writers often receive and even solicit peer response (in writers' groups, peer-reviewed journals or books, etc.) and that getting feedback from classmates and co-workers may be a regular part of their future academic and professional lives.

If students get a chance to talk through both the potential advantages and possible concerns about peer response, and if this discussion is intentionally paired with a training or modeling session, there is likely to be little resistance to the process and even some enthusiasm about it.

Preparing Students Carefully for Peer Response

The overview of peer response research shown in Appendix 4A demonstrates that, in most cases, students received training of some sort prior to their first peer feedback sessions. Researchers who have examined the effects of trained peer response have consistently found that students provide better quality feedback and that their affective responses to peer feedback are much better when they are prepared in advance for peer response (e.g., Berg, 1999; McGroarty & Zhu, 1997; Stanley, 1992). As noted by Stanley (1992),

> ... while peer evaluation has been accorded a place in ESL composition classrooms, productive group work has not always resulted ... Gere (1987) points to inadequate student preparation for group work as a major cause for unsuccessful peer evaluation sessions: "When I meet teachers who say, 'Oh, I tried writing groups and they didn't work,' I begin by asking about preparation." (p. 219)

However, a careful reading of the studies leads to the observation that "training" means different things in various contexts. In Stanley's (1992) study, the experimental ("coached") group received 7 hours of training. This preparation included careful examination of series of essay drafts written by students in a previous course "to pinpoint vague or unclear sections of text." Stanley noted that "By looking at succession of drafts, they saw each essay as a work in progress. As they read later drafts, they searched for evidence of reworkings and repairs" (p. 219). In addition, students were trained not only in *what* to look for, but *how* to give useful feedback. Stanley used extensive role-playing followed by whole-class discussion to explore what sorts of comments were most helpful (specific and short), what kinds of reader–writer interactions were most favorably received (frequent confirmation checks from reader to writer), and ways to express criticism tactfully. Stanley also described a technique known as a "fishbowl demonstration" (Lunsford, 1986), in which she and another instructor role-played a peer evaluation session as students read from their own copies of the draft under discussion.

Berg (1999), who also compared the effects of trained and untrained peer response, outlines an 11-step training process, with each step "ranging in time from 5 to 45 minutes each" (p. 223) (see Fig. 8.3). McGroarty and Zhu (1997), who studied the effects of peer response on L1 freshman writers, described a class conferencing procedure, repeated each time the students do peer response, that is a variation on the "fishbowl demonstration": A student volunteer reads his or her paper aloud as

---

1. Create a comfortable classroom environment.

2. Explain the role of peer response in the writing class.

3. Discuss how professional writers use peer response.

4. Share how you (the teacher) utilize peer response in your own writing/teaching.

5. Model peer response with the whole class using a sample text.

6. Discuss (in)appropriate vocabulary and expressions for peer feedback.

7. Introduce the peer response form.

8. Practice the process by having groups of students write a paragraph collaboratively and then having another group critique it for revision.

9. Facilitate conversations among readers, writers, and the teachers about the feedback process.

10. Discuss strategies for implementing peers' feedback in revision.

11. View and discuss video clips of a successful and an unsuccessful peer response session.

FIG. 8.3.   Peer response training steps. (Adapted from Berg, 1999, pp. 238–240.)

teacher and classmates listen and write down comments. Then the class discusses feedback points, articulates suggestions, and evaluates their own feedback (e.g., revising comments to make them clearer or more specific). A key variation in this process is that it is repeated several times throughout the semester so that students are reminded of the goals and strategies for effective peer response.

In other studies in which peer response preparation is described, techniques follow along the lines of the three studies just discussed, though typically the preparation is not so extensive as to time allowed and perhaps not as systematic and coherent. What most peer feedback preparation processes appear to have in common, though, are the following elements:

- Modeling of what to look for using sample student texts (usually not from the present group of students) and guided questions or peer feedback forms.
- Discussion of how to give feedback, including issues of sensitivity and tact as well as specificity and clarity.

Although peer feedback preparation will undoubtedly be more effective if extensive time is devoted to it (as in Stanley's study) and/or if the training steps are repeated systematically (as in McGroarty & Zhu's study), I have found that one 30 to 45 minute training session that incorporates discussion of the "whys, whats, and hows" of peer feedback as previously described, paired with careful structuring, monitoring, and follow-up of peer response sessions, has been adequate for my college students to engage in peer review that is both productive and enjoyable. I have been pleasantly surprised and gratified by their enthusiasm for, engagement in, and commitment to the process when care is taken to prepare them for it in advance.

Forming Pairs or Groups Thoughtfully

In the L2 peer response literature, writing groups range in size from 2 to 4 students. Many utilized dyads (pairs) of students, presumably because partners can give each other maximum time and attention. Others, including me, opt for slighter larger groups. In my opinion, the optimal writing group size is three, and if class numbers do not divide evenly by three, I might have a group or two with four members. I like the variety of viewpoints that three- or foursomes provide, and I have also found that students are a bit more comfortable in groups of threes than in pairs, which can be uncomfortably intimate in some cases (and may even be a problem for students from some cultural backgrounds especially if pairs are mixed as to gender). For time reasons, I prefer groups of three over groups of four if feasible, and I would never recommend a group larger than four.

Like many instructors, I also prefer writing groups that remain stable for the duration of the writing course. I typically assign these groups during the second week of the semester after getting to know the students a bit in class and reading a writing sample that they produced the first week. I mix students by language background, gender, and ability. I like to have stronger and weaker writers mixed. The weaker writers benefit from regularly reading the texts of more proficient writers, and the more advanced writers profit from the critical thinking required to give helpful feedback to their less able classmates. I once had a writing group composed of two "A" students and one "C" student. Over the course of the semester, the "C" student made dramatic progress. Late in the term, I complimented him on how well he was coming along. He immediately pointed to the other two members of his writing group and gave the credit to them, both to their helpful feedback and especially to being able to read their well-constructed texts over time.

Another benefit to having stable writing groups is that it can foster classroom community. I have my writing groups not only give peer feedback, but also discuss readings together, go to the library to do research together, and give group oral presentations. All of this collaborative work builds relationships, and I have had students comment that this was the only class at the university at which they had gotten to know classmates and made friends. I have even heard anecdotes indicating that some students still stayed in touch with members of their writing group several semesters after my class was over!

Possible drawbacks to set writing groups are student resistance and groups that have poor chemistry. Students may prefer to form their own groups and collaborate with their friends if they already know someone in the class. However, I feel strongly that it works better to have some objective criteria, as described, for forming groups, and I have also found that group work in college writing classes typically works better—as to students being engaged and on task—if they are *not* permitted to work only with "friends." I do, however, offer some opportunities throughout the course for students to work collaboratively with classmates outside of their writing groups, and in some cases

I allow them to choose their own partners or form their own groups. As to poor chemistry (students not liking or getting along with group members or simply not having productive interactions), I have never had significant problems with this if I am careful with preparation, structure, and monitoring of activities. However, if such a problem developed, I might consider changing the composition of groups at midterm.

Providing Structure for Peer Review Sessions

Along with careful preparation or training, probably the biggest factor in whether or not peer review sessions will be successful is the structure or guidelines provided by the instructor. Though some experts (particularly in L1 composition) urge that students simply be put into writing groups to "talk about each other's papers"—arguing that teacher structure of the writing group time is appropriative and imposes the teacher's Ideal Text (Brannon & Knoblauch, 1982; see also discussion in chapter 1) on the students—most agree that developing student writers are simply not capable of constructing useful responses without some guidance. There are a number of options and strategies for structuring peer response sessions. One suggestion that seems particularly valuable is to divide up the peer feedback time and ask one student in each group to serve as a timekeeper. That way, for example, if 45 minutes is allotted for writing groups to work, each member in a group of three would get approximately 15 minutes devoted to discussion of his or her paper.

The simplest way to structure peer response time is simply to write questions on the board or on an overhead for the students to discuss. A more effective alternative, in my view, is to have students read peers' papers silently and provide written responses on a peer feedback form, and then give them time to discuss feedback orally. Asking students to respond in writing has several important advantages: (a) It allows students more time to think and compose helpful feedback; (b) it gives the writer a record of what was said as she or he goes to revise; and (c) it allows the teacher to hold the students accountable for giving good feedback and to monitor the effectiveness of feedback sessions, both as to types of feedback given and as to its usefulness for subsequent revisions. On the other hand, it clearly will take more time (whether the written responses are assigned in or out of class) to have peers compose written feedback. Instructors will have to weigh the amount of time expended against the benefits, as outlined.

If a teacher does utilize a peer feedback form, there are several options to consider. Some ESL writing textbooks offer a "standard" peer feedback form that can be used every time peer response sessions take place. The advantage of this approach is that students become comfortable with the format and criteria for evaluation. On the other hand, it has been argued that peer feedback should be varied depending on the nature of the writing task and on other issues that have been discussed in class (Ferris & Hedgcock, 1998; Mittan, 1989). In Ferris and Hedgcock (1998), a sequence of three peer response forms is provided that illustrates how evaluation criteria can vary according to the type of assignment students have been given and the in-class instruction that has been provided (see Appendix 6A, pp. 194–196). A similar sequence is shown in Appendix 8A.

Designing peer feedback forms is more challenging than it may appear. It is important to have enough questions but not too many, to be clear and specific, to avoid yes–no questions, to require students to extract information from their peers' texts, and to facilitate a balance of praise and constructive criticism. Figure 8.4 shows an example of a peer response form that meets these criteria fairly well.

In addition to designing peer response forms that are responsive to the specific concerns of the class or assignment, another option is to have students utilize the

---

Assignment: Write an essay in which you examine the relationship between ideas in the reading and your own ideas and attitudes. Refer to one or more of the readings in Part Two of Guidelines (Spack, 1990; 1996).

Purpose: To show how the ideas of (an)other author(s) compare with your own ideas or experiences, or to show how his or her ideas have influenced your own thinking. You must explain and evaluate the author's ideas; **direct references to the reading(s)** (summary, paraphrase, or quotation) are **required**.

PEER RESPONSE FORM
Essay Assignment 2

Your Name: _____

Writer's Name: _____

1. What is the main idea of this essay? State it in your own words.

2. What article(s) does the writer discuss in this essay?

Author/Title:

Author/Title:

3. What ideas from the writer's own experience are given to discuss the article's ideas?

Idea from the Article	Idea from the Writer's Own Experience
a.	
b.	
c.	

4. What did you like best about this essay?

5. What are the *two specific areas* that need the most improvement?

FIG. 8.4.   A sample peer feedback form.

course grading criteria to give each other feedback. In chapter 6, a sample response checklist for teacher feedback was presented (Fig. 6.3); this is a checklist that was derived directly from the departmental grading criteria for one of the ESL writing courses I teach. When I last taught this course, during a 6-week summer session (see Ferris, 2001b, for a detailed description of this class), I utilized a version of this checklist not only for my own feedback, but also for peer feedback sessions. In addition to providing answers to questions on peer feedback forms, I had students complete the checklist and in some instances assign a number on the 1-to-6 grading scale. I found this combination of teacher/peer feedback using the same checklist to be tremendously successful. Not only did the students benefit from the repeated use of a consistent feedback tool, but they became quickly socialized to the grading criteria for the course and thus were more aware of the writing issues with which they had to grapple in order to succeed in the course. Between getting feedback from me that used the checklist, applying the tool to sample student essays, and then using it for evaluating peers' papers, the students rapidly became very proficient at giving excellent feedback that was not only clear and specific but also was extremely on-point as to the grading criteria for the course. As the course progressed, I also used the checklist for guided self-evaluation sessions leading to revisions. (See also White, 1999, for a discussion of using grading rubrics for feedback in L1 settings.) Appendix 8B shows a sample sequence of peer response activities leading to self-evaluation and revision.

Monitoring Peer Review Sessions

As students participate in peer review sessions, it is important for the instructor to strike the delicate balance of being obviously present in the room but not intrusive. If the teacher is too involved, there is a definite risk that students will simply wait for the teacher to come put his or her two cents in, rather than engaging seriously in the peer feedback task themselves. On the other hand, it is helpful for the teacher to occasionally listen in on peer review sessions so that students stay on task and especially so that the instructor can respond to any questions that might arise or deal with any interaction problems. My typical pattern is to leave the groups alone for an extended period of time (say 20–30 minutes), sitting quietly at the front of the room doing some work of my own. Then for the last 10 to 20 minutes of the peer review time, I might wander around to various groups, asking peers what they thought of each other's papers. Having spent some time reading papers and thinking about them, they usually have things to say. This is a good opportunity not only for me to connect with individual students but also to do on-the-spot assessment of how well students are handling the peer feedback task.

Holding Students Responsible
for Taking Peer Feedback Opportunities Seriously

If teachers seriously believe that peer feedback is valuable and if they devote considerable time to preparing students for it and scheduling it into class sessions, it is also important to build accountability mechanisms into the process. This can be done in a variety of ways.

1. After peer feedback sessions are over, give students a few minutes (say 5–10) to write individual responses about what they have experienced. Examples of how this can be structured are shown in Appendices 8A and 8B.
2. When students submit drafts and revisions for teacher feedback or grading, have them include peer feedback forms. In your own commentary, respond to some of the ideas the peers have given (your response could be one of agreement or disagreement).
3. Build peer feedback into the grading scheme. For instance, a number of points or a percentage of the grade could be allotted to students making a "good faith" effort to give their peers thoughtful feedback.
4. When students turn in revised papers after receiving peer feedback, ask them to compose a 1 to 2 page cover memo that details how they used peers' suggestions in revisions and/or explains why they chose not to incorporate these suggestions. (Make it clear that the final decisions about how to revise rest with them as the author, but that they need to at least justify why they chose to ignore a peer's comment.)

Besides communicating the value of peer feedback to students, these accountability suggestions have the added benefit of helping the teacher assess how well students are responding to peer feedback (both as to quality of feedback and affective response to it) so that adjustments can be made as necessary. The teacher may also wish to consider asking students to fill out a questionnaire at the end of the semester to express their opinions about how peer feedback has been for them during this writing class.

OTHER ALTERNATIVES

As technology becomes incorporated into composition instruction to greater degrees, it opens up other possible avenues for peer feedback. One already mentioned is e-mail, which not only solves the problem of students forgetting to bring copies of essay drafts for peer feedback, but also opens the way for highly motivated peers to have several rounds of feedback via e-mail. A possible downside of this is that teachers may not be able to monitor these exchanges; the instructor may wish to require that all e-mail exchanges be copied to him or her or printed out for inclusion with essay submissions. This requirement could also protect against possible abuses of the system, such as one student taking unfair advantage of peer group members by requesting excessive amounts of feedback or one student providing so much editing and advice to another that it becomes unclear which student is actually writing the paper.

Similarly, as more and more writing classes are conducted entirely or partially in a campus computer lab and/or through Web-based or Web-enhanced delivery systems, students will be able to engage in peer conferencing over local-area networks (LANs) or in real-time online discussions, rather than face-to-face. Although it is hard at this stage of technological evolution to assess what the effects of computer-based peer feedback as compared with in-person classroom-based peer response might be, one would imagine that there are drawbacks and benefits to each mode, and that these may vary according to individual students' personalities, learning styles, writing versus speaking ability, and comfort with the technology. For some L2 students, the ability to compose comments on the computer (where they can be read and edited) may relieve them of the added anxiety they may feel about their pronunciation, oral fluency, or aural comprehension skills. Others may find communicating via e-mail, the Web, or LANs too impersonal, slow, and disconnected, feeling that it deprives them of valuable opportunities for interaction, negotiation, and clarification. At this point, it is hard to know what to recommend to teachers except that they should consider both their own comfort and enthusiasm for technology as well as that of their students before making too many major changes in their peer response mechanisms.

A related issue is the very legitimate dislike that many students (or many people in general) have for working collaboratively. Some students truly enjoy the opportunity to interact with others about their writing, whereas others find it stressful or frustrating and may become resentful of it. In my view, the benefits of peer feedback are so considerable not only for individual writers but for the writing class as a whole that teachers should make a good faith attempt to present this strategy in such a way that students will at least be cooperative about trying it. If at midterm the instructor feels that peer feedback is doing more harm than good for some students, she or he could then offer the class the option of continuing to work with writing groups or spending that time in guided self-evaluation. If the class is split on this question, some could then work in groups and others could be allowed to work independently. Another way to address these individual differences is to vary class lessons in general so that there is a reasonable mix of whole-class, pair/small group, and individual work. If students are not constantly forced to work collaboratively, those who do not enjoy group work as much may not resent or resist it as much when the teacher does ask them to do it.

SUMMARY

Based both on my own teaching experience and on my careful reading of the research (discussed in chapters 4–5), I believe that peer feedback can be extremely valuable to L2 student writers. I personally cannot imagine teaching a writing course without using it extensively and regularly. However, I believe that careful planning by the instructor is the key variable to the success or lack thereof of peer review sessions. Specifically, I would make the following recommendations:

- Let students know from the first day that collaborative work and sharing of writing is going to be an integral part of the course. (I actually specify this in my course syllabus and suggest that if students are not comfortable with this, they enroll in another section of the course.)
- Prepare students for peer feedback by discussing its benefits and possible problems, showing them what to look for, and modeling the types of responses that are most appropriate and helpful. (It is also important to observe that a key type of "modeling" for peer response is the nature of the feedback given by the instructor in written commentary and in one-to-one writing conferences.)

- Assign set writing groups of 3 to 4 students, considering variables such as L1, writing ability, gender, and personality.
- Ask students to read group members' papers carefully and provide written comments before any oral discussion takes place.
- Give students peer feedback forms with questions that are clear and specific and that require students to be specific (not just answering "yes" or "no") and both positive and constructive.
- Consider pairing peer feedback questions with evaluation checklists tied specifically to course grading criteria.
- Help keep students on task by setting clear and adequate time limits, appointing timekeepers in each group, and checking occasionally to make sure groups are working effectively.
- Design accountability mechanisms so that the importance of peer feedback is modeled and students take the process seriously.
- Consider alternative forms of feedback (computer-based, self-evaluation) as needed and appropriate.

Like the other types of feedback discussed in this book, designing effective peer review sessions will take careful thought and planning by the instructor, starting with a syllabus design that privileges peer response and provides adequate time for it in the writing cycle and in the classroom. And, like written teacher commentary, conferences, and error correction, if the time and thought are expended, the potential payoffs are enormous. Rather than simply shrugging that "I tried writing groups and they didn't work," teachers should commit themselves to a conscientious effort to *make* them work. A mix of teacher feedback, peer response, and guided self-evaluation is key to students' overall progress as writers, and facilitating this mix may well be the most important thing we as L2 writing teachers can do.

APPENDIX 8A: PEER RESPONSE FORMS—A SAMPLE SEQUENCE

The peer feedback activities in this appendix were implemented in a university ESL writing course entitled "Writing for Proficiency." (See Ferris, 2001b, for more information about this course.)

Note: For Essay 1A, students read several essays on the topic of "Birth Order" from their textbook (Smalzer, 1996) and responded to the following prompt:

   Does birth order have an important influence on people's lives?

In addition, prior to this peer response activity, substantial work had been done on how to integrate ideas from other sources into one's own text. Question 2 below reflects that in-class emphasis.

PEER FEEDBACK DISCUSSION QUESTIONS (Essay 1A)

Writer's Name:_____

Partner's Name:_____

Instructions: You have read your partner's Essay 1A and evaluated it, using the Essay Evaluation Checklist (See Fig. 6.3). Now you will discuss your feedback together. The writer of the paper should take notes on this discussion in the space provided below.

1. Assignment: Did the writer do what the assignment asked? If yes, be specific about what s/he did. If no, be specific about what s/he did not do.

2. Response to Readings: Did the writer use the readings well? Specifically:

- Did references to readings ACCURATELY reflect what the authors said in their texts?
- Were summaries & paraphrases incorporated effectively and accurately (consider punctuation & verb tenses, too) into the writer's own text?

3. Positive Evaluations: Name at least two things you liked or that the writer did well in the essay.

4. Suggestions: Name at least two specific things that the writer might work on in the next essay draft.

SUMMARY/RESPONSE: Now you (the writer) will write a brief (1 paragraph) *summary* of your discussion. What were the main issues you and your partner discussed about your paper? End your paragraph with a 1-2 paragraph *reaction*. Do you agree or disagree with what your partner said? Do you think the feedback s/he gave will be helpful in writing your revision?

Note: For Essay 2A, students were given the option of writing on the topic of "work" or "manners," drawing on readings from their textbook (Smalzer, 1996). Extensive in-class work had been done on essay and paragraph organization patterns; Question 1 below reflects that emphasis. Question 2 reflects the earlier emphasis (see above) on incorporating readings into one's own text.

PEER FEEDBACK DISCUSSION QUESTIONS (Essay 2A)

Writer's Name:_____

Partner's Name:_____

Instructions: You have read your partner's Essay 2A and evaluated it, using the Essay Evaluation Checklist. Now you will discuss your feedback together. The writer of the paper should take notes on this discussion in the space provided below.

1. Does the essay follow standard essay organization patterns? Are there any specific areas (introduction, conclusion, individual body paragraphs) that could be better organized? Discuss them with your partner.

2. Response to Readings: Did the writer use the readings well? Specifically:

- Did references to readings ACCURATELY reflect what the authors said in their texts?
- Were summaries & paraphrases incorporated effectively and accurately (consider punctuation & verb tenses, too) into the writer's own text?

3. Positive Evaluations: Name at least two things you liked or that the writer did well in the essay.

4. Suggestions: Name at least two specific things that the writer might work on in the next essay draft.

SUMMARY/RESPONSE: Now you (the writer) will write a brief (1 paragraph) *summary* of your discussion. What were the main issues you and your partner discussed about your paper? End your paragraph with a 1-2 paragraph *reaction*. Do you agree or disagree with what your partner said? Do you think the feedback s/he gave will be helpful in writing your revision?

APPENDIX 8B: A PEER RESPONSE LESSON SEQUENCE

Step 1: Students wrote an in-class essay according to the instructions shown in the text box below.

You have read and discussed several texts on the issue of courtship and marriage. These readings focused on whether marriages should be arranged by families or by the individuals involved. Now respond to the following question:

When facing a major life decision, is it better to follow the advice of family and friends or to make your own choice?

You will need to write a clear, well developed persuasive essay which not only explains and supports your own position, but also defends your opinion against arguments opposing your viewpoint. References to the assigned readings are required.

Step 2: Students exchanged papers and had their partner score their essay, using the course grading criteria. They then completed the peer feedback activities below.

TIMED WRITING: PEER FEEDBACK ACTIVITIES

General Instructions: After you have read your partner's essay, completed the Essay Evaluation checklist, and assigned the score you think it should receive on the course grading criteria, discuss the following questions with your partner. Take notes on the discussion of **your** paper on this handout.

Your (Writer's) Name:_____

Partner's Name:_____

1. If your partner were a teacher grading this paper, what score did s/he think it should receive, and why? (Refer to specific course grading criteria).

2. Did the paper respond completely and appropriately to the assigned topic? Did it refer to readings accurately and effectively?

3. Was the essay well organized? Did it have all necessary elements of an academic essay? [introduction with thesis statement; body paragraphs with topic sentences, support, and summary sentences; conclusion with connection to thesis, summary of major support and general discussion of the importance of the topic to your life or to others]?

4. Did the essay consider both sides of the issue? If not, what might you have said? If yes, did you: (a) Write a thesis that expressed both sides? and/or (b) Write a paragraph or two that discussed the opposite side but still defended your own position?

Step 3: Still looking at the timed writing draft, students participated in a Peer Editing workshop, following the instructions given below.

TIMED WRITING: PEER EDITING WORKSHOP

Your Name:_____

Writer's Name:_____

<u>Instructions:</u> Read your partner's Timed Writing draft again, this time looking for any errors in grammar, vocabulary, punctuation, or spelling. <u>Underline</u> any errors you find, but **DO NOT** write any corrections! When you have finished, complete the chart below.

Error Type	# of Errors Found
Spelling	
Wrong Word or Word Form	
Noun Endings or Article Errors	
Verb Tense or Form Errors	
Sentence Structure Errors (missing words, extra words, run-ons, fragments)	
Punctuation Errors	

Step 4: After completing Steps 2-3 above and receiving separate teacher feedback on the timed writing drafts, students completed the activity below. They then revised the essay for inclusion in their final course portfolio.

TIMED WRITING: REACTION TO RESPONSES & REVISION PLANS

To prepare for your revision of your timed writing, complete the following activities.

A. Reaction to Responses. Reread your essay, along with your peer feedback forms and notes and your teacher feedback commentary. Jot down notes on the following issues:

- What comments do you agree with? Will you act on them in writing your revision?
- Are there any comments you do not understand? What will you do about them?
- Are there any comments you disagree with? What will you do about them?
- Now that you have reread your own essay, do you have any new ideas of your own for changes?

B. Revision Plans. Considering your answers in Part A, write down at least three steps you will take (or changes you will make) to improve your essay when you revise it. Be as specific as you can!

1.

2.

3.

REFERENCES

Allaei, S. K., & Connor, U. (1990). Using performative assessment instruments with ESL student writers. In L. Hamp-Lyons (Ed.), *Assessing second language writing in academic contexts* (pp. 227–240). Norwood, NJ: Ablex.

Anohui, A. (1993) *Think about editing.* Boston: Heinle & Heinle.

Anson, C. (1999). Talking about text: The use of recorded commentary in response to student writing. In R. Straub (Ed.), *A sourcebook for responding to student writing* (pp. 165–174). Creskill, NJ: Hampton Press.

Arndt, V. (1993). Response to writing: Using feedback to inform the writing process. In M. N. Brock & L. Walters (Eds.), *Teaching composition around the Pacific Rim: Politics & pedagogy* (pp. 90–116). Clevedon, England: Multilingual Matters.

Ashwell, T. (2000). Patterns of teacher response to student writing in a multiple-draft composition classroom: Is content feedback followed by form feedback the best method? *Journal of Second Language Writing, 9,* 227–258.

Atwell, N. (1998). *In the middle: New understandings about writing, reading, and learning* (2nd ed.). Portsmouth, NH: Boynton/Cook Heinemann.

Bates, L., Lane, J., & Lange, E. (1993). *Writing clearly: Responding to ESL compositions.* Boston: Heinle & Heinle.

Beason, L. (1993). Feedback and revision in writing across the curriculum classes. *Research in the Teaching of English, 27,* 395–421.

Belcher, D. D. (1988, March). *Is there an audience in the advanced EAP composition class?* Paper presented at the 22nd Annual TESOL Convention, Chicago, IL. (ERIC Document Reproduction Service No. ED 316 028)

Bell, J. H. (1991). Using peer response groups in ESL writing classes. *TESL Canada Journal, 8*(2), 65–71.

Berg, E. C. (1999). The effects of trained peer response on ESL students' revision types and writing quality. *Journal of Second Language Writing, 8,* 215–241.

Berger, V. (1990). The effects of peer and self-feedback. *CATESOL Journal, 3,* 21–35.

Bormann, E. G. (1975). *Discussion and group methods: Theory and practice.* New York: Harper & Row.

Brannon, L., & Knoblauch, C. H. (1982). On students' rights to their own texts: A model of teacher response. *College Composition and Communication, 33,* 157–166.

Brice, C. (1995, March). *ESL writers' reactions to teacher commentary: A case study.* Paper presented at the 30th Annual TESOL Convention, Long Beach, CA (ERIC Document Reproduction Service No. ED 394 312)

Brice, C., & Newman, L. (2000, September). *The case against grammar correction in practice: What do students think?* Paper presented at the Symposium on Second Language Writing, Purdue University, West Lafayette, IN.

Brown, H. D. (1994). *Principles of language learning and teaching* (3rd ed.). Englewood Cliffs, NJ: Prentice-Hall Regents.

Brown, J. D. (1988). *Understanding research in second language learning: A teacher's guide to statistics and research design.* Cambridge: Cambridge University Press.

Brown, J. D. (1991). Statistics as a foreign language—Part 1: What to look for in reading statistical language studies. *TESOL Quarterly, 25,* 569–586.

Bruffee, K. A. (1986). Social construction, language, and the authority of knowledge—A bibliographical essay. *College English, 48,* 773–790.

Carnicelli, T. (1980). The writing conference: A one-to-one conversation. In T. Donovan & B. McClelland (Eds.), *Eight approaches to teaching composition* (pp. 101–131). Urbana, IL: NCTE.

Carson, J. (1992). Becoming biliterate: First language influences. *Journal of Second Language Writing, 1,* 37–60.

Carson, J. G., & Nelson, G. L. (1994). Writing groups: Cross-cultural issues. *Journal of Second Language Writing, 3*(1), 17–30.

Carson, J. G., & Nelson, G. L. (1996). Chinese students' perceptions of ESL peer response group interaction. *Journal of Second Language Writing, 5*(1), 1–19.

Caulk, N. (1994). Comparing teacher and student responses to written work. *TESOL Quarterly, 28,* 181–188.

Chandler, J. (2000, March). *The efficacy of error correction for improvement in the accuracy of L2 student writing.* Paper presented at the AAAL Conference, Vancouver, BC.

Chaney, S. J. (1999). *The effect of error types on error correction and revision.* Unpublished master's thesis, California State University, Sacramento.

Chastain, K. (1990). Characteristics of graded and ungraded compositions. *Modern Language Journal, 74,* 10–14.

Cohen, A. (1987). Student processing of feedback on their compositions. In A. L. Wenden & J. Rubin (Eds.), *Learner strategies in language learning* (pp. 57–69). Englewood Cliffs, NJ: Prentice-Hall.

Cohen, A., & Cavalcanti, M. (1990). Feedback on written compositions: Teacher and student verbal reports. In B. Kroll (Ed.), *Second language writing: Research insights for the classroom* (pp. 155–177). Cambridge: Cambridge University Press.

Cohen, A. D., & Robbins, M. (1976). Toward assessing interlanguage performance: The relationship between selected errors, learners' characteristics, and learners' expectations. *Language Learning, 26,* 45–66.

Connor, U., & Asenavage, K. (1994). Peer response groups in ESL writing classes: How much impact on revision? *Journal of Second Language Writing, 3,* 257–276.

Conrad, S. M., & Goldstein, L. M. (1999). ESL student revision after teacher-written comments: Text, contexts, and individuals. *Journal of Second Language Writing, 8,* 147–180.

Corder, S. P. (1967). The significance of learners' errors. *IRAL, 5*(4), 161–170.

Cumming, A. (1985). Responding to the writing of ESL students. *Highway One, 8,* 58–78.

Davies, N. F., & Omberg, M. (1987). Peer group teaching and the composition class. *System, 15*(3), 313–323.

Doughty, C., & Williams, J. (Eds.) (1998). *Focus on form in classroom second language acquisition.* Cambridge: Cambridge University Press.

Elbow, P. (1973). *Writing without teachers.* Oxford: Oxford University Press.

Elbow, P. (1999). Options for responding to student writing. In R. Straub (Ed.), *A sourcebook for responding to student writing* (pp. 197–202). Creskill, NJ: Hampton Press.

Ellis, R. (1998). Teaching and research: Options in grammar teaching. *TESOL Quarterly, 32,* 39–60.

Emig, J. (1971). *The composing processes of twelfth graders.* Urbana, IL: National Council of Teachers of English.

Enginarlar, H. (1993). Student response to teacher feedback in EFL writing. *System, 21,* 193–204.

Eskey, D. E. (1983). Meanwhile, back in the real world.... Accuracy and fluency in second language teaching. *TESOL Quarterly, 17,* 315–323.

Faigley, L., & Witte, S. (1981). Analyzing revision. *College Composition and Communication, 32,* 400–414.

Fanselow, J. (1987). *Breaking rules: Generating and exploring alternatives in language teaching.* New York: Longman.

Fathman, A., & Whalley, E. (1990). Teacher response to student writing: Focus on form versus content. In B. Kroll (Ed.), *Second language writing: Research insights for the classroom* (pp. 178–190). Cambridge: Cambridge University Press.

Ferris, D. R. (1995a). Can advanced ESL students be taught to correct their most serious and frequent errors? *CATESOL Journal, 8*(1), 41–62.

Ferris, D. R. (1995b). Student reactions to teacher response in multiple-draft composition classrooms. *TESOL Quarterly, 29,* 33–53.

Ferris, D. R. (1995c). Teaching ESL composition students to become independent self-editors. *TESOL Journal, 4*(4), 18–22.

Ferris, D. R. (1997). The influence of teacher commentary on student revision. *TESOL Quarterly, 31,* 315–339.

Ferris, D. R. (1998). Student views of academic oral skills: A comparative needs analysis. *TESOL Quarterly, 32,* 289–318.

Ferris, D. R. (1999a). The case for grammar correction in L2 writing classes: A response to Truscott (1996). *Journal of Second Language Writing, 8,* 1–10.

Ferris, D. R. (1999b). One size does not fit all: Response and revision issues for immigrant student writers. In L. Harklau, K. Losey, & M. Siegal (Eds.), *Generation 1.5 meets college composition* (pp. 143–157). Mahwah, NJ: Lawrence Erlbaum Associates.

Ferris, D. R. (2001a). Teaching writing for academic purposes. In J. Flowerdew & M. Peacock (Eds.), *Research perspectives on English for academic purposes* (pp. 298–314). Cambridge: Cambridge University Press.

Ferris, D. R. (2001b). Teaching "writing for proficiency" in summer school: Lessons from a foxhole. In J. Murphy & P. Byrd (Eds.), *Understanding the courses we teach: Local perspectives on English language teaching* (pp. 328–345). Ann Arbor: University of Michigan Press.

Ferris, D. R., Chaney, S. J., Komura, K., Roberts, B. J., & McKee, S. (2000, March). *Perspectives, problems, & practices in treating written error.* Colloquium presented at International TESOL Convention, Vancouver, BC.

Ferris, D. R., & Hedgcock, J. S. (1998). *Teaching ESL composition: Purpose, process, & practice.* Mahwah, NJ: Lawrence Erlbaum Associates.

Ferris, D. R., & Helt, M. (2000, March). *Was Truscott right? New evidence on the effects of error correction in L2 writing classes.* Paper presented at AAAL Conference, Vancouver, BC.

Ferris, D. R., Pezone, S., Tade, C. R., & Tinti, S. (1997). Teacher commentary on student writing: Descriptions and implications. *Journal of Second Language Writing, 6,* 155–182.

Ferris, D. R., & Roberts, B. (2001). Error feedback in L2 writing classes: How explicit does it need to be? *Journal of Second Language Writing, 10,* 161–184.

Flower, L., & Hayes, J. (1981). A cognitive process theory of writing. *College Composition and Communication, 32,* 365–387.

Fox, L. (1992). *Focus on editing.* London: Longman.

Frantzen, D. (1995). The effects of grammar supplementation on written accuracy in an intermediate Spanish content course. *Modern Language Journal, 79,* 329–344.

Frantzen, D., & Rissell, D. (1987). Learner self-correction of written compositions: What does it show us? In B. VanPatten, T. R. Dvorak, & J. F. Lee (Eds.), *Foreign language learning: A research perspective* (pp. 92–107). Cambridge: Newbury House.

Freedman, S. W., & Katz, A. (1987). Pedagogical interaction during the composing process: The writing conference. In A. Matsuhasi (Ed.), *Writing in real time: Modeling production processes* (pp. 58–80). New York: Academic Press.

Freedman, S. W., & Sperling, M. (1985). Written language acquisition: The role of response and the writing conference. In S. W. Freedman (Ed.), *The acquisition of written language* (pp. 106–130). Norwood, NJ: Ablex.

Frodesen, J. (1991). Grammar in writing. In M. Celce-Murcia (Ed.), *Teaching English as a second or foreign language* (2nd ed., pp. 264–276). Boston: Heinle & Heinle.

Garrison, R. (1974). One-to-one tutorial instruction in freshman composition. *New Directions for Community Colleges, 2,* 55–84.

Gere, A. (1987). *Writing groups: History, theory, and implications.* Carbondale, IL: Southern Illinois University Press.

Goldstein, L., & Conrad, S. (1990). Student input and the negotiation of meaning in ESL writing conferences. *TESOL Quarterly, 24,* 443–460.

Grabe, W., & Kaplan, R. B. (1996). *Theory and practice of writing.* London: Longman.

Hafernik, J. J. (1984). The how and why of peer editing in the ESL writing class. *CATESOL Occasional Papers, 10,* 48–58. (ERIC Document Reproduction Service No. ED 253 064)

Hairston, M. (1986). On not being a composition slave. In C. W. Bridges (Ed.), *Training the new teacher of college composition* (pp. 117–124). Urbana, IL: NCTE.

Hedgcock, J., & Lefkowitz, N. (1992). Collaborative oral/aural revision in foreign language writing instruction. *Journal of Second Language Writing, 4,* 51–70.

Hedgcock, J., & Lefkowitz, N. (1994). Feedback on feedback: Assessing learner receptivity in second language writing. *Journal of Second Language Writing, 3,* 141–163.

Hedgcock, J., & Lefkowitz, N. (1996). Some input on input: Two analyses of student response to expert feedback on L2 writing. *Modern Language Journal, 80,* 287–308.

Hendrickson, J. M. (1978). Error correction in foreign language teaching: Recent theory, research, and practice. *Modern Language Journal, 62,* 387–398.

Hendrickson, J. M. (1980). The treatment of error in written work. *Modern Language Journal, 64,* 216–221.

Hillocks, G., Jr. (1986). *Research on written composition: New directions for teaching.* Urbana, IL: ERIC Clearinghouse on Reading and Communication Skills and the National Conference on Research in English.

Horowitz, D. (1986). Process not product: Less than meets the eye. *TESOL Quarterly, 20,* 141–144.

Huntley, H. S. (1992). *Feedback strategies in intermediate and advanced second language composition: A discussion of the effects of error correction, peer review, and student–teacher conferences on student writing and performance.* Washington, DC: ERIC/FLL, 1–18. (ERIC Document Reproduction Service No. ED 355 809)

Hvitfeldt, C. (1986). *Guided peer critique in ESL writing at the college level.* Paper presented at the Annual Meeting of the Japan Association of Language Teachers International Conference on Language Teaching and Learning, Seirei Gakuen, Hamamatsu, Japan. (ERIC Document Reproduction Service No. ED 282 438)

Hyland, F. (1998). The impact of teacher-written feedback on individual writers. *Journal of Second Language Writing, 7,* 255–286.

Jacobs, G. M., Curtis, A., Braine, G., & Huang, S. (1998). Feedback on student writing: Taking the middle path. *Journal of Second Language Writing, 7*, 307–318.

Jacobs, H. L., Zingraf, S., Wormuth, D., Hartfiel, V., & Hughey, J. (1981). *Testing ESL composition: A practical approach*. Rowley, MA: Newbury House.

Jacobs, S., & Karliner, A. (1977). Helping writers to think: The effect of speech roles in individual conferences on the quality of thought in student writing. *College English 38*, 489–505.

James, C. (1998). *Errors in language learning and use: Exploring error analysis*. London: Longman.

Johns, A. M. (1995). Genre and pedagogical purposes. *Journal of Second Language Writing, 4*, 181–190.

Jones, N. B. (1995). *Improving writing for international business through peer reviews*. Paper presented at the Malaysian English Language Teaching Association Biennial International Conference. (ERIC Document Reproduction Service No. ED 389 210)

Kepner, C. G. (1991). An experiment in the relationship of types of written feedback to the development of second-language writing skills. *Modern Language Journal, 75*, 305–313.

Komura, K. (1999). *Student response to error correction in ESL classrooms*. Unpublished master's thesis, California State University, Sacramento.

Knoblauch, C. H., & Brannon, L. (1981, Fall). Teacher commentary on student writing: The state of the art. *Freshman English News, 10*, 1–4.

Knoblauch, C. H., & Brannon, L. (1984). *Rhetorical traditions and the teaching of writing*. Upper Montclair, NJ: Boynton/Cook.

Krashen, S. D. (1982). *Principles and practices in second language acquisition*. Oxford: Pergamon Press.

Krashen, S. D. (1984). *Writing: Research, theory, and application*. Oxford: Pergamon Press.

Kroll, B. (1990). What does time buy? ESL student performance on home versus class compositions. In B. Kroll (Ed.), *Second language writing: Research insights for the classroom* (pp. 140–154). Cambridge: Cambridge University Press.

Lalande, J. F., II. (1982). Reducing composition errors: An experiment. *Modern Language Journal, 66*, 140–149.

Lam, C. Y. P. (1991). Revision processes of college ESL students: How teacher comments, discourse types, and writing tools shape revision. *Dissertation Abstracts International, 52*(12), 4248A.

Lane, J., & Lange, E. (1999). *Writing clearly: An editing guide* (2nd ed.). Boston: Heinle & Heinle.

Leki, I. (1990a). Coaching from the margins: Issues in written response. In B. Kroll (Ed.), *Second language writing. Research insights for the classroom* (pp. 57–68). Cambridge: Cambridge University Press.

Leki, I. (1990b). Potential problems with peer responding in ESL writing classes. *CATESOL Journal, 3*, 5–19.

Leki, I. (1991). The preferences of ESL students for error correction in college-level writing classes. *Foreign Language Annals, 24*, 203–218.

Leki, I. (1992). *Understanding ESL writers*. Portsmouth, NH: Boynton/Cook Heinemann.

Lightbown, P., & Spada, N. (1990). Focus on form and corrective feedback in communicative second language teaching: Effects on second language learning. *Studies in Second Language, 12*, 429–448.

Linden-Martin, M. (1997). *Hesitancy working with a peer: Comparison of two studies 1995 and 1996*. Paper presented at 31st Annual TESOL Convention, Orlando, FL.

Lockhart, C., & Ng, P. (1995a). Analyzing talk in ESL peer response groups: Stances, functions, and content, *Language Learning, 45*(4), 605–655.

Lockhart, C., & Ng, P. (1995b). Student stances during peer response in writing. In M. L. Tickoo (Ed.), *Reading and writing: Theory into practice* (pp. 118–132). SEAMEO Regional Language Centre: RELC.

Long, M. H., & Porter, P. A. (1985). Group work, interlanguage talk, and second language acquisition. *TESOL Quarterly, 19*(2), 207–227.

Lunsford, R. (1986). Planning for spontaneity in the writing classroom and a passel of other paradoxes. In C. Bridges (Ed.), *Training the new teacher of college composition* (pp. 95–108). Urbana, IL: NCTE.

Mangelsdorf, K. (1992). Peer reviews in the ESL composition classroom: What do the students think? *ELT Journal, 46*, 274–284.

Mangelsdorf, K., & Schlumberger, A. L. (1992). ESL student response stances in a peer-review task. *Journal of Second Language Writing, 1*(3), 235–254.

Marzano, R. J., & Arthur, S. (1977). *Teacher comments on student essays: It doesn't matter what you say.* (ERIC Document Reproduction Service No. ED 147 864)

McCurdy, P. (1992, March). *What students do with composition feedback.* Paper presented at the 27th Annual TESOL Convention, Vancouver, BC.

McGroarty, M. E., & Zhu, W. (1997). Triangulation in classroom research: A study of peer revision. *Language Learning, 47*(1), 1–43.

Mendonça, C. O., & Johnson, K. E. (1994). Peer review negotiations: Revision activities in ESL writing instruction. *TESOL Quarterly, 28*, 745–769.

Mittan, R. (1989). The peer review process: Harnessing students' communicative power. In D. M. Johnson & D. H. Roen (Eds.), *Richness in writing: Empowering ESL students* (pp. 207–219). New York: Longman.

Moore, L. (1986). Teaching students how to evaluate writing. *TESOL Newsletter, 20*(5), 23–24.

Moxley, J. (1989, Spring). Responding to student writing: Goals, methods, alternatives. *Freshman English News, 17*, 3–4, 9–10.

Nelson, G. L., & Carson, J. G. (1998). ESL students' perceptions of effectiveness in peer response groups. *Journal of Second Language Writing, 7*, 113–132.

Nelson, G. L., & Murphy, J. M. (1992). An L2 writing group: Task and social dimensions. *Journal of Second Language Writing, 1*(3), 171–193.

Nelson, G. L., & Murphy, J. M. (1993). Peer response groups: Do L2 writers use peer comments in revising their drafts? *TESOL Quarterly, 27*, 135–142.

Newkirk, T. (1995). The writing conference as performance. *Research in the Teaching of English, 29*, 193–215.

Patthey-Chavez, G. G., & Ferris, D. R. (1997). Writing conferences and the weaving of multi-voiced texts in college composition. *Research in the Teaching of English, 31*, 51–90.

Paulus, T. (1999). The effect of peer and teacher feedback on student writing. *Journal of Second Language Writing, 8*, 265–289.

Pica, T. (1984). Second language acquisition theory in the teaching of writing. *TESOL Newsletter, 18*(2), 5–6.

Polio, C. (1997). Measures of linguistic accuracy in second language writing research. *Language Learning, 47*, 101–143.

Polio, C., Fleck, C., & Leder, N. (1998). 'If only I had more time': ESL learners' changes in linguistic accuracy on essay revisions. *Journal of Second Language Writing, 7*, 43–68.

Radecki, P., & Swales, J. (1988). ESL student reaction to written comments on their written work. *System, 16*, 355–365.

Raimes, A. (1985). What unskilled ESL students do as they write: A classroom study of composing. *TESOL Quarterly, 19*, 229–258.

Raimes, A. (1992). *Grammar troublespots.* New York: St. Martin's Press.

Reid, J. (1993). *Teaching ESL writing.* Englewood Cliffs, NJ: Regents/Prentice Hall.

Reid, J. (1994). Responding to ESL students' texts: The myths of appropriation. *TESOL Quarterly, 28*, 273–292.

Reid, J. (1998a). "Eye" learners and "Ear" learners: Identifying the language needs of international student and U.S. resident writers. In P. Byrd & J. M. Reid (Eds.), *Grammar in the composition classroom: Essays on teaching ESL for college-bound students* (pp. 3–17). Boston: Heinle & Heinle.

Reid, J. (1998b). Responding to ESL student language problems: Error analysis and revision plans. In P. Byrd & J. M. Reid (Eds.), *Grammar in the composition classroom: Essays on teaching ESL for college-bound students* (pp. 118–137). Boston: Heinle & Heinle.

Rennie, C. (2000). *Error feedback in ESL writing classes: What do students really want?* Unpublished master's thesis, California State University, Sacramento.

Robb, T., Ross, S., & Shortreed, I. (1986). Salience of feedback on error and its effect on EFL writing quality. *TESOL Quarterly, 20*, 83–93.

Roberts, B. J. (1999). *Can error logs raise more than consciousness? The effects of error logs and grammar feedback on ESL students' final drafts.* Unpublished master's thesis, California State University, Sacramento.

Rothschild, D., & Klingenberg, F. (1990). Self and peer evaluation of writing in the intensive ESL classroom. *TESL Canada Journal, 8*(1), 52–65.

Russikoff, K., & Kogan, S. (1996, March). *Feedback on ESL writing.* Paper presented at the 31st Annual TESOL Convention, Chicago, IL.

Saito, H. (1994). Teachers' practices and students' preferences for feedback on second language writing: A case study of adult ESL learners. *TESL Canada Journal, 11*(2), 46–70.

Schmid, L. M. (1999). *The effects of peer response on essay drafts.* Unpublished master's thesis, California State University, Sacramento.

Schwartz, B. (1993). On explicit and negative data effecting and affecting competence and linguistic behavior. *Studies in Second Language Acquisition, 15*, 147–163.

Semke, H. (1984). The effects of the red pen. *Foreign Language Annals, 17*, 195–202.

Sheppard, K. (1992). Two feedback types: Do they make a difference? *RELC Journal, 23*, 103–110.

Silva, T. (1988). Comments on Vivian Zamel's "Recent research on writing pedagogy." *TESOL Quarterly, 22*, 517–519.

Silva, T. (1993). Toward an understanding of the distinct nature of L2 writing: The ESL research and its implications. *TESOL Quarterly, 27*, 657–677.

Silva, T. (1997). On the ethical treatment of ESL writers. *TESOL Quarterly, 31*, 359–363.

Silva, T., Leki, I., & Carson, J. (1997). Broadening the perspective of mainstream composition studies: Some thoughts from the disciplinary margins. *Written Communication, 14*, 398–428.

Sommers, N. (1980). Revision strategies of student writers and experienced adult writers. *College Composition and Communication, 31*, 378–388.

Sommers, N. (1982). Responding to student writing. *College Composition and Communication, 33*, 148–156.

Spack, R. (1988). Initiating ESL students into the academic discourse community: How far should we go? *TESOL Quarterly, 22*, 29–51.

Spack, R. (1996). *Guidelines: A cross-cultural reading/writing text* (2nd ed.). New York: St. Martin's Press.

Spack, R. (1997). The rhetorical construction of multilingual students. *TESOL Quarterly, 31*, 765–774.

Sperling, M. (1991). Dialogues of deliberation: Conversation in the teacher–student writing conference. *Written Communication, 8*, 131–162.

Sperling, M. (1994). Constructing the perspective of teacher-as-reader: A framework for studying response to student writing. *Research in the Teaching of English, 28*, 175–207.

Sperling, M., & Freedman, S. W. (1987). A good girl writes like a good girl: Written responses to student writing. *Written Communication, 4*, 343–369.

Stanley, J. (1992). Coaching student writers to be effective peer evaluators. *Journal of Second Language Writing, 1*(3), 217–233.

Straub, R. (1996). The concept of control in teacher response: Defining the varieties of directive and facilitative commentary. *College Composition and Communication, 47*, 223–251.

Straub, R. (1997). Students' reactions to teacher comments: An exploratory study. *Research in the Teaching of English, 31*, 91–119.

Straub, R. (1999). *A sourcebook for responding to student writing.* Creskill, NJ: Hampton Press.

Straub, R., & Lunsford, R. F. (1995). *Twelve readers reading: Responding to college student writing.* Creskill, NJ: Hampton Press.

Truscott, J. (1996). The case against grammar correction in L2 writing classes. *Language Learning, 46,* 327–369.

Truscott, J. (1999). The case for "the case for grammar correction in L2 writing classes": A response to Ferris. *Journal of Second Language Writing, 8,* 111–122.

VanPatten, B. (1988). How juries get hung: Problems with the evidence for a focus on form in teaching. *Language Learning, 38,* 243–260.

Villamil, O. S., & de Guerrero, M. C. M. (1996). Peer revision in the L2 classroom: Social-cognitive activities, mediating strategies, and aspects of social behavior. *Journal of Second Language Writing, 5*(1), 51–76.

Vygotsky, L. (1986). *Thought and language* (A. Kozulin, Trans. & Ed.). Cambridge, MA: MIT Press. (Original work published 1962)

Walker, C. P., & Elias, D. (1987). Writing conference talk: Factors associated with high- and low-rated writing conferences. *Research in the Teaching of English, 21,* 266–285.

Weaver, C. (1996). *Teaching grammar in context.* Portsmouth, NH: Boynton/Cook Heinemann.

White, E. M. (1999). Using scoring guides to assess writing. In R. Straub (Ed.), *A sourcebook for responding to student writing* (pp. 203–212). Creskill, NJ: Hampton Press.

Zamel, V. (1982). Writing: The process of discovering meaning. *TESOL Quarterly, 16,* 195–209.

Zamel, V. (1983). The composing processes of advanced ESL students: Six case studies. *TESOL Quarterly, 17,* 165–187.

Zamel, V. (1985). Responding to student writing. *TESOL Quarterly, 19,* 79–102.

Zamel, V. (1987). Recent research on writing pedagogy. *TESOL Quarterly, 21,* 697–715.

Zhang, S. (1995). Reexamining the affective advantage of peer feedback in the ESL writing class. *Journal of Second Language Writing, 4,* 209–222.

Zhang, S. (1999). Thoughts on some recent evidence concerning the affective advantage of peer feedback. *Journal of Second Language Writing, 8,* 321–326.

Author Index

Subject Index